Everyman, I will go with thee,
and be thy guide

THE EVERYMAN
LIBRARY

*The Everyman Library was founded by J. M. Dent
in 1906. He chose the name Everyman because he wanted
to make available the best books ever written in every
field to the greatest number of people at the cheapest possible
price. He began with Boswell's 'Life of Johnson',
his one-thousandth title was Aristotle's 'Metaphysics',
by which time sales exceeded forty million.*

*Today Everyman paperbacks remain true to
J. M. Dent's aims and high standards, with a wide range
of titles at affordable prices in editions which address
the needs of today's readers. Each new text is reset to give
a clear, elegant page and to incorporate the latest thinking
and scholarship. Each book carries the pilgrim logo,
the character in 'Everyman', a medieval morality play,
a proud link between Everyman
past and present.*

William Shakespeare

MACBETH

Edited by
JOHN F. ANDREWS
Foreword by
ZOE CALDWELL

EVERYMAN
J. M. DENT · LONDON
CHARLES E. TUTTLE
VERMONT

First published in Everyman by J. M. Dent 1993
Published by permission of GuildAmerica Books, an imprint
of Doubleday Book and Music Clubs, Inc.
Reissued 1996
Reprinted 1998, 1999, 2000

J. M. Dent
Orion Publishing Group
Orion House
5 Upper St Martin's Lane, London WC2H 9EA
and
Tuttle Publishing
Airport Industrial Park
364 Innovation Drive
North Clarendon VT 05759-9436, USA

Photoset by Deltatype Ltd, Ellesmere Port, Cheshire
Printed in Great Britain by
The Guernsey Press Co. Ltd, Guernsey, C.I.

British Library Cataloguing-in-Publication Data is
available upon request.

ISBN 0 460 87182 X

CONTENTS

Note on the Author and Editor vii

Chronology of Shakespeare's Life and Times viii

Foreword to Macbeth *by Zoe Caldwell* xiii

Editor's Introduction to Macbeth xv

The Text of the Everyman Shakespeare xxiii

MACBETH 1

Perspectives on Macbeth 187

Suggestions for Further Reading 205

Plot Summary 209

Acknowledgements 213

NOTE ON THE AUTHOR AND EDITOR

WILLIAM SHAKESPEARE is held to have been born on St George's Day, 23 April 1564. The eldest son of a prosperous glove-maker in Stratford-upon-Avon, he was probably educated at the town's grammar school.

Tradition holds that between 1585 and 1592, Shakespeare first became a schoolteacher and then set off for London. By 1595 he was a leading member of the Lord Chamberlain's Men, helping to direct their business affairs, as well as being a playwright and actor. In 1598 he became a part-owner of the company, which was the most distinguished of its age. However, he maintained his contacts with Stratford, and his family seem to have remained there. From about 1610 he seems to have grown increasingly involved in the town's affairs, suggesting a withdrawal from London. He died on 23 April 1616, in his 53rd year, and was buried at Holy Trinity Church on the 25th.

JOHN F. ANDREWS has recently completed a 19-volume edition *The Guild Shakespeare*, for the Doubleday Book and Music Clubs. He is also the editor of a 3-volume reference set, *William Shakespeare: His World, His Work, His Influence*, and the former editor (1974–85) of the journal *Shakespeare Quarterly*. From 1974–1984, he was Director of Academic Programs at the Folger Shakespeare Library in Washington and Chairman of the Folger Institute.

CHRONOLOGY OF SHAKESPEARE'S LIFE

Year[1]	Age	Life
1564		Shakespeare baptised 26 April at Stratford-upon-Avon
1582	18	Marries Anne Hathaway
1583	19	Daughter, Susanna, born
1585	21	Twin son and daughter, Hamnet and Judith, born
1590–1	26	*The Two Gentlemen of Verona* & *The Taming of the Shrew*
1591	27	*2 & 3 Henry VI*
1592	28	*Titus Andronicus* & *1 Henry VI*
1592–3		*Richard III*
1593	29	*Venus and Adonis* published
1594	30	*The Comedy of Errors. The Rape of Lucrece* published
1594–5		*Love's Labour's Lost*
1595	31	*A Midsummer Night's Dream, Romeo and Juliet,* & *Richard II.* An established member of Lord Chamberlain's Men
1596	32	*King John.* Hamnet dies
1596–7		*The Merchant of Venice* & *1 Henry IV*

1 It is rarely possible to be certain about the dates at which plays of this period were written. For Shakespeare's plays, this chronology follows the dates preferred by Wells and Taylor, the editors of the Oxford Shakespeare. Publication dates are given for poetry and books.

Year	Literary Context	Historical Events
1565–7	Golding, Ovid's *Metamorphoses*, tr.	Elizabeth I reigning
1574	*A Mirror for Magistrates* (3rd ed.)	
1576	London's first playhouse built	
1578	John Lyly, *Euphues*	
1579	North, Plutarch's *Lives*, tr.	
	Spenser, *Shepherd's Calender*	
1587	Marlowe, *I Tamburlaine*	Mary Queen of Scots executed
	Holinshed's *Chronicles* (2nd ed.)	
1588		Defeat of Spanish Armada
1589	Kyd, *Spanish Tragedy*	Civil war in France
	Marlowe, *Jew of Malta*	
1590	Spenser, *Faerie Queene*, Bks I–III	
1591	Sidney, *Astrophel and Stella*	Proclamation against Jesuits
1592	Marlowe, *Dr Faustus* & *Edward II*	Scottish witchcraft trials
		Plague closes theatres from June
1593	Marlowe killed	
1594	Nashe, *Unfortunate Traveller*	Theatres reopen in summer
1594–6		Extreme food shortages
1595	Sidney, *Defence of Poetry*	Riots in London
1596		Calais captured by Spanish
		Cadiz expedition

Year	Age	Life
1597	33	Buys New Place in Stratford
1597–8		*The Merry Wives of Windsor* & *2 Henry IV*
1598	34	*Much Ado About Nothing*
1598–9		*Henry V*
1599	35	*Julius Caesar*. One of syndicate responsible for building the Globe in Southwark, where the Lord Chamberlain's Men now play
1599–1600		*As You Like It*
1600–1		*Hamlet*
1601	37	*Twelfth Night*. His father is buried in Stratford
1602	38	*Troilus and Cressida*. Invests £320 in land near Stratford[2]
1603	39	*Measure for Measure*. The Lord Chamberlain's Men become the King's Men. They play at court more than all the other companies combined
1603–4		*Othello*
c.1604	40	Shakespeare sues Philip Rogers of Stratford for debt
1604–5		*All's Well That Ends Well*
1605	41	*Timon of Athens*. Invests £440 in Stratford tithes
1605–6		*King Lear*
1606	42	*Macbeth* & *Antony and Cleopatra*
1607	43	*Pericles*. Susanna marries the physician John Hall in Stratford
1608	44	*Coriolanus*. The King's Men lease Blackfriar's, an indoor theatre. His only grandchild is born. His mother dies
1609	45	*The Winter's Tale*. 'Sonnets' and 'A Lover's Complaint' published
1610	46	*Cymbeline*
1611	47	*The Tempest*
1613	49	*Henry VIII*. Buys houses in London for £140
1613–14		*The Two Noble Kinsmen*
1616	52	Judith marries Thomas Quiney, a vintner, in Stratford. On 23 April he dies, and is buried two days later
1623	59	Publication of the First Folio. His wife dies in August

2 A schoolmaster would earn around £20 a year at this time.

Year	Literary Context	Historical Events
1597	Bacon's *Essays*	
1598	Marlowe and Chapman, *Hero and Leander* Jonson, *Every Man in his Humour*	Rebellion in Ireland
1599	Children's companies begin playing George Dekker's *Shoemaker's Holiday*	Essex fails in Ireland
1601	'War of the Theatres' Jonson, *Poetaster*	Essex rebels and is executed
1602		Tyrone defeated in Ireland
1603	Florio, Montaigne's *Essays*, tr.	Elizabeth I dies, James I accedes Raleigh found guilty of treason
1604	Marston, *The Malcontent*	Peace with Spain
1605	Bacon's *Advancement of Learning*	Gunpowder plot
1606	Jonson's *Volpone*	
1607	Tourneur, *The Revenger's Tragedy*, published	Virginia colonized Enclosure riots
1609		Oath of allegiance Truce in Netherlands
1610	Jonson, *Alchemist*	
1611	Authorised Version of the Bible Donne, *Anatomy of the World*	
1612	Webster, *White Devil*	Prince Henry dies
1613	Webster, *Duchess of Malfi*	Princess Elizabeth marries
1614	Jonson, *Bartholomew Fair*	
1616	Folio edition of Jonson's plays	

Biographical note, chronology and plot summary compiled by John Lee, University of Bristol, 1993.

I came back from six weeks in India, centred and sane. Two weeks later I was involved in a benighted production of *Macbeth* and all health vanished. What is it about that play? I had been warned by a very distinguished member of the theatre profession that *Macbeth* was not only unlucky but a source of strange evil. 'How silly!' I thought – and jumped right in.

This was not my production; I had not cast it, nor had any influence on the design; and in three weeks it was to open on Broadway. The company, playing eight performances a week and having already played eight weeks on the road with two different directors, was in no mood for a fresh face. So I thought I'd simply read the text and find out where the play was being 'helped'. We actors and directors seem to feel it our duty to help William Shakespeare more than any other playwright. I know of no playwright who needs our help less!

Shakespeare has given us a short, sharp, riveting play about a splendid man's total destruction, a fate brought about by his becoming addicted to evil. Could anything be more timely? And to get us ready for such excitement, the playwright brings us all to attention by a crack of thunder, a bolt of lightning, and a brief exchange between three witches telling us that Macbeth is their target. Why Macbeth? Because he is the brightest and the best. The one with the most to lose.

'Brave', 'valiant', 'noble', 'worthy' Macbeth. The King loves him, the soldiers admire and respect him, he has close good friends and an adoring wife. His castle even has a pleasant seat. And he has a crucial element for evil: a human flaw. In his case, vaulting ambition. Banquo would have been of no use to the witches.

I became aware that the Scotland, or Scot lands, in this play is not an established country but a series of fiefdoms gathered together by Duncan the King and desperately keeping attackers at bay. The bloodline is in fact created by Duncan in front of us early in the play, making the prophecy of 'King hereafter' impossible for Macbeth without murder. Macbeth is a renowned killer when we first meet him, and he is given great honours and promotions for it. So the witches couldn't have better material to work on.

Having read the witches' prophecies, Lady Macbeth knows what they will do to her husband. And yet, knowing how strangely ill-equipped he is to pursue his ambition ruthlessly, she does the most extraordinary thing. She calls on the spirits of the dark to take away what is most precious to her – her womanliness, her femininity – so that she may be strong enough to give her husband what he desires.

Godless images, images of chaos, of blood, of dark, permeate the play. But what truly stunned me while working on it was the daring way Shakespeare presents us *not* with an evil man but with a man who, while we are watching, removes himself from all human contact. 'Laugh to scorn the power of man' sends chills up my spine; for if that advice is followed, a man will surely become alone and ultimately powerless.

And that is what Macbeth becomes. The final sweep of the play has at its centre a lonely, slightly mad, desolate figure. With any luck, we weep. The fact that he speaks some of the most profoundly beautiful speeches in the English language while letting us see his blasted soul doesn't hurt. It is, I think, disconcerting for an audience that has come to see the wicked Macbeths at play to be confronted with such lucid understanding of human frailties. Sometimes the audience rejects the tragedy. But it is our job to follow step-by-step what Shakespeare has written and let the play do the work.

So why did all health vanish? Because I couldn't clear the path sufficiently for Mr Shakespeare. Why is it the 'bad luck play'? You find out for yourself.   *Zoe Caldwell*

Zoe Caldwell has played most of the female roles in the Shakespearean canon – with Cleopatra a personal favourite. Among her directorial credits is an acclaimed production of *Macbeth* on Broadway in 1988.

It is difficult to imagine a work of greater dramatic intensity than *Macbeth*. It portrays the most violent of passions. It makes extraordinary demands upon the audience's emotions. It raises fundamental questions about what it means to be human. And it suggests that the beginning of wisdom – and the antidote to those excesses that promote self-destruction – is a judgement tempered by humility, compassion, and a sense of cosmic awe.

Background

When Shakespeare wrote *Macbeth*, probably in 1605–6, he wove into a coherent tragedy of ambition several strands of scattered narrative from the 1587 edition of Raphael Holinshed's *Chronicles of England, Scotland, and Ireland*. For the title character, for example, the playwright combined elements of two episodes in Holinshed: Donwald's murder of King Duff (a crime largely instigated by Donwald's wife, and one that takes place in Donwald's castle while the King sleeps peacefully as a guest), and Macbeth and Banquo's rebellion against a Duncan who is venial and weak rather than saintly and meek as in Shakespeare. In Holinshed the Duncan who is slain by Macbeth and his allies can be construed as exceeding his authority as an elected monarch when he declares his son Malcolm to be the presumptive heir to the throne. And in Holinshed, once Duncan is removed from power and Macbeth receives 'by common consent' the 'investure of the kingdome according to the accustomed maner', the new king reigns successfully and responsibly for a decade before he degenerates into the despot that Shakespeare's Macbeth becomes almost as soon as he seizes the crown.

At the same time that Shakespeare sullied the reputations of Macbeth and his Lady, he transformed Banquo from a rebel and fellow assassin into a nobleman who explicitly rejects the course his companion chooses. The playwright's reasons for the alteration were probably twofold. First, he knew that the monarch he served (and who was now the official patron of Shakespeare's acting company, known formally as 'His Majesty's Servants' and informally as 'the King's Men') claimed descent from the legendary Banquo. Second, he knew that that same monarch would expect to see the progenitor of the Stuart dynasty represented as a loyal subject of his duly anointed lord.

There is a good possibility that Shakespeare's drama was first presented before King James at Hampton Court on 7 August 1606, when the King was entertaining the visiting King Christian of Denmark. If so, that fact would account for several features of *Macbeth* that appear designed to reflect the King's tastes and interests.

One such feature is the play's emphasis on the supernatural. During the period when he ruled solely as James VI of Scotland (he became James I of England when he was invited to succeed Elizabeth I after her death on 24 March 1603), the King had written a book on *Daemonologie* (published in London in 1599), and had administered capital punishment to women his courts found guilty of engaging in witchcraft.

A second feature is the play's stress on the kind of 'equivocation' (II.iii.9–13, 34–41; V.v.41–43) that undermines trust and threatens to dis-join the very 'Frame of things' (III.ii.16). On 5 November 1605 England had been stunned by the discovery of a conspiracy to blow up the Houses of Parliament in an effort to assassinate the king and his ministers. The Gunpowder Plot was widely perceived as a Satanic device to overthrow the true religion and return the British Isles to the corruptions of Catholicism, and that view was strongly reinforced by the testimony of a Jesuit priest who was convicted on 28 March 1606 of having been a party to the plot. Father Henry Garnet offered as his chief defence the argument that he was guilty of nothing more than 'equivocation' (speaking in a manner intended to mislead the hearer), and that equivocation was ethically and theologically permissible, even under oath, 'if just necessity so require'.

A third feature is the play's comparative brevity. As Kenneth.

Muir points out in his introduction to the Arden edition of *Macbeth* (London: Methuen, 1979), 'Shakespeare was probably in Oxford in the summer of 1605, and he would then have heard that James I, on the occasion of his visit in August, approved of Matthew Gwinn's *Tres Sibyllae*, with its allusions to his ancestry, and that he disliked long plays' (p. xix). Over the years many scholars have suggested that the version of *Macbeth* that appeared in the 1623 First Folio (the only text of the play that survives) was one that had been cut for presentation before the king. Perhaps so, but a close examination of the tragedy will show that it works extraordinarily well as it stands; there is no need to hypothesize the previous existence of scenes not included in the text that has come down to us.

Comment on the Play

Actors customarily refer to *Macbeth* as 'the Scottish Play', and so potent are the superstitions traditionally attached to it that even today many theatre professionals refuse to incur the risk of mentioning it by name. Like Marlowe's *Doctor Faustus* and Shakespeare's own *Richard III*, it is a script that requires its performers to utter blasphemies and engage in traffic with the agents of blackest Night. Like *Richard II* and *Julius Caesar*, it focuses on regicide. Like *Hamlet* and *King Lear*, it forces the audience to ponder cosmic questions, matters of 'deepest consequence'. But for all its correspondence with these and other exemplars of Renaissance stagecraft, *Macbeth* is in one respect unique: it alone is widely believed to carry a curse.

It would be fruitless to try and dispel the aura that surrounds this bloody piece of work. Every thespian can recount mishaps attributable to encounters with Shakespeare's most metaphysical tragedy; every director can detail the disasters that have plagued productions. At the same time, however, and more to the point, everyone knows that the demonic lore associated with *Macbeth* is an ineradicable aspect of the mystique this magnificent drama has always held for players and playgoers alike.

From Richard Burbage's original rendering of the title part (either at Hampton Court or at Shakespeare's Globe, where

Macbeth was probably being staged at least as early as 1607, though the earliest surviving record of a performance there dates from the spring of 1611, when Dr Simon Forman entered an account of it in his manuscript 'Booke of Plaies and Notes thereof') to recent revivals in theatres and on cinema and television screens around the world, the role of Macbeth has inspired a regal procession of memorable performances. But if the play's four centuries have seen many eminent actors essay the title role, they have bequeathed an equally imposing succession of Ladies to urge the warlike Thane towards the 'Golden Round' (I.v.30) for which both characters lust.

Nor is it difficult to understand why the dramatis personae of Macbeth and his wife have proven so enduring. In the hero's aspiration for the crown, Shakespeare depicts a 'vaulting Ambition' (I.vii.27) so primal as to rival the insurrection of Lucifer. In Macbeth's assassination of his beneficent king, the playwright details an act of treachery so egregious that it can be exceeded only by Judas' betrayal of *his* Lord. In the reign of terror that ensues in the aftermath of the slaying, Shakespeare portrays the desperation of a dictator so obsessed with safeguarding his throne that he becomes another Herod (Matthew 2:16–18), slaughtering innocent children and their mothers in a frantic but futile effort to arrest the future and trammel up 'the Life to come' (I.vii.7). Meanwhile, in the noctural vigils of Macbeth's Lady,* the playwright displays the torments of an accomplice so incarnardined with guilt that, like Pontius Pilate, she must ultimately forgo any hope of ever cleansing her hands again.

This is a world of heightened dimensions, and its poetry is at times so opulent that, like the verbal music of *Othello*, it can be described as operatic. The atmosphere is so overcharged with passion and violence, so redolent of damnation, that it would not be inappropriate to refer to it as Shakespeare's answer to Dante's *Inferno*.

But if we conclude that Shakespeare's object in this tragedy is to engulf us in the maelstroin Macbeth and his wife stir up for

---

* As noted in *The Text of the Everyman Shakespeare* (p. xxxvi), 'Lady Macbeth' does not appear by that name in the original text of the play.

themselves and for the kingdom they usurp, we should bear in mind that much of the play's effect derives from our initial view of 'Noble Macbeth' (I.ii.69) as a splendid warrior whose valour in the service of his monarch has just earned him a new title. When we see the hero with Banquo on the blasted heath, rapt in speculation about the Witches' prophecy that he will be 'King hereafter' (I.iii.48), we should avoid presuming too quickly that 'Brave Macbeth' (I.ii.16) is foreordained to prove a villain. It is true that he is being singled out for the 'supernatural Soliciting' of the 'weyward Sisters' (I.iii.128, 130). And it is clear that in his opening scenes with his Lady (I.v. and I.vii) the Thane is all too receptive to her interpretation of what it means to be a 'Man' in such a situation. But up to the moment when he irrevocably determines to don a 'False Face' to 'hide what the False Heart doth know' (I.vii.82), Macbeth remains capable of saying 'We will proceed no further in this Business' (l.vii.31).

That he eventually does not say no to temptation is what the play is all about. And nowhere else in all the world's dramatic literature can we find so profound an analysis of what it means to choose evil and consign one's self to perdition.

By giving us an opportunity to observe Macbeth before he succumbs to the promptings of his unruly pride, Shakespeare introduces us to a man not all that different from ourselves, a human being with those frailties we can identify. We meet the hero when he can properly be designated as Banquo's 'Noble Partner' (I.iii.52), and at this juncture the only distinction between the two warriors is that Banquo doesn't permit his curiosity about the Witches' prophecies to blind him to the commonplace that 'oftentimes, to win us to our Harm, / The Instruments of Darkness tell us Truths' (I.iii.121–22).

By showing us the exchanges with Macbeth's Lady that follow, Shakespeare depicts the psychology of seduction. As the Thane's 'Desire' supplants his 'Judgement' (I.vii.41, 8), he finds that a proposition he initially dismissed as unthinkable begins to assume an air of inevitability. Once his wife persuades him to 'screw' his 'Courage to the Sticking Place' (I.vii.60), Macbeth's 'Heat-oppressed Brain' (II.i.38) produces a somnambulistic state in which first an imagined dagger and then a tolling bell summon him to an act from which his whole being would otherwise recoil.

From this point on we are made privy to a study in the deterioration of humanity. In Shakespeare's time 'conscience' was indistinguishable from what we now call 'consciousness', and what Macbeth experiences in the wake of his crime is a process by which both are corrupted beyond reclamation.

Almost immediately Macbeth's homicidal narcosis yields to evasion: 'I am afraid', he says, 'to think what I have done'. Evasion leads to a willed suppression of self-knowledge: 'To know my Deed, 'Twere best not know my Self' (II.ii.48, 69–70). From there Shakespeare charts a steady decline to that hardening of the moral sense wherein the most brutal murders become virtually automatic – what Macbeth calls the 'Firstlings of my heart' (IV.i. 146). Eventually the man whose nature was thought 'too full o' th' Milk of Humane Kindness' (I.v.19) acknowledges that he has 'almost forgot the Taste of Fears' (V.v.9) or any other human feeling. And by the end of the play (V.v.24–28) he is left with the nihilistic observation that

> Life's but a walking Shadow, a poor Player,
> That struts and frets his Hour upon the Stage
> And then is heard no more; it is a Tale
> Told by an Idiot, full of Sound and Fury
> Signifying nothing.

Moments after this speech we hear Macbeth 'wish th' Estate of the World were now undone', and it dawns on us that, having wagered his soul to gain the whole world (Matthew 16:26), he finally and ironically ends up with neither.

The disintegration of Macbeth's Lady follows a different course. Whereas her husband is passive in his initial encounter with evil suggestion, she is aggressive. At the beginning Macbeth pays at least some heed to his doubts; without hesitation his wife invokes demonic aid to transform herself into an unreflective, unfeeling 'Knife' to be employed in the 'Night's great Business' (I.v. 54, 70). Following the murder of Duncan, true to her resolve, she endeavours to prevent Macbeth from considering the deed too deeply: 'What's done is done' (III.ii.12), she says matter-of-factly. But after the Banquet Scene (III.iv), where she makes an admirable attempt to preserve decorum in the face of her husband's agitation on seeing the ghost of Banquo, she largely disappears from view. Macbeth ceases to confide in her, and when at last we look in on her again in the Sleepwalking Scene (V.i), we realize that the madness she has sought to prevent in her husband has taken possession of her instead. The conscience she has tried to thwart now drives her to despair with its insistence that 'What's done cannot be undone' (V.i.76).

Happily, there is more to this dramatic action than the two central figures. While Shakespeare focuses most of our attention on the Macbeths' ruses to escape retribution for their misdeeds, he makes us increasingly aware of another realm beyond the claustrophobic cauldron their castle has become. We see 'Sinful Macduff' roused by the fate of his family to 'Dispute it like a Man' and become a minister of 'the Powres above' (IV.iii.223, 219, 237). We witness Malcolm's emergence as the true scion of a father who had embodied all the 'King-becoming Graces' (IV.iii.91). We receive a much-needed reminder that 'Angels are Bright still, though the Brightest fell' (IV.iii.22). And finally with the removal of the usurper whose name has now become identical with 'Tyrant', we observe that it is still possible for a sick society to purge itself of 'the Evil' (IV.iii.146) and assert, at least for a while, that 'the Time is Free' (V.vii.84).

It is a mark of the modernity of *Macbeth* that any optimism we may feel about the 'Measure, Time, and Place' to be ushered in at Scone (V.vii.102–4) is secured at the price of one of the most wrenching experiences the theatre can afford.

John F. Andrews

THE TEXT OF THE EVERYMAN SHAKESPEARE

Background

THE EARLY PRINTINGS OF SHAKESPEARE'S WORKS

Many of us enjoy our first encounter with Shakespeare when we are introduced to *Julius Caesar* or *Macbeth* at school. It may therefore surprise us that neither of these tragedies could have been read, let alone studied, by most of the playwright's contemporaries. Along with seventeen other titles that never saw print during Shakespeare's lifetime, they made their inaugural appearance as 'literary' works seven years after his death, in the 1623 collection we know today as the First Folio.

The Folio contained thirty-six titles in all. Of these, half had been issued previously in the small paperbacks we now refer to as quartos.* Like several of the plays first published in the Folio, the most trustworthy of the quarto printings appear to have been set either from the dramatist's own manuscripts or from faithful copies of them. It's not impossible that the poet himself prepared some of them for the press, and it's intriguing to imagine him reviewing proof-pages as the words he'd written for actors to speak and embody were being transposed into the type that readers would filter through their eyes, minds, and imaginations. But, alas, there's no indisputable evidence that Shakespeare had any direct involvement with the publication of these early texts of his plays.

What about the plays that appeared in print for the first time in the Folio? Had Shakespeare taken any steps to give them the permanency of book form before he died in 1616? We don't know. All we can say is that when he became fatally ill in 1616,

---

* Quartos derived their name from the four-leaf units of which these small books were comprised: large sheets of paper that had been folded twice after printing to yield four leaves, or eight pages. Folios, volumes with twice the page-size of quartos, were put together from two-leaf units: sheets that had been folded once after printing to yield four pages.

Shakespeare was denied any opportunities he might have taken to ensure that his 'insubstantial Pageants' survived their creator, who was now slipping into the 'dark Backward and Abysm of Time'.

Fortunately, two of the playwright's colleagues felt an obligation, as they put it, 'to procure his Orphans Guardians'. Sometime after Shakespeare's death John Heminge and Henry Condell made arrangements to preserve his plays in a manner that would keep them vibrant for posterity. They dedicated their endeavour to two noblemen who had helped England's foremost acting company through some of its most trying vicissitudes. They solicited several poetic tributes for the volume, among them a now-famous eulogy by fellow writer Ben Jonson. They commissioned a portrait of Shakespeare to adorn the frontispiece. And they did their utmost to display the author's dramatic works in a style that would both dignify them and and make them accessible to 'the great Variety of Readers'.

As they prepared Shakespeare's plays for the compositors who would set them in stately Folio columns, Heminge and Condell (or editors designated to carry out their wishes) revised and augmented many of the entrances, exits, and other stage directions in the manuscripts. They divided most of the plays into acts and scenes.* For a number of plays they appended 'Names of the Actors', or casts of characters. Meanwhile they made every effort to ensure that the Folio printers had reliable copy-texts for each of the titles: authoritative manuscripts for the plays that had not been published previously, and good quarto printings (annotated in some instances to insert staging details, mark script changes, and add supplementary material) for those issued prior to the Folio. For several titles they supplied texts that were substantively different from, if not always demonstrably superior to, the quarto versions that preceded them.

Like even the most accurate of the earlier printings, the Folio collection was flawed by minor blemishes. But it more than fulfilled the purpose of its generous-minded compilers: 'to keep

---

* The early quartos, reflecting the unbroken sequence that probably typified Elizabethan and Jacobean performances of the plays, had been printed without the structural demarcations usual in Renaissance editions of classical drama.

the memory of so worthy a Friend and Fellow alive as was our Shakespeare'. In the process it provided a publishing model that remains instructive today.

MODERN EDITIONS OF THE PLAYS AND POEMS

When we compare the First Folio and its predecessors with the usual modern edition of Shakespeare's works, we're more apt to be impressed by the differences then by the similarities. Today's texts of Renaissance drama are normally produced in conformity with twentieth-century standards of punctuation and usage; as a consequence they look more neat, clean, and, to our eyes, 'right' than do the original printings. Thanks to an editorial tradition that extends back to the early eighteenth century, most of the rough spots in the early printings of Shakespeare have long since been smoothed away. Textual scholars have ferreted out redundancies and eradicated inconsistencies. They have emended what they've perceived to be errors and oversights in the author's playscripts, and they have systematically attended to what they've construed as misreadings by the copyists and compositors who transmitted those playscripts to posterity. They've added '[Within]' brackets and other theatrical notations. They've revised stage directions they've judged incomplete or inadequate in the initial printings. They've regularized disparities in the speech headings. They've gone back to the playwright's sources and reinstated the proper forms for many of the character and place names a presumably hasty or inattentive author got 'wrong' as he conferred identities on his dramatis personae and stage locales. They've replaced obsolete words like *bankrout* with their modern heirs (in this case *bankrupt*). And in a multitude of other ways they've accommodated Shakespeare to the tastes, interests, and expectations of latter-day readers.

The results, on the whole, have been splendid. But interpreting the artistic designs of a complex writer is always problematical, and the task is especially challenging when that writer happens to have been a poet who felt unconstrained by many of the 'rules' that more conventional dramatists respected. The undertaking becomes further complicated when new rules, and new criteria of linguistic and social correctness, are imposed by subsequent generations of artists and critics.

To some degree in his own era, but even more in the neoclassical period (1660–1800) that came in its wake, Shakespeare's most ardent admirers thought it necessary to apologize for what Ben Jonson hinted at in his allusion to the 'small Latin, and less Greek' of an untutored prodigy. To be sure, the 'sweet Swan of Avon' sustained his popularity; in fact his esteem rose so steadily that by the end of the eighteenth century he'd eclipsed Jonson and his other coevals and become the object of universal Bardolatry. But in the theatre most of his plays were being adapted in ways that were deemed advisable to tame their supposed wildness and bring them into conformity with the taste of a society that took pride in its refinement. As one might expect, some of the attitudes that induced theatre proprietors to metamorphose an unpolished poet from the provinces into something closer to an urbane man of letters also influenced Shakespeare's editors. Persuaded that the dramatist's works were marred by crudities that needed expunging, they applied their ministrations to the canon with painstaking diligence.

Twentieth-century editors have moved away from many of the presuppositions that guided a succession of earlier improvers. But a glance at the textual apparatus accompanying virtually any modern edition of the plays and poems will show that emendations and editorial procedures deriving from such forebears as the sets published by Nicholas Rowe (1709), Alexander Pope (1723–25, 1728), Lewis Theobald (1733, 1740, 1757), Thomas Hanmer (1743–45, 1770–71), Samuel Johnson (1765), Edward Capell (1768), and George Steevens (1773) retain a strong hold on today's renderings. The result is a 'Shakespeare' who offers the tidiness we've come to expect in our libraries of classical authors, but not necessarily the playwright a 1599 reader of the Second Quarto of *Romeo and Juliet* would recognize as a contemporary.

OLD LIGHT ON THE TOPIC

Over the last two decades we've learned from art curators that paintings by old Masters such as Michelangelo and Rembrandt look much brighter when centuries of grime are removed from their surfaces – when hues dulled with soot and other extraneous matter are restored to their pristine luminosity. Conductors like Christopher Hogwood have shown the aesthetic rewards to be gained from a return to the scorings and instruments with which Renaissance and Baroque musical compositions were first presented. Twentieth-century experiments in the performance of Shakespeare's plays have shown that an open, multi-level stage analogous to that on which the scripts were originally enacted does more justice to their dramaturgical techniques than does a proscenium auditorium devised for works that came later in the development of Western theatre. And archaeological excavations in London's Bankside have revealed that the foundations of playhouses such as the Rose and the Globe look rather different from what many historians had expected. And we're now learning from a close scrutiny of Shakespeare's texts that they too look different, and function differently, when we accept them for what they are and resist the impulse to 'normalize' features that strike us initially as quirky, unkempt, or unsophisticated.

The Aims that Guide the Everyman Text

Like other modern editions of Shakespeare's plays and poems, *The Everyman Shakespeare* owes an incalculable debt to the scholarship that has led to so many excellent renderings of his works. But in an attempt to draw fresh inspiration from the spirit that animated those remarkable achievements at the outset, the *Everyman* edition departs in a number of respects from the usual post-Folio approach to the presentation of Shakespeare's texts.

RESTORING SOME OF THE NUANCES OF
RENAISSANCE PUNCTUATION

In its punctuation *Everyman* tries to give equal emphasis to sound and sense. In places where Renaissance practice calls for heavier punctuation than we'd normally employ – to mark the caesural pause in the middle of a line of verse, for instance – *Everyman* sometimes retains commas that other modern editions omit. Meanwhile, in places where current practice usually calls for the inclusion of commas – after vocatives and interjections such as 'O' and 'alas', say, or before 'Madam' or 'Sir' in phrases such as 'Ay Madam' or 'Yes Sir' – *Everyman* follows the original printings and omits them.

Occasionally the absence of a comma has a significant bearing on what an expression means, or can mean. At one point in *Othello*, for example, Iago tells The Moor 'Marry patience' (IV.i.90). Inserting a comma after 'Marry', as most of today's editions do, limits Iago's utterance to one that says 'Come now, have patience.' Leaving the clause as it stands in the Folio, the way the *Everyman* text does, permits Iago's words to have the additional, agonizingly ironic sense 'Be wed to Patience'.

The early texts generally deploy, exclamation points quite sparingly, and the *Everyman* text follows suit. *Everyman* also follows the early editions, more often than not, when they use question marks in places that seem unusual by current standards: at the ends of what we'd normally treat as exclamations, for example, or at the ends of interrogative clauses in sentences that we'd ordinarily denote as questions in their entirety.

The early texts make no orthographic distinction between simple plurals and either singular or plural possessives, and there are times when the context doesn't indicate whether a word spelled *Sisters*, say, should be rendered *Sisters*, *Sisters'*, or *Sister's* in today's usage. In such situations the *Everyman* edition prints the words in the form modern usage prescribes for plurals.

REVIVING SOME OF THE FLEXIBILITY OF RENAISSANCE SPELLING

Spelling had not become standardized by Shakespeare's time, which meant that many words could take a variety of forms. Like James Joyce and some of the other innovative prose and verse stylists of our own century, Shakespeare revelled in the freedom a largely unanchored language provided, and with that in mind *Everyman* retains original spelling forms (or adaptations of those forms that preserve their key distinctions from modern spellings) whenever there is any reason to suspect that they might have a bearing on how a word was intended to be pronounced or on what it meant, or could have meant, in Shakespeare's day. When there is any likelihood that multiple forms of the same word could be significant, moreover, the *Everyman* text mirrors the diversity to be found in the original printings.

In many cases this practice affects the personalities of Shakespeare's characters. One of the heroine's most familiar questions in *Romeo and Juliet* is 'What's in a Name?' For two and a half centuries readers – and as a consequence actors, directors, theatre audiences, and commentators – have been led to believe that Juliet was addressing this query to a Romeo named 'Montague'. In fact 'Montague' *was* the name Shakespeare found in his principal source for the play. For reasons that will become apparent to anyone who examines the tragedy in detail, however, he changed his protagonist's surname to 'Mountague', which plays on both 'mount' and 'ague' (fever). Setting aside an editorial practice that began with Lewis Theobald in the middle of the eighteenth century, *Everyman* resurrects the name Shakespeare himself gave Juliet's lover.

Readers of *The Merchant of Venice* in the *Everyman* edition will be amused to learn that the character modern editions usually identify as 'Lancelot' is in reality 'Launcelet', a name that calls attention to the clown's lusty 'little lance'. Like Costard in *Love's Labour's Lost*, another stage bumpkin who was probably played by the actor Will Kemp, Launcelet is an upright 'Member of the Commonwealth'; we eventually learn that he's left a pliant wench 'with Child'.

Readers of *Hamlet* will find that 'Fortinbras' (as the name of the Prince's Norwegian opposite is rendered in the First Folio and in most modern editions) appears in the earlier, authoritative 1604 Second Quarto of the play as 'Fortinbrasse'. In the opening scene of that text a surname that meant 'strong in arms' in French is introduced to the accompaniment of puns on *brazen*, in the phrase 'brazon Cannon', and on *metal*, in the phrase 'unimprooued mettle'. In the same play readers of the *Everyman* text will encounter 'Ostricke', the ostrich-like courtier who invites the Prince of Denmark to participate in the fateful fencing match that draws *Hamlet* to a close. Only in its final entrance direction for the obsequious fop does the Second Quarto call this character 'Osric, the name he bears in all the Folio text's references to him and in most modern editions of Shakespeare's most popular tragedy.

Readers of the *Everyman* text of *Macbeth* will discover that the fabled 'Weird Sisters' appear only as the 'weyward' or 'weyard' Sisters. Shakespeare and his contemporaries knew that in his *Chronicles of England, Scotland, and Ireland* Raphael Holinshed had used the term 'weird sisters' to describe the witches who accost Macbeth and Banquo on the heath; but because he wished to play on *wayward*, the playwright changed their name to *weyward*. Like Samuel Johnson, who thought punning vulgar and lamented Shakespeare's proclivity to seduction by this 'fatal Cleopatra', Lewis Theobald saw no reason to retain the playwright's 'weyward' spelling of the witches' name. He thus restored the 'correct' form from Holinshed, and editors ever since have generally done likewise.

In many instances Renaissance English had a single spelling for what we now define as two separate words. For example, *humane* combined the senses of 'human' and 'humane' in modern English. In the First Folio printing of *Macbeth* the protagonist's wife expresses a concern that her husband is 'too full o'th' Milke of humane kindnesse'. As she phrases it, *humane kindnesse* can mean several things, among them 'humankind-ness', 'human kindness', and 'humane kindness'. It is thus a reminder that to be true to his or her own 'kind' a human being must be 'kind' in the sense we now attach to 'humane'. To disregard this logic, as the protagonist and his wife will soon prove, is to disregard a principle as basic to the cosmos as the laws of gravity.

In a way that parallels *humane*, *bad* could mean either 'bad' or 'bade', *borne* either 'born' or 'borne', *least* either 'least' or 'lest', *lye* either 'lie' or 'lye', *powre* either 'pour' or 'power', *then* either 'than' or 'then', and *tide* either 'tide' or 'tied'.

There were a number of word-forms that functioned in Renaissance English as interchangeable doublets. *Travail* could mean 'travel', for example, and *travel* could mean 'travail'. By the same token *dear* could mean *dear* and vice-versa, *dew* could mean *due*, *hart* could mean *heart*, and (as we've already noted) *mettle* could mean *metal*.

A particularly interesting instance of the equivocal or double meanings some word-forms had in Shakespeare's time is *loose*, which can often become either 'loose' or 'lose' when we render it in modern English. In *The Comedy of Errors* when Antipholus of Syracuse compares himself to 'a Drop / of Water that in the Ocean seeks another Drop' and then says he will 'loose' himself in quest of his long-lost twin, he means both (a) that he will release himself into a vast unknown, and (b) that he will lose his own identity, if necessary, to be reunited with the brother for whom he searches. On the other hand, in *Hamlet* when Polonius says he'll 'loose' his daughter to the Prince, he little suspects that by so doing he will also lose his daughter.

In some cases Shakespeare employs word-forms that can be translated into words we wouldn't think of as related today: *sowre*, for instance, which can mean 'sour', 'sower', or 'sore', depending on the context. In other cases he uses forms that do have modern counterparts, but not counterparts with the same potential for multiple connotation. For example, *onely* usually means 'only' in the modern sense; but occasionally Shakespeare gives it a figurative, adverbial twist that would require a nonce word such as 'one-ly' to replicate in current English.

In a few cases Shakespeare employs word-forms that have only seeming equivalents in modern usage. For example, *abhominable*, which meant 'inhuman' (derived, however incorrectly, from *ab*, 'away from', and *homine*, 'man') to Shakespeare and his contemporaries, is not the same word as our *abominable* (ill-omened, abhorrent). In his advice to the visiting players Hamlet complains about incompetent actors who imitate 'Humanity so abhominably' as to make the characters they depict seem unrecognizable as men. Modern readers who don't realize the distinction between Shakespeare's word and our own, and who see *abominable* on the page before them, don't register the full import of the Prince's satire.

Modern English treats as single words a number of word-forms that were normally spelled as two words in Shakespeare's time. What we render as *myself*, for example, and use primarily as a reflexive or intensifying pronoun, is almost invariably spelled *my self* in Shakespeare's works; so also with *her self*, *thy self*, *your self*, and *it self* (where *it* functions in the way that *its* does today).

Often there is no discernible difference between Shakespeare's usage and our own. At other times there is, however, as we are reminded when we come across a phrase such as 'our innocent self' in *Macbeth* and think how strained it would sound in modern parlance, or when we note how naturally the self is objectified in the balanced clauses of the Balcony Scene in *Romeo and Juliet*:

> Romeo, doffe thy name,
> And for thy name, which is no part of thee,
> Take all my selfe.

Yet another manifestation of the differences between Renaissance orthography and our own can be exemplified with words such as *today*, *tonight* and *tomorrow*, which (unlike *yesterday*) were treated as two words in Shakespeare's time. In *Macbeth* when the Folio prints 'Duncan comes here to Night', the unattached *to* can function either as a preposition (with *Night* as its object, or in this case its destination) or as the first part of an infinitive (with *Night* operating figuratively as a verb). Consider the ambiguity a Renaissance reader would have detected in the original publication of one of the most celebrated soliloquies in all of Shakespeare:

> To morrow, and to morrow, and to morrow,
> Creeps in this petty pace from day to day,
> To the last syllable of Recorded time:
> And to all our yesterdayes, have lighted Fooles
> The way to dusty death.

Here, by implication, the route 'to morrow' is identical with 'the way to dusty death', a relationship we miss if we don't know that for Macbeth, and for the audiences who first heard these lines spoken, *to morrow* was not a single word but a potentially equivocal two-word phrase.

RECAPTURING THE ABILITY TO HEAR WITH OUR EYES

When we fail to recall that Shakespeare's scripts were designed initially to provide words for people to hear in the theatre, we sometimes overlook a fact that is fundamental to the artistic structure of a work like *Macbeth*: that the messages a sequence of sounds convey through the ear are, if anything, even more significant than the messages a sequence of letters, punctuation marks, and white spaces on a printed page transmit through the eye. A telling illustration of this point, and of the potential for ambiguous or multiple implication in any Shakespearean script, may be found in the dethronement scene of *Richard II*. When Henry Bullingbrook asks the king if he is ready to resign his crown, Richard replies 'I, no no I; for I must nothing be.' Here the punctuation in the 1608 Fourth Quarto (the earliest text to print this richly complex passage) permits each *I* to signify either 'ay' or 'I' (*I* being the usual spelling for 'ay' in Shakespeare's time). Understanding *I* to mean 'I' permits additional play on *no*, which can be heard (at least in its first occurrence) as 'know'. Meanwhile the second and third soundings of *I*, if not the first, can also be heard as 'eye'. In the context in which this line occurs, that sense echoes a thematically pertinent passage from Matthew 18:9: 'if thine eye offend thee, pluck it out'.

But these are not all the implications *I* can have here. *I* can also represent the Roman numeral for '1', which will soon be reduced, as Richard notes, to 'nothing' (o), along with the speaker's title, his worldly possessions, his manhood, and eventually his life. In Shakespeare's time, to become 'nothing' was, *inter alia*, to be emasculated, to be made a 'weaker vessel' (1 Peter 3:7) with 'no thing'. As the Fool in *King Lear* reminds another monarch who has abdicated his throne, a man in want of an 'I' is impotent, 'an O without a Figure' (I.iv.207). In addition to its other dimensions, then, Richard's reply is a statement that can be formulated mathematically, and in symbols that anticipate the binary system behind today's computer technology: '1, o, o, 1, for 1 must o be.'

Modern editions usually render Richard's line 'Ay, no; no, ay; for I must nothing be.' Presenting the line in that fashion makes good sense of what Richard is saying. But as we've seen, it doesn't make total sense of it, and it doesn't call attention to Richard's paradoxes in the same way that hearing or seeing three undifferentiated *I*'s is likely to have done for Shakespeare's contemporaries. Their culture was more attuned than ours is to the oral and aural dimensions of language, and if we want to appreciate the special qualities of their dramatic art we need to train ourselves to 'hear' the word-forms we see on the page. We must learn to recognize that for many of what we tend to think of as fixed linkages between sound and meaning (the vowel 'I', say, and the word 'eye'), there were alternative linkages (such as the vowel 'I' and the words 'I' and 'Ay') that could be just as pertinent to what the playwright was communicating through the ears of his theatre patrons at a given moment. As the word *audience* itself may help us to remember, people in Shakespeare's time normally spoke of 'hearing' rather than 'seeing' a play.

In its text of *Richard II*, the *Everyman* edition reproduces the title character's line as it appears in the early printings of the tragedy. Ideally the orthographic oddity of the repeated *I*'s will encourage today's readers to ponder Richard's utterance, and the play it epitomizes, as a characteristically Shakespearean enigma.

OTHER ASPECTS OF THE EVERYMAN TEXT

Now for a few words about other features of the *Everyman* text.

One of the first things readers will notice about this edition is its bountiful use of capitalized words. In this practice as in others, the *Everyman* exemplar is the First Folio, and especially the works in the Folio sections billed as 'Histories' and 'Tragedies'.* *Everyman* makes no attempt to adhere to the Folio printings with literal exactitude. In some instances the Folio capitalizes words that the *Everyman* text of the same passage lowercases; in other instances *Everyman* capitalizes words not uppercased in the Folio. The objective is merely to suggest something of the flavour, and what appears to have been the rationale, of Renaissance capitalization, in the hope that today's audiences will be made continually aware that the works they are contemplating derive from an earlier epoch.

* The quarto printings employ far fewer capital letters than does the Folio. Capitalization seems to have been regarded as a means of recognizing the status ascribed to certain words (*Noble*, for example, is almost always capitalized), titles (not only King, Queen, Duke, and Duchess, but Sir and Madam), genres (tragedies were regarded as more 'serious' than comedies in more than one sense), and forms of publication (quartos, being associated with ephemera such as 'plays', were not thought to be as 'grave' as the folios that bestowed immortality on 'works', writings that, in the words of Ben Johnson's eulogy of Shakespeare, were 'not of an age, but for all time').

Readers will also notice that instead of cluttering the text with stage directions such as '[Aside]' or '[To Rosse]', the *Everyman* text employs unobtrusive dashes to indicate shifts in mode of address. In an effort to keep the page relatively clear of words not supplied by the original printings, *Everyman* also exercises restraint in its addition of editor-generated stage directions. Where the dialogue makes it obvious that a significant action occurs, the *Everyman* text inserts a square-bracketed phrase such as '[Fleance escapes.]'. Where what the dialogue implies is subject to differing interpretations, however, the *Everyman* text provides a facing-page note to discuss the most plausible inferences.

Like other modern editions, the *Everyman* text combines into 'shared' verse lines (lines divided among two or more speakers) many of the part-lines to be found in the early publications of the plays. One exception to the usual modern procedure is that *Everyman* indents some lines that are not components of shared verses. At times, for example, the opening line of a scene stops short of the metrical norm, a pentameter (five-foot) or hexameter (six-foot) line comprised predominantly of iambic units (unstressed syllables followed by stressed ones). In such cases *Everyman* uses indentation as a reminder that scenes can begin as well as end in mid-line (an extension of the ancient convention that an epic commences *in medias res*, 'in the midst of the action'). *Everyman* also uses indentation to reflect what appear to be pauses in the dialogue, either to allow other activity to transpire (as happens in *Macbeth*, II.iii.87, when a brief line 'What's the Business?' follows a Folio stage direction that reads 'Bell rings. Enter Lady.') or to permit a character to hesitate for a moment of reflection (as happens a few seconds later in the same scene when Macduff responds to a demand to 'Speak, speak' with the reply 'O gentle Lady, / 'Tis not for you to hear what I can speak').

Everyman preserves many of the anomalies in the early texts. Among other things, this practice pertains to the way characters are depicted. In *A Midsummer Night's Dream*, the ruler of Athens is usually identified in speech headings and stage directions as 'Theseus', but sometimes he is referred to by his title as 'Duke'. In the same play Oberon's merry sprite goes by two different names: 'Puck' and 'Robin Goodfellow'.

Readers of the *Everyman* edition will sometimes discover that characters they've known, or known about, for years don't appear in the original printings. When they open the pages of the *Everyman* edition of *Macbeth*, for example, they'll learn that Shakespeare's audiences were unaware of any woman with the title 'Lady Macbeth'. In the only authoritative text we have of the Scottish tragedy, the protagonist's spouse goes by such names as 'Macbeth's Lady', 'Macbeth's Wife', or simply 'Lady', but nowhere is she listed or mentioned as 'Lady Macbeth'. The same is true of the character usually designated 'Lady Capulet' in modern editions of *Romeo and Juliet*. 'Capulet's Wife' makes appearances as 'Mother', 'Old Lady', 'Lady', or simply 'Wife'; but she is never called 'Lady Capulet', and her husband never treats her with the dignity such a title would connote.

Rather than 'correct' the grammar in Shakespeare's works to eliminate what modern usage would categorize as solecisms (as when Mercutio says 'my Wits faints' in *Romeo and Juliet*), the *Everyman* texts leaves it intact. Among other things, this principle applies to instances in which archaic forms preserve idioms that differ slightly from related modern expressions (as in the clause 'you are too blame', where 'too' functions as an adverb and 'blame' is used, not as a verb, but as an adjective roughly equivalent to 'blameworthy').

Finally, and most importantly, the *Everyman* edition leaves unchanged any reading in the original text that is not manifestly erroneous. Unlike other modern renderings of Shakespeare's works, *Everyman* substitutes emendations only when obvious problems can be resolved by obvious solutions.

The *Everyman* Text of *Macbeth*

Our only textual authority for *Macbeth* is the version of the play that appeared in the 1623 First Folio. Most scholars believe that the printers' copy for the Folio text was either a theatre promptbook or a manuscript that closely reflected the author's own hand.

The *Everyman* text produces the act and scene divisions supplied by the editors of the First Folio. Most of today's editions divide into three scenes (V.vii, V.iii, V.ix) what the Folio prints as Act V, scene vii; the *Everyman* text leaves V.vii as it appears in the Folio.

In a handful of instances the *Everyman* edition adopts the emendations to be found in other modern texts. In II.iii.38, 39, for example, *Everyman* alters the Folio's 'to' to 'too'. In III.ii.43, *Everyman* alters 'born' to 'borne'; in III.vi.24 it alters 'Sonnes' to 'Son'; in IV.ii.40 it alters 'by' to 'buy'; in IV.iii.133 it alters 'they' to 'thy'; in IV.iii.160 it alters 'nor' to 'not'; and in V.i.1 it alters 'too' to 'two'. In many passages the *Everyman* text makes slight modifications in the Folio's punctuation. In a number of instances, moreover, and not always in ways that coincide with the practice of other modern editions, the *Everyman* text alters the verse alignment to be found in the Folio printing.

Of far more moment than what *Everyman* alters, however, is what it leaves unaltered. Most of the *Everyman* readings that depart from the usual modern renderings of the text are discussed in the facing-page notes to this edition. For an important one that isn't, let's focus on the Folio printing of one of Macbeth's most critical soliloquies (I.vii.2–10).

> If th' Assassination
> Could trammel vp the Consequence, and catch
> With his surcease, Successe: that but this blow
> Might be the be all, and the end all. Heere,
> But heere, vpon this Banke and Schoole of time,
> Weel'd iumpe the life to come. But in these Cases,
> We still have iudgement heere, that we but teach
> Bloody Instructions, which being taught, returne
> To plague th'Inuenter.

Since Theobald's texts in the middle of the eighteenth century, virtually all editions have emended 'Schoole' to 'shoal', assuming that Macbeth is referring to a treacherous shallow, a sandbar near the bank of a river. That is almost certainly an aspect of what Macbeth is thinking about, but the third sentence in this passage makes it clear that he is also pondering the kind of 'Schoole' and 'Banke' (bench) that one connects with a room to 'teach' various kinds of 'Instructions.'

As it happens, the words *school* and *shoal* were comparable to such pairings as *travail* and *travel* in Shakespeare's day: they were not the readily distinguishable words that they have become since the seventeenth century. As evidence we need go no farther than to what modern dictionaries list as one definition of *shoal*: 'school' in the sense that pertains to a school of fish. *School* and *shoal* could have been pronounced interchangeably in Renaissance England. And their subsequent histories will probably seem less mysterious if we consider what's happened to *schedule*, a word that is now pronounced 'shedule' in the United Kingdom and 'skedule' in the United States.

A spelling that editors for the last two centuries have perceived as marking a distinction, then (the meaning, if not the sounds, of *school*, as opposed to those now associated with *shoal*), would probably have been taken for granted in the playwright's time as simply another word-form with a range of possibilities that extended beyond what later English usage would permit to it.

So what is a modern edition to do in a case such as this? Here as elsewhere, the *Everyman* text takes the easy route: it merely retains the spelling form that occurs in the earliest authoritative printing of Shakespeare's play.

In the selection of instances that follow, the *Everyman* text preserves Folio readings in ways that set it apart from most modern editions of *Macbeth*. For each passage the first entry, set in boldface type, is the *Everyman* reading; the second is the emendation usually adopted in today's editions. For some word-forms that occur more than once, this list records only the initial instance.

I.i.4 **Battaile's** battle's
I.ii.3 **Serieant** sergeant 13 **Gallowgrosses** gallowglasses 14 **Quarry** quarry 15 **Shew'd** Show'd 21 **bad** bade 26 **Thunders** thunders breaking
I.iii.24 **tost** toss'd 30 **weyward** weird 37 **soris** Forres 46 **hail** hail, 55 **wrapt** rapt 89 **Rebels** rebels' *or* rebel's 94 **make** make, 95 **Death**, death. 96 **Can** came 98 **powr'd** pour'd 100 **Onely** only 100 **harrold** herald 109 **loose** lose 133 **Heir** hair
I.iv.1 **Or** Are 45 **Herbenber** harbinger
I.v.19 **Humane** human 27 **High** Hie 28 **powre** pour 30 **impeides** impedes 33 **to Night** tonight 49 **Hit** it 65 **Matters, to beguile the Time** matters: to beguile the time, 72 **Masterdome** masterdom

I.vi.0 S.D. **Hoboys** hautboys **4 Barlet** martlet **5 Mansonry** mansionry **6 Jutty Frieze** jutty, frieze **9 must** most **18 Maiesty** majesty **19 Ermites** hermits **25 ever,** ever

I.vii.5 **End-all. Here** end-all, here **6 School** shoal **21 borne** born **22 Cherubin** cherubins **23 Curriors** curriers **28 other** other – **43 Esteem?** esteem, **47 no** do **68 lyes** lies

II.i.54 **Sides** strides **55 sowre** sure **56 they may** way they **62 Knell** knell

II.ii.13 **Husband?** husband! **14 schream** scream **17 I** Ay **34 Sleeve** sleave **53 guild** gild **55 appalls** appals **59 incarnadine** incarnadine **60 Green one, Red** green one red **66 then?** then! **59 least** lest

II.iii.18 **rost** roast **23 anon, I** anon! I **25 lye** lie **67 fevorous** feverous **85 Sprights** sprites

II.iv.7 **travailing** travelling **16 flong** flung **21 Why** Why, **28 raven** ravin **37 Wall may** Well, may

III.i.68 **Seeds** seed **69 come Fate** come, Fate, **74 Speeches:** speeches? **77 self.** self? **78 past** pass'd **92 clipt** clept **109 spight** spite

III.ii.7 **then** than

III.iii.7 **end** and **16 Rayne** rain

III.iv.8 **Harts'** hearts' **13 then** than **56 I** Ay **57 Divel** Devil **76 Times** time **89 him we thirst** him, we thirst **102 Desart** desert **142 indeed** in deed

III.v.2 **are?** are, **26 slights** sleights **32 Mortals** mortals' **38 their** the

IV.i.18 **powreful** powerful **23 Witches** witch's **24 salt Sea** salt-sea **43 Inchanting** Enchanting **46 Open Locks** Open, locks **50 ere** e'er **58 Germain** germens **58 altogether** all together **62 Masters** masters' **67 deaftly** deftly **79 borne** born **81 live Macduff** live, Macduff **97 Byrnan** Birnam **97 high plac'd** high-plac'd **118 Eight** eighth **129 Antique** antic **140 Word:** word

IV.ii.10 **diminitive** diminutive **14 Cooz** Cuz **41 withal** with all **65 thus – Me thinks** thus, methinks **68 Whether** Whither **79 Shag-ear'd** shag-hair'd

IV.iii.4 **Birthdome** birthdom **15 discern** deserve **34 affear'd** affeer'd **107 accust** accus'd *or* accurs'd **110 Knees, then** knees than **234 Time** tune

V.i.29 **I** Ay **43 fear? Who** fear who

V.ii.1 **Powre** power **10 unruff** unrough **28 pour we in** pour we, in **64 Ones** ones

V.iii.21 **dis-eat** dis-seat **26 steed** stead **39 Cure of** Cure her of **52 pristive** pristine **57 I** Ay

V.v.2 **still, they come.** still 'They come!' **49 Bell, blow** Bell! Blow

V.vi.4 **Battell** battle

V.vii.6 **hoter** hotter

MACBETH

NAMES OF THE ACTORS

DUNCAN [Duncane], King of Scotland

MALCOLM
DONALBAIN
} Duncan's Sons

MACBETH
BANQUO
} Generals of the King's Army

MACDUFF
LENOX
ROSSE
MENTETH
ANGUS
CATHNESS
} Noblemen of Scotland

FLEANCE, Son to Banquo

SEYWARD, Earl of Northumberland,
General of the English Army

YOUNG SEYWARD, his Son

SEYTON, an Officer attending on Macbeth

MACBETH'S LADY

MACDUFF'S LADY

BOY, Son to Macduff

THREE WITCHES, the Weyward Sisters
HECAT
Three other WITCHES
APPARITIONS

CAPTAIN [Serieant]
PORTER
OLD MAN
Three MURDERERS
ENGLISH DOCTOR
SCOTTISH DOCTOR
GENTLEWOMAN, attending on Macbeth's Lady

LORDS
GENTLEMEN
OFFICERS
SOLDIERS
ATTENDANTS
MESSENGERS

4

I.i   The play opens at some unspecified setting in Scotland.

3   **Hurly-burly** tumultuous conflict; 'Broil' or battle (I.ii.6).
       Battaile both (a) army (battalion), and (b) battle.

4   **lost and won** lost by one side, won by the other. The Witch's
       phrasing also hints that in some sense the outcome of 'the
       Battle' may be ambiguous: it may be 'lost' by those who
       appear to win, and 'won' by those who appear to lose. The
       same notion is implicit in 'Fair is Foul, and Foul is Fair' (line
       9) and in the phrase 'Doubtful it stood' (I.ii.7).

6   **Heath** an expanse covered only by heather and other small
       shrubs.

8   **I come** The wording in the Folio could be interpreted to mean
       either (a) '[Yes,] I'm coming', or (b) 'Ay, come'. What modern
       editions render as *ay* is almost always spelled *I* in the early
       texts.
       Gray-Malkin grey cat. The Witch is probably addressing her
       familiar (a demonic spirit in the form of a cat).
       Padock toad (another familiar).
       anon immediately, right away. What the Witches probably
       mean is that Padock calls 'Anon', telling the Witches to come
       with him. Most editors reassign 'Padock calls' to the Second
       Witch, and 'anon' to the Third Witch.

9   **Fair . . . Fair** what appears beautiful and good is ugly and evil,
       and vice versa. This line anticipates Macbeth's observation
       about the weather in I.iii.36. It also introduces one of the
       major themes of the tragedy.

I.ii   This scene takes place at or near the King's military camp in
       Scotland.

S.D.   **Alarum within** a trumpet call to arms, sounded off stage.

2   **Revolt** rebellion against the King's authority.

3   **Serieant** sergeant. The Folio spelling suggests that the word is
       here to be pronounced with three syllables, and possibly with
       an *i* or *y* rather than a *j* sound; compare *Norweyan* (line 31).
       Originally, *sergeant* meant 'servant', and in Shakespeare's
       time the designation was compatible with the title 'Captain'
       (line 7).

5   **'Gainst my Captivity** to prevent my being taken.

ACT I

Scene 1

Thunder and Lightning. Enter three Witches.

1 WITCH   When shall we three meet again?
  In Thunder, Lightning, or in Rain?
2 WITCH   When the Hurly-burly's done,
  When the Battaile's lost and won.
3 WITCH   That will be ere the set of Sun.   5
1 WITCH   Where's the place?
2 WITCH   Upon the Heath.
3 WITCH   There to meet with Macbeth.
1 WITCH   I come, Gray-Malkin.
ALL   Padock calls anon.
  Fair is Foul, and Foul is Fair;
  Hover through the Fog and filthy Air.   *Exeunt.*   10

Scene 2

*Alarum within. Enter King, Malcolm, Donalbain, Lenox, with
Attendants, meeting a bleeding Captain.*

KING   What Bloody Man is that? He can report,
  As seemeth by his Plight, of the Revolt
  The newest State.
MALCOLM   This is the Serieant,
  Who like a good and hardy Soldier fought
  'Gainst my Captivity. – Hail, brave Friend: 5
  Say to the King the knowledge of the Broil
  As thou didst leave it.

9 **choke their Art** keep each other from swimming effectively. Later Macbeth and his Lady will 'cling together' in a way that illustrates this line.

10 **to that** to that end; in keeping with that purpose.

11–12 **The . . . him** Here *multiplying* suggests 'procreative' or 'rapidly reproducing'; and *swarm upon him* hints at both (a) multiple demon possession, and (b) the swarming of flies or hornets (the forces 'suppli'd' to Macdonwald).

13 **Kerns** Irish footsoldiers with light weapons and armour.
Gallowgrosses gross (sizeable and numerous) galloglasses; soldiers armed with battle-axes.

14 **Fortune . . . smiling** Fortune now smiling (like a fickle whore) on the quarry it has marked as its victim for damnation (if *his* means 'its', as it often does). Most editors substitute *quarrel* for the Folio's *quarry*. *Shew'd* means 'showed'.

18 **smok'd . . . Execution** steamed with blood from its work.

19 **Minion** favourite, darling.

21 **Which** either (a) Macbeth (if *which* means 'who'), or (b) Macbeth's sword. *Bad* (line 21) means 'bade'.

22 **unseam'd . . . Chops** opened up a seam from the navel to the jaws. Compare *seem'd* (line 27, echoing lines 2, 48).

25–28 **As . . . swells** Just as a red Sunrise disperses ('shipwrecks') storms and deadly thunder [but portends more of the same], so from the same source that promised comfort we received discomfort instead. The Captain appears to be alluding to the proverb 'Red sky at morning, sailor's warning'. For those loyal to the King, Macbeth's bloody emergence was a welcome relief, one that spelled doom for the rebellious Macdonwald; but it soon gave way to a new 'Discomfort' that swelled up like another storm.

31 **surveying Vantage** looking over the situation and seeing an opening.

32 **furbish'd** polished; new or refurbished.

33 **Dismay'd** both (a) intimidated and (b) debilitated (literally, 'deprived of might').

35 **As Sparrows Eagles** as much as sparrows frighten eagles.

CAPTAIN   Doubtful it stood,
  As two spent Swimmers that do cling together
  And choke their Art. The merciless Macdonwald
  (Worthy to be a Rebel, for to that   10
  The multiplying Villainies of Nature
  Do swarm upon him) from the Western Isles
  Of Kerns and Gallowgrosses is suppli'd,
  And Fortune, on his damned Quarry smiling,
  Shew'd like a Rebel's Whore. But all's too
      weak: 15
  For Brave Macbeth (well he deserves that Name),
  Disdaining Fortune, with his brandish'd Steel,
  Which smok'd with bloody Execution
  (Like Valor's Minion), carv'd out his Passage
  Till he fac'd the Slave,   20
  Which nev'r shook Hands, nor bad Farewell to
      him,
  Till he unseam'd him from the Nave to th' Chops,
  And fix'd his Head upon our Battlements.
KING   O valiant Cousin, worthy Gentleman.
CAPTAIN   As whence the Sun 'gins his Reflection,   25
  Shipwracking Storms, and direful Thunders,
  So from that Spring, whence Comfort seem'd to
      come,
  Discomfort swells: mark, King of Scotland,
      mark,
  No sooner Justice had, with Valour arm'd,
  Compell'd these skipping Kerns to trust their
      Heels   30
  But the Norweyan Lord, surveying Vantage,
  With furbish'd Arms and new Supplies of Men,
  Began a fresh Assault.
KING   Dismay'd not this
  Macbeth and Banquo?
CAPTAIN   Yes,
  As Sparrows Eagles, or the Hare the Lion.   35

36 **say sooth** speak truly.

37 **As ... Cracks** like cannons loaded with double rounds of firepower.

39-40 **Except ... Golgotha** unless they intended to bathe themselves in blood or make the field as memorable as Golgotha (Calvary), 'the place of a skull' (Mark 15:22).

43 **So ... Wounds** your words adorn you as much as do your wounds.

45 **Thane** an ancient Anglo-Saxon title for a knight or baron who held lands and in exchange provided military services for the King (compare V.vii.91–93).

47 **that seems to** who appears ready to. See lines 2, 22, 27.

51 **fan ... cold** fan, and thus cool, the heat of our men's courage. Compare *Antony and Cleopatra*, II.ii.207–10.

52 **terrible** terrifying.

54 **a dismal Conflict** an ominous assault. See III.v.21.

55 **Bellona's Bridegroom** the new husband of the Goddess of War (here referring to Macbeth).
lapp'd in Proof enfolded in armour of proven mettle.

56 **Self-comparisons** a self that defied and matched (compared with) him in every respect. Like 'rebellious Arm' (line 57), this image hints at more equivalence than the speaker intends; it suggests that Macbeth has the potential to be 'disloyal' too.

58 **Curbing ... Spirit** restraining his overweening ambition.

If I say sooth, I must report they were
As Cannons over-charg'd with double Cracks,
So they doubly redoubled Strokes upon the Foe.
Except they meant to bathe in reeking Wounds,
Or memorize another Golgotha,   40
I cannot tell; But I am Faint,
My Gashes cry for help.

KING   So well thy Words become thee as thy
   Wounds:
They smack of Honour both. – Go get him Surgeons.

                              [*Exit Captain, attended.*]

                  Enter Rosse and Angus.

– Who comes here?

MALCOLM   The worthy Thane of Rosse.   45

LENOX   What a Haste looks through his Eyes?
   So should he look that seems to speak things
      strange.

ROSSE   God save the King.

KING   Whence cam'st thou, worthy Thane?

ROSSE   From Fife, great King,
   Where the Norweyan Banners flout the Sky   50
   And fan our People cold.
   Norway himself, with terrible Numbers,
   Assisted by that most disloyal Traitor,
   The Thane of Cawdor, began a dismal Conflict,
   Till that Bellona's Bridegroom, lapp'd in
      Proof,   55
   Confronted him with Self-comparisons,
   Point against Point, rebellious Arm 'gainst
      Arm,
   Curbing his lavish Spirit; and to conclude,
   The Victory fell on us.

KING   Great Happiness.

60 **craves Composition** begs for terms that will resolve the conflict. The literal meaning of *Composition* is 'putting together'.

61 **deign** condescend to allow.

62 **Saint Colme's Inch** Inchcolm, an island in the Firth of Forth.

63 **Dollars** a denomination in use in Norway from the early years of the sixteenth century. Dollars or their equivalent were also to be found in Spain and Germany in Shakespeare's time. Compare *The Tempest*, II.i.14–18, where *Dollar* plays on *Dolor*.

64–65 **No . . . Interest** No longer shall that Thane of Cawdor deceive me in those matters that are closest to my heart. Subsequent developments will render these words ironic.

66 **pronounce . . . Death** sentence him to immediate execution.

69 **What . . . won** The King's words echo the Witch's reference to a battle that is 'lost and won' (I.i.4). They also hint that Macbeth has inherited all that goes with the 'former Title' of 'that Thane of Cawdor'. Compare lines 52–58.

I.iii We now meet the Witches on the 'Heath' referred to in I.i.6.

4 **mounch'd** munched.

5 **Aroint** avaunt; begone.
   Rump-fed Ronyon swine-fattened scab of a person.

6 **Aleppo** a city in Turkey. Compare *Othello*, V.ii.346.
   Master . . . Tiger captain of the ship known as the *Tiger*.

9 **I'll do** I'll perform my mischief. The Witch pledges to avenge herself on the Sailor's Wife by afflicting the woman's husband at sea. It was commonly believed that Witches could use sieves as boats. Witches were also credited with the ability to inhabit animals such as rats, usually deforming them in the process. Compare I.i.8.

13 **have . . . other** will control all the remaining winds.

ROSSE   That now Sweno, the Norways' King, craves
  Composition: 60
 Nor would we deign him Burial of his Men
 Till he disbursed, at Saint Colme's Inch,
 Ten thousand Dollars to our general use.
KING No more that Thane of Cawdor shall deceive
 Our Bosom Interest.   65
 Go pronounce his present Death,
 And with his former Title greet Macbeth.
ROSSE I'll see it done.
KING What he hath lost, Noble Macbeth hath won.
             Exeunt.

Scene 3

Thunder. Enter three Witches.

1 WITCH Where hast thou been, Sister?
2 WITCH   Killing Swine.
3 WITCH Sister, where thou?
1 WITCH A Sailor's Wife had Chestnuts in her Lap,
 And mounch'd, and mounch'd, and mounch'd.
  'Give me,' quoth I.
 'Aroint thee, Witch,' the Rump-fed Ronyon
  cries.   5
 Her Husband's to Aleppo gone, Master o' th'
  Tiger;
 But in a Sieve I'll thither sail
 And like a Rat without a Tail
 I'll do, I'll do, and I'll do.
2 WITCH I'll give thee a Wind.   10
1 WITCH Th'art kind.
3 WITCH And I another.
1 WITCH I my self have all the other,

14 **And ... blow** as well as the seaports from which they blow [thereby preventing ships from entering them].

15 **All ... know** all the directions from which they come.

16 **Card** both (a) chart (navigating map), and (b) compass.

17 **drain him** deprive him of fresh water [by keeping his ship at sea] and enervate him.

19 **Penthouse Lid** eyelid (here likened to the sloping roof of a penthouse). Lines 18–19 will be echoed in II.ii.32–37.

20 **Forbid** both (a) prohibited from arriving safely on land, and (b) under a spell or curse. Compare line 44.

22 **peak** grow peaked; become emaciated; 'pine'.

23 **Though ... lost** though we do not have the power to destroy his boat completely. Compare I.i.4 and I.ii.69.

30 **weyward** both (a) wayward (lawless, evil and misleading), and (b) fatal (from the Anglo-Saxon *wyrd*, which meant 'fate' or 'destiny'). Later the word will be spelled *weyard*. Modern editions normally print *weird*.

31 **Posters of** swift journeyers over. As they speak lines 30–35 the Sisters turn 'about' in a pattern that will 'make up nine' and thus wind up (put into effect) the 'Charm' they cast for Macbeth.

36 **Foul and Fair** both (a) changeable, and (b) combining opposing features. Compare I.i.9.

3? **call'd** said to be.
Soris Most editors emend to *Forres*, the Scottish castle referred to at this point in Holinshed's *Chronicles of England, Scotland, and Ireland*.

40 **aught** anything.

42 **choppy** both (a) cracked, chapped, and (b) skinny and angular. *Forbid* (line 44) echoes line 20.

And the very Ports they blow,
All the Quarters that they know,   15
I' th' Shipman's Card.
I'll drain him dry as Hay;
Sleep shall neither Night nor Day
Hang upon his Penthouse Lid.
He shall live a Man Forbid: 20
Weary Sev'nnights, nine times nine,
Shall he dwindle, peak, and pine.
Though his Bark cannot be lost,
Yet it shall be Tempest-tost.
Look what I have.
2 WITCH   Shew me, shew me.   25
1 WITCH   Here I have a Pilot's Thumb,
Wrack'd as Homeward he did come.   *Drum within.*
3 WITCH   A Drum, a Drum:
Macbeth doth come.
ALL   The weyward Sisters, Hand in Hand,   30
Posters of the Sea and Land,
Thus do go, about, about,
Thrice to thine, and thrice to mine,
And thrice again, to make up nine.
Peace, the Charm's wound up.   35

       Enter Macbeth and Banquo.

MACBETH   So Foul and Fair a Day I have not seen.
BANQUO   How far is't call'd to Soris? What are these,
So Wither'd and so Wild in their Attire,
That look not like th' Inhabitants o' th' Earth
And yet are on't? – Live you, or are you aught   40
That Man may question? You seem to understand
   me,
By each at once her choppy Finger laying
Upon her skinny Lips. You should be Women,
And yet your Beards forbid me to interpret
That you are so.

46 **hail** both (a) salute, greet, and (b) health (from a related Anglo-Saxon word, *hale*, that means 'whole'). Most editors place commas after this word; but there are ambiguities in the original phrasing that become obscured when commas are added. Among other things, the First Witch's greeting may mean 'Let all salute Macbeth' (or 'Everyone salutes Macbeth'), or 'health to you as Thane of Glamis' (Macbeth's present title). Compare I.ii.67.

49 **start** react involuntarily, act startled.

50 **Fair** (a) good, (b) beautiful, and (c) favourable. Compare I.i.9 and I.iii.36. *Fair* echoes *fear* (line 49).

51 **Fantastical** imaginary; the product of our fantasies.

52 **shew** show; appear to be. But *shew* can also mean 'display' and 'eschew' (shun, avoid). Compare I.ii.14–15.

53 **Grace** favour (as distinguished from Providence).

54 **Noble Having** noble possessions. Banquo refers to the two titles attributed to Macbeth in lines 46–47.

55 **wrapt withal** both (a) clothed in, and (b) rapt (in a reverie) over. Compare line 140; also see I.ii.55.

58–59 **who . . . Hate** What Banquo says discriminates him from Macbeth, whose 'start' *does* suggest 'fear' (line 49), and who *will* later 'beg' the Witches' 'Favours'.

64 **Not . . . Happier** The Witch's words play ambiguously on two senses of *happy*: (a) fortunate in worldly 'Having' (line 54), and (b) blessed by Heaven (that is, truly fortunate).

65 **get** beget; be the progenitor of.

68 **imperfect** incomplete; riddling, equivocal in potential meaning. *Imperfect* can also refer to actors or 'Speakers' who have not completely mastered their lines and thus deliver them haltingly, incorrectly, or fragmentarily.

69 **Sinel** Macbeth's father.

MACBETH   Speak if you can: what are you?   45

1 WITCH   All hail Macbeth, hail to thee Thane of
    Glamis.

2 WITCH   All hail Macbeth, hail to thee Thane of
    Cawdor.

3 WITCH   All hail Macbeth, that shalt be King
    hereafter.

BANQUO   Good Sir, why do you start, and seem to
    fear
  Things that do sound so Fair? – I' th' name of
    Truth,   50
  Are ye Fantastical, or that indeed
  Which outwardly ye shew? My Noble Partner
  You greet with present Grace and great
    Prediction
  Of Noble Having and of Royal Hope,
  That he seems wrapt withal; to me you speak
    not.   55
  If you can look into the Seeds of Time
  And say which Grain will grow and which will
    not,
  Speak then to me, who neither beg nor fear
  Your Favours nor your Hate.

1 WITCH   Hail.   60

2 WITCH   Hail.

3 WITCH   Hail.

1 WITCH   Lesser than Macbeth, and Greater.

2 WITCH   Not so Happy, yet much Happier.

3 WITCH   Thou shalt get Kings, though thou be
    none.   65
  So all hail Macbeth and Banquo.

1 WITCH   Banquo and Macbeth, all hail.

MACBETH   Stay, you imperfect Speakers, tell me
    more.
  By Sinel's death, I know I am Thane of Glamis;
  But how of Cawdor? The Thane of Cawdor lives   70

71 **prosperous** healthy, prospering. Evidently Macbeth does not yet know of Cawdor's treason, or of what has happened to the Thane.

72 **Stands . . . Belief** is no more credible. The literal meaning of *Prospect* is 'forward looking'. Macbeth's phrasing hints at the kinds of 'standing up' that will become associated with two manifestations of the proud human will: (a) the passions rebelling against reason, and (b) political insurrection.

73 **No** Modern usage would call for *any* here.

74 **owe** both (a) own, possess, and (b) are indebted for.
strange Here, as is often the case in Shakespeare, *strange* has numinous implications: it hints at that which inspires awe.

75 **blasted** blighted, barren; cursed.

79 **Corporal melted** physical dissolved. *Corporal* anticipates I.vii.80.

82 **the Insane Root** the kind of root that induces insanity. Macbeth is probably thinking of hemlock or henbane. But audiences familiar with 1 Timothy 6: 1–10 might also have heard an echo of the warning that 'the love of money is the root of all evil'. The biblical admonition occurs in a passage that warns against all forms of covetousness (love of 'gain'), including those that tempt servants to rebel against their masters. It reminds believers to be 'content' with 'food and raiment'. For 'they that will be rich fall into temptation and a snare, and into many foolish and hurtful lusts, which drown men in destruction and perdition.' Compare IV.iii.76–86.

88 **Success** victory in the recent battle. Rosse's words are a reminder that Macbeth has just learned of even more 'Success' (and succession) to come.

89 **Thy . . . Fight** what you did personally in the fight against the rebels. Again Rosse's phrasing can be interpreted in a way that links Macbeth with 'the Rebels Fight'; compare I.ii.52–58. *Contend* echoes I.ii.7–9, 25–33, 52–58.

93 **in . . . Ranks** in the midst of the mighty enemy forces.

94–95 **Nothing . . . Death** not at all frightened of those whom you turned into disfigured, dead images of their living selves.

95–96 **as thick . . . with post** as rapidly as witnesses with reports of your feats can ride post-horses post-haste. Compare line 31.

A prosperous Gentleman; and to be King
Stands not within the Prospect of Belief
No more than to be Cawdor. Say from whence
You owe this strange Intelligence, or why
Upon this blasted Heath you stop our Way   75
With such prophetic Greeting. Speak, I charge
   you.   *Witches vanish.*
BANQUO   The Earth hath Bubbles as the Water
   has,
And these are of them. Whither are they
   vanish'd?
MACBETH   Into the Air: and what seem'd Corporal
   melted,
As Breath into the Wind. Would they had stay'd.   80
BANQUO   Were such things here as we do speak
   about?
Or have we eaten on the Insane Root
That takes the Reason Prisoner?
MACBETH   Your Children shall be Kings.
BANQUO   You shall be King.
MACBETH   And Thane of Cawdor too: went it not so?   85
BANQUO   To th' self-same Tune, and Words.

Enter Rosse and Angus.

                   Who's here?
ROSSE   The King hath happily receiv'd, Macbeth,
The News of thy Success; and when he reads
Thy personal Venture in the Rebels Fight,
His Wonders and his Praises do contend   90
Which should be thine or his. Silenc'd with
   that
In viewing o'er the rest o' th' self-same Day
He finds thee in the stout Norweyan Ranks
Nothing afeard of what thy self didst make
Strange Images of Death, as thick as Tale   95

98   **powr'd**   poured. But this spelling form could also be used for 'powered'. Compare I.v.28, IV.i.18.

100   **onely**   only, solely. So also in I.iv.20.
        harrold   both (a) herald, and (b) harrow (plead for).

102   **Earnest**   down payment, foretaste.

104   **Addition**   title. Compare *Othello*, III.iv.184.

106–7 **dress . . . Robes**   invest me in apparel that belongs to someone else. Compare lines 52–55, 142–44.

107   **Who**   he who.

109   **loose**   both (a) lose, and (b) loosen and discard.
        combin'd   in league; conspiring. Compare I.ii.60.

110   **line**   support. Here *line* hints at both (a) the lining that reinforces a garment, and (b) the lining of a person's pockets with money.

112   **Wrack**   wreck, destruction. Compare I.ii.25–28.

115   **behind**   beyond; yet to come.

118   **trusted home**   allowed to be thrust as far as it will go.

119   **enkindle**   enflame, incite, provoke.

121   **to win . . . Harm**   to persuade us to do what is harmful to us. Lines 118–24 may be spoken in soliloquy.

123   **honest Trifles**   trivial truths. Compare the phrasing in *Othello*, III.iii.312–14.

Came post with post, and every one did bear
Thy Praises in his Kingdom's great Defence,
And powr'd them down before him.

ANGUS   We are sent
To give thee, from our Royal Master, Thanks,
Onely to harrold thee into his Sight,   100
Not pay thee.

ROSSE   And for an Earnest of a greater Honour,
He bad me, from him, call thee Thane of Cawdor,
In which Addition hail, most worthy Thane,
For it is thine.

BANQUO   — What, can the Devil speak true?   105

MACBETH   The Thane of Cawdor lives: why do you
    dress me
In borrowed Robes?

ANGUS   Who was the Thane lives yet,
But under heavy Judgement bears that Life
Which he deserves to loose. Whether he was
    combin'd
With those of Norway, or did line the Rebel   110
With hidden Help and Vantage, or that with both
He labour'd in his Country's Wrack, I know not;
But Treasons Capital, confess'd and prov'd,
Have overthrown him.

MACBETH   — Glamis and Thane of Cawdor:
The Greatest is behind. — Thanks for your Pains.   115
— Do you not hope your Children shall be Kings
When those that gave the Thane of Cawdor to me
Promis'd no less to them?

BANQUO   That trusted home
Might yet enkindle you unto the Crown
Besides the Thane of Cawdor. But 'tis Strange: 120
And oftentimes, to win us to our Harm,
The Instruments of Darkness tell us Truths,
Win us with honest Trifles, to betray's

124   **In deepest Consequence**   in the matters of profound significance that follow. See the note to *Othello*, I.i.120.

126–   **As . . . Theme**   Macbeth's phrasing derives from dramatic
27   terminology. But *swelling Act* also hints at both tumescence and pregnancy; it thus relates to 'Seeds of Time' (line 56) and to the imagery of line 72.

128   **Soliciting**   enticing, suggesting. Compare Desdemona's remarks in *Othello*, III.iii.26–28.

130   **Earnest of Success**   Macbeth alludes to the news of lines 102–5. *Earnest* echoes line 102.

133   **unfix my Heir**   Macbeth means 'make my hair stand on end'. But the Folio spelling hints that another consequence of the 'Horrid Image' to which his imagination is yielding will be to make him heirless. Compare lines 63–65.

134   **seated**   firmly fixed; enthroned. Compare *settl'd* in I.vii.79.
   knock . . . Ribs   Macbeth suggests that his throbbing heart is either demanding his attention or seeking a way to escape its ribcage. His phrasing anticipates II.ii.54–72.

135–   **Present . . . Imaginings**   My fear of the consequences of what I
36   am contemplating is less powerful than the imaginings themselves. Macbeth's syntax is 'wrought' (line 147).

137   **My . . . Fantastical**   my thought, in which murder is still but a fantasy rather than a fully realized intention.

138   **Shakes . . . Man**   causes such an insurrection in my own body politic. Compare *Julius Caesar*, II.i. 62–68.

138–   **that . . . not**   that my normal mental and emotional operations
40   are so choked by my 'Horrible Imaginings' that nothing seems real to me but what is not [yet] real. Compare I.ii.7–9.

140   **rapt**   enraptured; taken captive by a 'Surmise'.

142–   **New . . . Use**   Banquo compares Macbeth to a man who
44   has just been given new apparel, and who will need to wear it for a while before it fits his form properly.
   Cleave can mean both 'cling' and 'split open' (compare I.ii.22).

147   **Give . . . Favour**   please pardon my inattentiveness.

In deepest Consequence.
— Cousins, a Word, I pray you.
MACBETH   — Two Truths are told,   125
As happy Prologues to the swelling Act
Of the Imperial Theme. — I thank you, Gentlemen.
— This supernatural Soliciting
Cannot be Ill, cannot be Good. If Ill,
Why hath it given me Earnest of Success,   130
Commencing in a Truth? I am Thane of Cawdor.
If Good, why do I yield to that Suggestion
Whose Horrid Image doth unfix my Heir
And make my seated Heart knock at my Ribs
Against the use of Nature? Present Fears   135
Are less than Horrible Imaginings.
My Thought, whose Murther yet is but
     Fantastical,
Shakes so my Single State of Man that Function
Is smother'd in Surmise, and nothing is
But what is not.
BANQUO   Look how our Partner's rapt.   140
MACBETH   — If Chance will have me King, why
     Chance may Crown me
Without my Stir.
BANQUO   New Honours come upon him,
Like our strange Garments, cleave not to their
     Mould
But with the aid of Use.
MACBETH   — Come what come may,
Time, and the Hour, runs through the roughest
     Day.   145
BANQUO   Worthy Macbeth, we stay upon your Leisure.
MACBETH   Give me your Favour: my dull Brain was
     wrought
With things forgotten. Kind Gentlemen, your
     Pains

151 **at more Time**   when we have more leisure at our disposal.

152 **The . . . it**   our having thought about it in the meantime.

153 **free**   open, unrestrained; frank (as in I.iv.5).

I.iv This scene appears to take place at the same site as I.ii. Most editors place it in the King's palace at Forres, but lines 41–42 suggest that Duncan is still away from his own residence and thus in need of a night's lodging at Macbeth's castle in Inverness.

1 **Or**   or are. Most editors emend *Or* to *Are*.

2 **Those in Commission**   those assigned to perform the execution.

10–11 **To . . . Trifle**   to cast off the most precious thing he owned as if it were nothing important. Malcolm's words echo I.iii.120–24, and they remind us that Macbeth is considering a deed that will place at risk the dearest thing *he* possesses: his immortal soul. Here as in line 22 *ow'd* conveys the notion that what a human being 'owns' in this world is actually 'owed' to Heaven. The erstwhile Thane of Cawdor, who had forgotten that truth in his rebellion against God's deputy (Romans 13:1–7), has come to see his error. His death has thus been 'studied' (line 9): informed by a repentant awareness of the crimes he has committed against both God and man. It has thereby become an instance in which something 'Foul' has turned out to be 'Fair' (the gateway to Heaven for a redeemed sinner). Cawdor has 'lost and won' (I.i.4) in the sense defined in John 12:24–25. See I.iii.64, and compare *Henry VIII*, IV.ii.64–68.

11–12 **There's . . . Face**   there is no skill that allows one to construe (interpret) the thoughts of a person by looking at his face. The King plays on another sense of *Construction* when he uses the word *built* in the next line. Compare *Twelfth Night*, III.i.124. *Art* echoes I.ii.7–9.

14 **An absolute Trust**   The King is now placing complete confidence in another Thane of Cawdor whose 'Face' appears fair (I.i.9). *Trust* recalls I.iii.118–20.
    Cousin   Macbeth and Duncan were both grandsons of King Malcolm.

Are regist'red where every Day I turn
The Leaf to read them. Let us toward the King.   150
– Think upon what hath chanc'd; and at more
     Time,
The Interim having weigh'd it, let us speak
Our free Hearts each to other.
BANQUO   Very gladly.
MACBETH   Till then enough. – Come, Friends.   *Exeunt.*

Scene 4

Flourish. Enter King, Lenox, Malcolm,
Donalbain, and Attendants.

KING   Is Execution done on Cawdor? Or not
   Those in Commission yet return'd?
MALCOLM   My Liege,
   They are not yet come back. But I have spoke
   With one that saw him die, who did report
   That very frankly he confess'd his Treasons,   5
   Implor'd your Highness' Pardon, and set forth
   A deep Repentance. Nothing in his Life
   Became him like the leaving it. He died
   As one that had been studied in his Death
   To throw away the dearest thing he ow'd   10
   As 'twere a careless Trifle.
KING   There's no Art
   To find the Mind's Construction in the Face:
   He was a Gentleman on whom I built
   An absolute Trust.

       Enter Macbeth, Banquo, Rosse, and Angus.

              O worthiest Cousin,

15 **The . . . Ingratitude** Duncan is speaking hyperbolically here; he means that he's too much in Macbeth's debt to avoid feeling guilty about the tardiness and inadequacy of any thanks he can bestow.

16 **before** in advance, ahead. The King doesn't realize that Macbeth is even further 'before' him in another sense.

19–20 **That . . . mine** so that it might have been possible for me to thank and reward you in proportion to your unmatchable deservings. *Due* (deserving) anticipates *doing* and *Duties*.

22 **owe** both (a) owe you as your subject, and (b) own up to.

23 **part** role (an acting metaphor). Compare I.iii.68, 125–27.

27 **Safe . . . Honour** that promotes your safety and is in keeping with the love and reverence we owe you.

28 **plant thee** Duncan refers to the new 'garden' in which he has installed Macbeth: the thaneship of Cawdor. His imagery echoes I.iii.56–59, 75, 82–83.

29 **full of Growing** prosper as bounteously as possible. Duncan's phrasing is an inadvertent reminder of the 'swelling' to which Macbeth has referred in I.iii.125–27.

31 **enfold** embrace. The King's verb is a reminder of the sheepfold and of the tradition likening a monarch to a good shepherd.

33–35 **My . . . Sorrow** My abundant joys, lavish in their overflowing harvest, seek to disguise themselves in 'drops' (tears) that would normally signify 'Sorrow'.

36 **whose . . . Nearest** whose birth places you nearest to the throne.

37 **establish our Estate** designate as my heir. Compare lines 131–35.

40 **invest him onely** attire him alone. Compare I.iii.106–7, 142–44.

41 **Signs** insignia, visible tokens and manifestations.

43 **Bind . . . you** make us even more deeply indebted to you [by hosting us].

The Sin of my Ingratitude even now   15
Was heavy on me. Thou art so before
That swiftest Wing of Recompense is slow
To overtake thee. Would thou hadst less
   deserv'd,
That the Proportion both of Thanks and Payment
Might have been mine; onely I have left to say,   20
More is thy Due than more than All can pay.
MACBETH   The Service, and the Loyalty I owe,
  In doing it pays it self. Your Highness' part
  Is to receive our Duties; and our Duties
  Are to your Throne and State Children and
    Servants,   25
  Which do but what they should by doing every
    thing
  Safe toward your Love and Honour.
KING   Welcome hither:
  I have begun to plant thee, and will labour
  To make thee full of Growing. – Noble Banquo,
  That hast no less deserv'd, nor must be known   30
  No less to have done so, let me enfold thee
  And hold thee to my Heart.
BANQUO   There if I grow,
  The Harvest is your own.
KING   My plenteous Joys,
  Wanton in Fulness, seek to hide themselves
  In drops of Sorrow. Sons, Kinsmen, Thanes,   35
  And you whose Places are the Nearest, know
  We will establish our Estate upon
  Our eldest, Malcolm, whom we name hereafter
  The Prince of Cumberland; which Honour must
  Not unaccompanied invest him onely,   40
  But Signs of Nobleness, like Stars, shall shine
  On all Deservers. – From hence to Inverness,
  And bind us further to you.

44 **The ... you** that time spent in rest becomes onerous labour when it is not dedicated to your service. *Rest* plays on 'remainder'.

45 **Herbenger** harbinger, forerunner; one who arranges lodging and shelter.

49 **fall down** see my hopes for the Crown defeated. Macbeth fails to note that to 'o'erleap' in this case is to 'fall down'.

50 **Stars** Macbeth addresses the Heavens that look down on mankind. He echoes what the King has just said about the 'Stars' he will bestow 'on all Deservers' (lines 41–42).

52 **wink** shut itself (so as not to see).

58 **It ... Kinsman** He is an incomparable kinsman. Duncan refers to what Macbeth has done to preserve the kingdom; he little suspects how 'peerless' Macbeth aspires to become.

I.v This scene takes place at Inverness in Macbeth's castle.

1 **Success** victory. Compare I.iii.87–8, 130–31.

2 **perfect'st Report** most reliable testimony. See I.iii.68.

3 **Mortal Knowledge** the kind of knowledge mere humans possess. *Mortal* can also mean 'deadly' or 'fatal', of course, and that sense will prove applicable in more ways than one.

6 **rapt** caught up in meditation. Compare I.iii.53–55, 140. Macbeth describes a state of ecstasy (literally, being 'beside one's self') that is etymologically related to *rape* or 'seizure by force'. More than he now realizes, Macbeth has 'eaten on the Insane Root / That takes the Reason Prisoner' (I.iii.82–83). His mind is 'hurt' (II.ii.36).

7 **Missives** messengers.

9 **weyward Sisters** ministers of Destiny. See the note to I.iii.30.

MACBETH   The Rest is Labour which is not us'd
    for you:
  I'll be my self the Herbenger, and make joyful   45
  The hearing of my Wife with your Approach:
  So humbly take my Leave.
KING   My worthy Cawdor.
MACBETH   — The Prince of Cumberland: that is
    a Step
  On which I must fall down, or else o'erleap,
  For in my Way it lies. — Stars, hide your Fires;   50
  Let not Light see my black and deep Desires.
  The Eye wink at the Hand; yet let that be
  Which the Eye fears, when it is done, to see.   *Exit.*
KING   True, worthy Banquo: he is full so Valiant,
  And in his Commendations I am fed: 55
  It is a Banquet to me. Let's after him,
  Whose Care is gone before to bid us Welcome:
  It is a peerless Kinsman.   *Flourish. Exeunt.*

Scene 5

Enter Macbeth's Wife alone with a Letter.

LADY   'They met me in the Day of Success; and I
  have learn'd, by the perfect'st Report, they
  have more in them than Mortal Knowledge.
  When I burnt in Desire to question them
  further, they made themselves Air, into   5
  which they vanish'd. Whiles I stood rapt
  in the Wonder of it, came Missives from the
  King, who all hail'd me Thane of Cawdor, by
  which Title before these weyward Sisters
  saluted me, and referr'd me to the coming   10
  on of Time with "Hail King that shalt be!"
  This have I thought good to deliver thee,

13 **Partner** fellow partaker. Compare I.iii.140.

14 **loose** lose; be deprived of (as in I.iii.109).
the ... Rejoicing the joys to which you are now entitled.
Compare I.iv.21–27, 33–43.

18 **fear thy Nature** have doubts about your disposition.

19 **Humane** both (a) human, and (b) humane.

20 **catch ... Way** seize hold of the quickest means or route to
'Greatness' (line 15). *Way* echoes I.iii.75–76, I.iv.50; *nearest*
recalls I.iv.36 and suggests that one means of catching 'the
nearest Way' will be for Macbeth to 'catch' those 'nearest' to
the throne. *Catch* anticipates I.vii.3.

22 **The ... it** the evil that needs to serve such high designs.
Macbeth's Lady doesn't realize that he is already infected with
'Illness'; see I.iii.132–40 and I.v.6.
highly both (a) earnestly, and (b) ambitiously. Here *high* hints
at *hie*, to suggest a third sense, (c) hastily.

23 **holily** righteously. Compare I.iii.141–42.

24 **wouldst wrongly win** you would like to obtain that to which
you are not entitled. Now that Duncan has named his son
Prince of Cumberland, Macbeth is no longer a potential heir
to the Crown (I.iv.37–39, 48–50).

26–27 **that ... undone** that which you fear to do more than you wish
it not to be done. Compare I.iii.135–36, I.iv.50–53.

27 **High** hie, hasten; but with wordplay similar to that in line 22.

28 **powre ... Ear** The Folio's *powre* combines two senses: (a)
pour, and (b) power. Compare I.iii.98 and IV.i.18. The Lady's
imagery hints at the kind of poisoning that proved fatal to the
Prince of Denmark's father (see *Hamlet*, I.v.35–37, 58–69).
Compare *Othello*, II.iii.368.

31 **Metaphysical** supernatural (literally, 'beyond the physical'),
exceeding nature.

31–32 **doth ... withal** appears determined to crown you with. *Seem*
recalls I.ii.2, 22, 27, 48.

35 **inform'd for Preparation** told me so that I could prepare for
the visit.

my dearest Partner of Greatness, that thou
might'st not loose the Dues of Rejoicing by
being ignorant of what Greatness is promis'd   15
thee. Lay it to thy Heart, and farewell.'
Glamis thou art, and Cawdor, and shalt be
What thou art promis'd. Yet do I fear thy
    Nature:
It is too full o' th' Milk of Humane Kindness
To catch the nearest Way. Thou wouldst be
    Great,   20
Art not without Ambition, but without
The Illness should attend it. What thou
    wouldst highly,
That wouldst thou holily; wouldst not play
    False,
And yet wouldst wrongly win. Thou'dst have,
    great Glamis,
That which cries 'Thus thou must do if thou
    have it,'   25
And that which rather thou dost fear to do
Than wishest should be undone. High thee
    hither,
That I may powre my Spirits in thine Ear
And chastise with the Valour of my Tongue
All that impeides thee from the Golden Round   30
Which Fate and Metaphysical Aid doth seem
To have thee crown'd withal.

Enter Messenger.

         – What is your Tidings?
MESSENGER   The King comes here to Night.
LADY   Thou'art mad to say it.
Is not thy Master with him? Who, were't so,
Would have inform'd for Preparation.   35

39 **Give him Tending** attend to his needs; help him recover his breath. *Tending* resonates with lines 22, 43.

40 **Raven** a bird of evil omen, usually regarded as portending death. Compare *Hamlet*, III.i.276–79.

41 **Entrance** here to be pronounced 'én-ter-ánce'.

43 **Mortal Thoughts** both (a) the thoughts of mortals, and (b) thoughts of mortality (murder). Compare line 3.

44 **Crown** top of the head; but with a reminder of 'the Golden Round' (line 30, the Crown).

46 **Remorse** compassion, sympathy, pity. *Stop* echoes I.iii.75.

47 **compunctious** literally, pricking or stinging (here associated with 'Nature' or conscience); penetrating the thickness.

48 **Shake . . . Purpose** interfere with my dire intentions. *Shake* echoes I.iii.138.

49 **Th' . . . Hit** the decision to effect 'my fell Purpose' and the 'Hit' (blow or 'Wound', line 54) that results. *Hit* (a fencing term) is also a variant spelling for *it*. *Effect* can also refer to the 'Wound' the 'Hit' effects.

50 **for Gall** in exchange for bitter bile.
   murth'ring Ministers instruments of murder; murderous agents of Hell.

51 **sightless** invisible. But the Lady also wishes to become 'sightless' (unseeing) and unseen (lines 52–56).

53 **pall thee** (a) enshroud yourself; (b) make yourself appalling.
   dunnest duskiest, with a hint of 'done-est' (most done).

60 **Instant** the 'Present' the Lady wishes to make 'ignorant' (ignoring) or 'sightless'.

MESSENGER   So please you, it is true: our Thane
   is coming.
One of my Fellows had the Speed of him,
Who, almost dead for Breath, had scarcely more
Than would make up his Message.
LADY   Give him Tending:
He brings great News.   *Exit Messenger.*
               – The Raven himself is hoarse   40
That croaks the fatal Entrance of Duncan
Under my Battlements. – Come, you Spirits
That tend on Mortal Thoughts, unsex me here,
And fill me from the Crown to the Toe, top-full
Of direst Cruelty. Make thick my Blood,   45
Stop up th' Access and Passage to Remorse,
That no compunctious Visitings of Nature
Shake my fell Purpose, nor keep Peace between
Th' Effect and Hit. Come to my Woman's Breasts
And take my Milk for Gall, you murth'ring
   Ministers,   50
Where-ever in your sightless Substances
You wait on Nature's Mischief. Come, thick
   Night,
And pall thee in the dunnest Smoke of Hell,
That my keen Knife see not the Wound it makes,
Nor Heaven peep through the Blanket of the
   Dark,   55
To cry 'Hold, hold.'

Enter Macbeth.

           – Great Glamis, worthy Cawdor,
Greater than both by the all-hail hereafter.
Thy Letters have transported me beyond
This ignorant Present, and I feel now
The Future in the Instant.
MACBETH   My dearest Love,   60
Duncan comes here to Night.

64–65 **Your . . . Time**   What Macbeth's Lady appears to mean is 'your face, my lord, is like a book where men men may read matters new to them to while away the time'. But what she really has in mind is a fair face that is estranged from the foul heart behind it and can deceive others. Compare I.iv.11–12.

66 **Look . . . Time**   adopt a face that befits the occasion.

68 **the . . . under't**   The ultimate source for the Lady's image is the form that Satan took in the Garden of Eden; see Genesis 3:1. But in books such as Geffrey Whitney's *Source of Emblems* (1586), Elizabethans would have observed pictures of vipers lurking beneath strawberries and other flowering plants. Compare *Othello*, III.iii.423–24.

70 **great Business**   important undertaking. Like many of the Lady's expressions in I.vi, this phrase hints at the 'keen Knife' a woman who has invoked demonic assistance to 'unsex' her and swell her up with manly 'Cruelty' might wish to wield (or take into her waiting 'Dispatch') in a 'Hit' that will allow her to 'feel now / The Future in the Instant'. Here as elsewhere, Shakespeare employs the imagery of sexual arousal to suggest the perverse, anti-procreative ways in which 'the flesh lusteth against the Spirit' (Galatians 5:17) in a woman who seems hellbent on making herself barren of every impulse that promotes fruitfulness. Compare I.iii.125–27.

73 **Onely**   only; with wordplay on the upright number 1, and the 'solely sovereign Sway and Masterdome' it signifies to the Lady. *Masterdome* (masterdom, mastery) suggests a phallic crown as well as a crown for a monarch's 'dome' (head).
   look up clear   maintain a Heaven-directed, benign 'Favour'.

I.vi   This scene begins at dusk at the entrance to Macbeth's castle.

S.D.   **Hoboys**   hautboys, oboes.

4 **Barlet**   Most editors emend to *martlet* (martin). But *Barlet* may be a variant on a dialectal form such as *barnlet* (barn swallow).

4–5 **approve . . . Mansonry**   prove by his nest-building. Duncan's words recall his observation in I.iv.11–14.

6 **No Jutty Frieze**   [there is] no projecting roofline border or frieze-lined upper storey.

7 **Coign of Vantage**   corner offering an advantageous 'Seat' (situation). *Seat* (line 1) echoes I.iii.132–35.

LADY   And when goes hence?
MACBETH   To morrow, as he purposes.
LADY   O never
  Shall Sun that Morrow see.
  Your Face, my Thane, is as a Book, where Men
  May read Strange Matters, to beguile the Time.   65
  Look like the Time, bear Welcome in your Eye,
  Your Hand, your Tongue: look like th' innocent
    Flower,
  But be the Serpent under't. He that's coming
  Must be provided for: and you shall put
  This Night's great Business into my Dispatch,   70
  Which shall to all our Nights and Days to come
  Give solely sovereign Sway and Masterdome.
MACBETH   We will speak further.
LADY   Onely look up clear:
  To alter Favour ever is to fear.
  Leave all the rest to me.   *Exeunt.*   75

Scene 6

Hoboys and Torches. Enter King, Malcolm, Donalbain,
Banquo, Lenox, Macduff, Rosse, Angus, and Attendants.

KING   This Castle hath a pleasant Seat: the Air
  Nimbly and sweetly recommends it self
  Unto our gentle Senses.
BANQUO   This Guest of Summer,
  The Temple-haunting Barlet, doth approve
  By his loved Mansonry that th' Heaven's Breath   5
  Smells wooingly here. No Jutty Frieze,
  Buttress, nor Coign of Vantage, but this Bird

34

8   **pendant**   dependent or suspended.
       procreant Cradle   nest for the breeding of offspring. In view of
              what Macbeth's Lady has said in I.v.40–56, Duncan's
              observations about this fruitful, 'Temple-haunting' bird
              remind us once again that what appears 'Fair' may be 'Foul'
              (I.i.9) in the world of the Macbeths.

11–12 **The . . . Love**   The love that attaches itself to us is sometimes an
              inconvenience, but we are nevertheless grateful for it because
              of the bond it represents. What this gracious guest doesn't
              realize is that he will bring 'Trouble' in a way his hosts can
              little imagine as they plot 'Trouble' for him.

13–14 **How . . . Trouble**   how you shall pray 'God yield (reward) us'
              for the effort you go to, and thank me for the 'Trouble' that
              yields you Heaven's reward for your bounty.

20   **rest your Ermites**   will ever be your hermits (those who
              consecrate their lives to praying for you). *Rest* echoes
              I.iv.44–45 and I.v.75.

22   **his Purveyor**   the one who preceded him (see I.iv.45, 56–57)
              and prepared things for his arrival. *Home* recalls I.iii.118–20.

26   **in Compt**   in account, as something for which we stand in your
              debt. Compare the references to 'owing' in I.iii.74 and
              I.iv.10–11, 22–23; and see *Othello*, V.ii.267.

27   **make their Audit**   render up their account for an auditing (to
              determine whether they have been faithful stewards).
              Macbeth's Lady alludes to such passages as Matthew
              25:14–30 and Luke 12:42–54. By implication, she
              acknowledges that her duty to the King is rooted in her
              relationship to God.

Hath made his pendant Bed and procreant Cradle,
Where they must breed and haunt: I have observ'd
The Air is delicate.

Enter Lady.

KING   See, see, our honour'd Hostess: 10
The Love that follows us sometime is our Trouble,
Which still we thank as Love. Herein I teach you
How you shall bid God-eyld us for your Pains
And thank us for your Trouble.
LADY   All our Service
In every Point twice done, and then done double,   15
Were poor and single Business to contend
Against those Honours deep and broad wherewith
Your Maiesty loads our House: for those of old,
And the late Dignities heap'd up to them,
We rest your Ermites.
KING   Where's the Thane of Cawdor?   20
We cours'd him at the Heels, and had a purpose
To be his Purveyor: but he rides well,
And his great Love (sharp as his Spur) hath
      holp him
To his Home before us. Fair and Noble Hostess,
We are your Guest to Night.
LADY   Your Servants ever,   25
Have theirs, themselves, and what is theirs in
      Compt,
To make their Audit at your Highness' pleasure,
Still to return your own.
KING   Give me your Hand:
Conduct me to mine Host. We love him highly,
And shall continue our Graces towards him.   30
By your leave, Hostess.   *Exeunt.*

I.vii   This scene takes place somewhat later within Macbeth's castle.

3   **trammel . . . Consequence**   gather up into a net everything that will follow as a result.

4   **his Surcease**   both (a) its cessation, and (b) Duncan's death.
     Success   a successful achievement of its purpose. Macbeth's phrasing provides an ironic reminder that the kind of success he desires is a wanton violation of due succession. See I.v.1.

6   **Bank and School**   bench and schoolroom (with earthly life viewed as a preparation for eternity). See lines 7–10, where Macbeth notes that by committing murder he will 'teach' others to 'plague' the perpetrator. There is wordplay on the kind of bank (shore) or *shoal* (shelf or sandbar) that the fishermen of 'Time' must negotiate if they hope to return successfully with their 'catch' (line 3). Compare I.iii.13–24.

7   **jump**   Macbeth probably means 'risk'; but to make the gamble worth it, he must assume that it is somehow possible to 'leap over' eternity. Compare I.iv.48–50.

8   **here**   in this life (as opposed to 'the Life to come').

11   **Commends th' Ingredience**   offers the ingredients.
     poison'd Chalice   Macbeth's image recalls what happened to Claudius in *Hamlet* (see IV.vii.155–58, V.ii.337–39).

15   **shut**   bar. Macbeth alludes to the sacred bonds that oblige a host to protest his guest from all harm.

17   **borne his Faculties**   carried himself in his role as King.
     meek   an echo of Matthew 5:5, 'Blessed are the meek'.

18   **clear**   pure, innocent. Compare I.v.73, where 'look up clear' suggests a pretence of looking up to Heaven (see Psalm 121:1), with a clear (true) countenance.

20   **taking off**   both (a) removal, and (b) divestiture. See I.iv.40.

22   **Striding the Blast**   astride the gust caused by the trumpet's blast. *Blast* recalls I.iii.75.
     Cherubin   cherubim; angels.

23   **sightless Curriers**   invisible couriers (messengers who curry, ride hastily). Compare I.v.45–60.

Scene 7

Hoboys. Torches. Enter a Sewer, and divers Servants with Dishes and Service over the Stage. Then enter Macbeth.

MACBETH   If it were done when 'tis done, then
   'twere well
If it were done quickly. If th' Assassination
Could trammel up the Consequence, and catch,
With his Surcease, Success; that but this Blow
Might be the Be-all and the End-all. Here,   5
But here, upon this Bank and School of Time,
We'd jump the Life to come. But in these Cases
We still have Judgement here, that we but teach
Bloody Instructions, which, being taught, return
To plague th' Inventor. This even-handed Justice   10
Commends th' Ingredience of our poison'd
   Chalice
To our own Lips. He's here in double Trust:
First, as I am his Kinsman and his Subject,
Strong both against the Deed; then as his Host,
Who should against his Murtherer shut the Door,   15
Not bear the Knife my self. Besides, this Duncane
Hath borne his Faculties so meek, hath been
So clear in his great Office, that his Virtues
Will plead like Angels, Trumpet-tongu'd against
The deep Damnation of his taking off;   20
And Pity, like a naked new-borne Babe,
Striding the Blast, or Heaven's Cherubin, hors'd
Upon the sightless Curriors of the Air,
Shall blow the horrid Deed in every Eye,

38

25-27 **I ... Ambition** Macbeth's description of himself as the rider of
a leaping steed continues the imagery of lines 5-7 and 21-23.
Meanwhile *Spur*, *prick*, and *onely* recall the phrasing in
I.v.69-73 and I.vi.22-24. Macbeth has no basis for revenge;
his only motive is the kind of aspiration that prompted
Lucifer to rebel against his Lord in Heaven (Isaiah 14:12-15).

31 **proceed** go forward. **Business** echoes I.v.70.

33 **sorts** ranks and degrees. *Golden Opinions* is a reminder of the
'Golden Round' (I.v.30), the crown.

36 **dress'd** both (a) appareled, and (b) addressed (directed).
Compare I.iii.55, 106-7, 140-44; I.iv.31-32, 39-42; and
I.vii.20.

37 **so ... pale** with a sickly hangover that turns it cowardly.

42 **Ornament of Life** another term for 'the Golden Round'.
Account (line 39) echoes I.vi.14-20, 25-28.

44-45 **Letting ... Adage** Allowing the servant who says 'I dare not'
to be the one who attends to 'I would' – and thus permitting
yourself to be an illustration of the adage that 'The cat would
eat fish, and would not wet her feet'.

46 **become** befit, adorn. Macbeth's phrasing recalls I.ii.44-45 and
I.iv.7-8. Compare *adhere* (line 52), 'cleave to'.

47 **no** Here *no* functions as an emphatic double negative and
means 'any', as in I.iii.73. Most editions emend to *do*.

48 **break** broach, open up; disclose.

That Tears shall drown the Wind. I have no Spur   25
To prick the Sides of my Intent, but onely
Vaulting Ambition, which o'erleaps it self,
And falls on th' other.

Enter Lady.

                       – How now? What News?
LADY   He has almost supp'd: why have you left the
   Chamber?
MACBETH   Hath he ask'd for me?
LADY   Know you not he has?   30
MACBETH   We will proceed no further in this
   Business:
   He hath honour'd me of late, and I have bought
   Golden Opinions from all sorts of People,
   Which would be worn now in their newest Gloss,
   Not cast aside so soon.
LADY   Was the Hope drunk   35
   Wherein you dress'd your self? Hath it slept
      since?
   And wakes it now to look so green, and pale,
   At what it did so freely? From this Time
   Such I account thy Love. Art thou affear'd
   To be the same in thine own Act, and Valour,   40
   As thou art in Desire? Wouldst thou have that
   Which thou esteem'st the Ornament of Life,
   And live a Coward in thine own Esteem?
   Letting 'I dare not' wait upon 'I would'
   Like the poor Cat i' th' Adage.
MACBETH   Prythee peace: 45
   I dare do all that may become a Man;
   Who dares no more is none.
LADY   What Beast was't then
   That made you break this Enterprise to me?
   When you durst do it, then you were a Man;

51   **more the Man**   Just as Macbeth's Lady has attempted to elevate herself in the recognized hierarchy by changing herself into a more man-like woman (I.v.42–56), she now seeks to transform her husband into a more masculine version of 'Man', in effect a superman.

52   **Did . . . both**   did they conform to (fit) your desires, and yet you would create such an occasion. Compare I.iii.142–44.

53   **Fitness**   convenience; coming together. Here 'their Fitness' is in apposition to (stands for) 'that'. It hints at the same genital and copulative implications as 'Sticking Place' (line 60). Compare *Othello*, III.iii.241.

60   **screw . . . Sticking Place**   This famous image refers to the crossbow, on which a soldier screwed a device to 'bend up' (line 79) the cord until the taut bowstring caught in a notch (the sticking-place) to indicate that the weapon was ready to discharge its arrow. It also alludes to fitting a man's 'corporal Agent' (line 80) to the 'Act and Valour' his 'Desire' prompts him to (lines 40–41). Meanwhile it can also describe an impediment; compare I.iii.70–76, I.vii.1–7.

62   **Whereto the rather**   to which all the more readily.

63   **Chamberlains**   personal servants of the bedchamber.

64   **Wassel**   both (a) wassailing, carousing and (b) the spiced drink with which wassailers cheered 'be hale'. Compare I.iii.46.
   convince   vanquish, overcome (the original Latin sense).

65   **Warder**   guard, protector [at the entrance to].

66   **Receit**   receipt, receptacle (receiver).

67   **Limbeck**   alembic; the upper chamber of a still (here corresponding to the part of the brain where Reason resided) to which the vapours rose in the distillation process. *Lyes* (line 68) can mean both *lies* (*lie* in modern usage) and *lyes* (urinates, as in II.iii.24–28).

71   **spungy**   spongy; saturated with the fumes of alcohol.

72   **Quell**   kill. Both words derived from the Anglo-Saxon *cwellan*.
   onely   only (as in line 67); with the same phallic implications as in I.v.73 and I.vii.26.

73   **Compose**   make, mould (with wordplay on hard-tempered *Mettle/Metal*); 'put together'. Compare I.ii.60.

And to be more than what you were, you would   50
Be so much more the Man. Nor Time, nor Place
Did then adhere, and yet you would make both:
They have made themselves, and that their
   Fitness now
Does unmake you. I have given Suck, and know
How tender 'tis to love the Babe that milks me;   55
I would, while it was smiling in my Face,
Have pluck'd my Nipple from his Boneless Gums,
And dash'd the Brains out, had I so sworn as you
Have done to this.

MACBETH   If we should fail?

LADY   We fail?
But screw your Courage to the Sticking Place   60
And we'll not fail. When Duncan is asleep
(Whereto the rather shall his Day's hard
   Journey
Soundly invite him), his two Chamberlains
Will I with Wine and Wassel so convince
That Memory, the Warder of the Brain,   65
Shall be a Fume, and the Receit of Reason
A Limbeck onely. When in Swinish Sleep
Their drenched Natures lyes as in a Death,
What cannot you and I perform upon
Th' unguarded Duncan? What not put upon   70
His spungy Officers? Who shall bear the Guilt
Of our great Quell.

MACBETH   Bring forth Men-children onely:
For thy undaunted Mettle should compose
Nothing but Males. Will it not be receiv'd,
When we have mark'd with Blood those sleepy two   75
Of his own Chamber, and us'd their very Daggers,
That they have done't?

LADY   Who dares receive it other,
As we shall make our Griefs and Clamour roar
Upon his Death?

79–80 **I . . . Feat** Macbeth's imagery echoes lines 60–61. In the process it reminds us that 'Doubtful it stood' (I.ii.7) with Macbeth before his wife helped him 'screw' his 'Courage to the Sticking Place'. Lines 81–82 recall I.v.64–68, 73–75.

MACBETH   I am settled, and bend up
Each corporal Agent to this terrible Feat.   80
Away, and mock the Time with Fairest Show:
False Face must hide what the False Heart doth
        know.   *Exeunt.*

II.i   This scene takes place in an inner court of Macbeth's castle.

1   **How ... Night** how far gone is the night? Banquo and his son are trying to keep themselves from going to sleep, and Banquo wants to know what time it is. Compare III.iv.124.

3   **she** the Moon, here associated with the Goddess Diana.

4   **Husbandry in Heaven** thrifty household management in the skies.
   Candles stars. This image anticipates V.v.23.

6   **heavy Summons** Banquo uses a legal term (referring to an order to appear in court) to describe the heavy eyelids that are calling him to sleep. His words sound ominous, and they will prove prophetic. *Lies* (*lyes* in the Folio) echoes I.vii.68.

7   **Merciful Powers** Banquo addresses the Holy Spirit and Heaven's angels.

8   **cursed Thoughts** It is not clear whether Banquo means (a) the impulse to commit a crime that will make the 'weyward Sisters' predictions come to pass (as III.i.6–10 might suggest), or (b) apprehensions about another man who is also having 'cursed Thoughts' at this moment (compare I.iii.125–40, I.vii.1–28). Unlike his 'Partner' (I.iii.140), Banquo calls on Heaven to assist him in fighting off temptation (see Matthew 6:13). As Angelo points out in *Measure for Measure*, ''Tis one thing to be Tempted, . . . Another thing to Fall' (II.i.17–18). In Mark 14:38, Jesus tells his disciples, 'Watch ye and pray, lest ye enter into temptation.'

11   **Rest** This word recalls I.iv.44, I.vi.20.

12   **He ... Pleasure** he has been pleased to an unusual degree.

13   **great ... Offices** lavish gifts to the servants who maintain your kitchens and other domestic departments.

14   **withal** with. Banquo probably hands Macbeth 'This Diamond' as he speaks this line.

15   **shut up** has concluded the evening. Compare I.vii.15.

16   **Being unprepar'd** since we did not have time to prepare properly for the roles suddenly thrust upon us.

17   **Our ... Defect** what we would have wished to do was restricted by our lack of supplies.

ACT II

Scene 1

Enter Banquo and Fleance, with a Torch before him.

BANQUO   How goes the Night, Boy?
FLEANCE   The Moon is down: I have not heard the
  Clock.
BANQUO   And she goes down at Twelve.
FLEANCE   I take't 'tis later, Sir.
BANQUO   Hold, take my Sword. There's Husbandry in
  Heaven: Their Candles are
  All out. Take thee that too.   5
  A heavy Summons lies like Lead upon me,
  And yet I would not sleep. – Merciful Powers,
  Restrain in me the cursed Thoughts that Nature
  Gives way to in Repose.

      Enter Macbeth, and a Servant with a Torch.

  – Who's there?
MACBETH   A Friend.   10
BANQUO   What, Sir, not yet at Rest? The King's abed.
  He hath been in unusual Pleasure, and
  Sent forth great Largess to your Offices.
  This Diamond he greets your Wife withal,
  By the name of 'Most kind Hostess', and shut up   15
  In measureless Content.
MACBETH   Being unprepar'd,
  Our Will became the Servant to Defect,

18 **Which . . . wrought** which would otherwise have manifested itself without restraint. Lines 17–18 hint at the workings of Macbeth's 'Will' in I.iii–vii.

21 **entreat . . . serve** beg an hour to serve us. See I.iii.151–53.

24 **cleave . . . Consent** adhere to my viewpoint. Macbeth's phrasing is couched in ambiguity. *Consent* literally means 'feel or perceive with', and Macbeth appears to be saying no more than that he hopes that he will be able to continue relying on Banquo's support and confidence. *Cleave* echoes I.iii.142–44; it also recalls I.vii.35–36, 46, 51–54.

25–26 **So . . . it** so long as I lose no honour in my efforts to increase it. Compare I.vii.31–35, 46–51.

27 **My . . . clear** my heart free from disloyalty and my allegiance to the King pure. Compare I.vii.16–20.

28 **Good Repose** This benediction, which reminds us of the 'cursed' repose of lines 7–9, will prove ironic in numerous ways. *Repose* recalls line 11.

30 **Drink** Macbeth probably refers to a posset – a sweet, warm nightcap of spiced wine (or ale) and milk. See II.ii.6–8.

35 **Fatal Vision** the kind of vision induced by Fate. Macbeth refers to an apparition that he regards as substantial ('palpable', line 39), though supernatural – capable of being felt as well as seen (line 36). He goes on to contrast it with the kind of 'Dagger' that 'the Mind' (line 37) itself can conjure up: an insubstantial hallucination as 'false' (misleading) as a mirage. *Feeling* echoes I.v.52–60.
sensible perceptible. Compare I.iii.135–40.

38 **Heat-oppressed** fevered. Compare I.vii.63–67.

41 **Thou marshall'st** you conduct. A marshal was an official who escorted guests to their places at ceremonial occasions. *Way* recalls I.v.19–20.

Which else should free have wrought.

BANQUO   All's well.
I dreamt last Night of the three weyward
    Sisters:
To you they have shew'd some Truth.

MACBETH   I think not of them.   20
Yet when we can entreat an Hour to serve,
We would spend it in some Words upon that Business,
If you would graunt the Time.

BANQUO   At your kind'st Leisure.

MACBETH   If you shall cleave to my Consent, when
    'tis,
It shall make Honour for you.

BANQUO   So I lose none   25
In seeking to augment it, but still keep
My Bosom franchis'd and Allegiance clear,
I shall be counsell'd.

MACBETH   Good Repose the while.

BANQUO   Thanks, Sir: the like to you.

                                        Exit [with Fleance].

MACBETH   – Go bid thy Mistress, when my Drink
    is ready,   30
She strike upon the Bell. Get thee to Bed.

                                        Exit [Servant].

Is this a Dagger which I see before me,
The Handle toward my Hand? – Come, let me
    clutch thee:
I have thee not, and yet I see thee still.
Art thou not Fatal Vision, sensible   35
To Feeling as to Sight? Or art thou but
A Dagger of the Mind, a false Creation
Proceeding from the Heat-oppressed Brain?
I see thee yet, in Form as palpable
As this which now I draw.   40
Thou marshall'st me the way that I was going,
And such an Instrument I was to use.

45 **Dudgeon** handle. Originally the word referred to a wooden hilt.
Gouts drops.

47 **informs** literally, in-forms; creates internal images.

48 **one half World** the half of the globe that is now in darkness.

49 **Nature seems dead** Banquo and Fleance have spoken similarly in lines 1–5. Compare I.iv.50–53, I.v.42–63, and I.vii.16–25.

51 **Pale Hecat's Off'rings** the sacrificial offerings to Hecat, the Goddess of Witchcraft. One reason Hecat is here called 'Pale' is that in one of her aspects she was the Goddess of the Moon. *Pale* recalls I.vii.37 and anticipates II.ii.61–62.

54 **Tarquin's ravishing Sides** the profile of the rapist Tarquin (who assaulted the chaste Lucrece). Most editors emend the Folio's *sides* to *strides*; but *sides* (an echo of I.vii.26) may involve wordplay on the Latin word *sidus*, 'star', which could refer to the Moon. Macbeth's imagery associates the 'stealthy' movements of 'Murther' with 'Pale Hecat'. Murder is summoned to action ('Alarum'd', line 52) by 'the Wolf', a 'Sentinel' whose 'Howl' is often associated with the Moon – now 'down' (line 1) to conceal Hecat's influence. Compare *A Midsummer Night's Dream*, V.i.375–91.

55 **sowre** both (a) sour (morose, sorrowful, gloomy), and (b) sore. Most editors emend to *sure*.

57 **prate of** blab about. Macbeth's words echo Luke 19:37–40, where the Pharisees tell Jesus to rebuke his disciples for referring to him as King; he replies that 'if these should hold their peace, the stones would immediately cry out'.

59–60 **Whiles . . . gives** As long as I stand here mouthing threats, Duncan continues to live: cold words cannot inflame deeds. Compare IV.i.144–53.

— Mine Eyes are made the Fools o' th' other
    Senses,
Or else worth all the rest. — I see thee still,
And on thy Blade and Dudgeon, Gouts of Blood,   45
Which was not so before. — There's no such
    thing:
It is the bloody Business which informs
Thus to mine Eyes. Now o'er the one half World
Nature seems dead, and wicked Dreams abuse
The Curtain'd Sleep; Witchcraft celebrates   50
Pale Hecat's Off'rings; and wither'd Murther,
Alarum'd by his Sentinel, the Wolf,
Whose Howl's his Watch, thus with his stealthy
    Pace,
With Tarquin's ravishing Sides, towards his
    Design
Moves like a Ghost. — Thou sowre and firm-set
    Earth,   55
Hear not my Steps, which they may walk, for
    fear
Thy very Stones prate of my where-about,
And take the present Horror from the Time
Which now suits with it. — Whiles I threat, he
    lives:
Words to the Heat of Deeds too cold Breath
    gives.   *A Bell rings.*   60
I go, and it is done: the Bell invites me.
— Hear it not, Duncan, for it is a Knell,
That summons thee to Heaven, or to Hell.   *Exit.*

II.ii   This scene takes place, after a brief interval, in the same setting.

2   **quench'd**   doused their flame. See I.vii.35–38 and 61–70.

3   **fatal Bellman**   Macbeth's Lady compares the screech-owl's ominous cry to the watchman's handbell at midnight before an execution to warn the condemned prisoners to prepare their souls for the Last Judgement. For Macbeth's 'bold' Lady 'the stern'st Goodnight' (line 4) is merely a signal that her husband is 'about' an execution of his own.

5   **surfeited Grooms**   the 'quench'd' Chamberlains (line 2). See I.vii.61–70. *Doors* recalls I.vii.14–16 and II.i.14–16.

6   **mock their Charge**   make a mockery of their responsibilities (as guardians of the sleeping King).
       drugg'd their Possets   laced their bedtime potation with enough alcohol to put them into a drunken slumber. See II.i.30.

7–8   **That . . . die**   that the forces of life and death are in contention to determine whether they will wake up again or sleep forever.

10–11 **th' . . . us**   if we are caught attempting to commit murder, having failed to carry it off successfully, we will be undone. What will eventually become clear is that it is 'the Deed', not the temptation or 'th' Attempt', that confounds the Macbeths; see the note to II.i.8. It is ironic that Macbeth's Lady should use *confound* here; the word's literal meaning is 'pour together', and it serves as a reminder that 'the surfeit'd Grooms' are not the only ones in Macbeth's castle whose rational faculties are too 'Drunk' to function normally. Macbeth's Lady has invoked demonic aid to thicken her blood, replace the 'Milk of Humane Kindness' with 'Gall', and fill herself with 'direst Cruelty' (I.v.19, 42–52); meanwhile, she has poured her spirits into Macbeth's ear (I.v.28) to drug him. See 1 Thessalonians 5:1–24.

15   **Crickets**   Like the screech-owl's 'scream', the 'cry' of crickets was thought to bode death.

Scene 2

Enter Lady.

LADY   That which hath made them Drunk hath made
   me Bold;
  What hath quench'd them hath given me Fire.
   Hark, peace:
  It was the Owl that shriek'd, the fatal Bellman,
  Which gives the stern'st Goodnight. He is about
   it,
  The Doors are open: and the surfeited Grooms   5
  Do mock their Charge with Snores. I have drugg'd
   their Possets,
  That Death and Nature do contend about them
  Whether they live or die.

Enter Macbeth.

MACBETH   Who's there? What ho?
LADY   Alack, I am afraid they have awak'd,
  And 'tis not done: th' Attempt, and not the
   Deed,   10
  Confounds us. Hark: I laid their Daggers
   ready,
  He could not miss 'em. Had he not resembled
  My Father as he slept, I had done't. – My Husband?
MACBETH   I have done the Deed: didst thou not hear
  a Noise?
LADY   I heard the Owl schream, and the Crickets
  cry.   15
  Did not you speak?
MACBETH   When?

18   **This . . . Sight**   The usual interpretation of this line is that
       Macbeth suddenly notices his bloodstained hands.

25   **As**   as if.
       Hangman's Hands   After the executioner hanged his victims, he
       was responsible for quartering (cutting up) their bodies.

27   **Consider . . . deeply**   Don't think about your reaction so
       profoundly. For Macbeth's Lady, it is essential to keep the
       conscience in a narcotized, non-reflective condition.

31   **After these ways**   about in this manner. *Ways* echoes II.i.41.
       so . . . Mad   if we do so, we will go insane.

34   **ravell'd Sleeve**   tangled, frayed, or unknitted (loose-threaded)
       sleeve. Most editors emend the Folio's *sleeve* to *sleave* (a word
       that can mean 'skein' or 'slender filament', but one that can
       also refer to 'rough silk'). *Sleave* may be one of Macbeth's
       meanings, but *Sleeve* (which can refer to a protective shield
       for the arm as well as to a portion of one's upper garment) fits
       the context equally well.

35   **The . . . Life**   Here *Death* appears to refer to both 'Sleep' (the
       'rest' at the end of all one's days) and 'Care' (the worries that
       can make a 'Day's Life' seem like 'Death'). Compare lines
       49–52.

36   **Balm**   a fragrant healing ointment. Balm was used to anoint the
       heads of monarchs (see *Richard II*, III.ii.55); it is thus a telling
       reminder of the Macbeths' own 'hurt Minds' that a man who
       has just murdered a king now feels a need for such 'Blessing'
       (line 29). See the notes to I.v.6, 22, 59, and II.i.28.
       second Course   a culinary metaphor, comparing sleep to the
       second (and most nourishing) course of a meal. Compare the
       Witch's remarks in I.iii.17–22. *Labours* recalls I.iv.44 and
       I.vi.20.

LADY   Now.
MACBETH   As I descended?
LADY   I.
MACBETH   Hark, who lies i' th' second Chamber?
LADY   Donalbain.
MACBETH   This is a Sorry Sight.
LADY   A Foolish Thought, to say a Sorry Sight.
MACBETH   There's one did laugh in's Sleep, and
   one cried 'Murther,'   20
  That they did wake each other. I stood and
   heard them;
  But they did say their Prayers and address'd
   them
  Again to Sleep.
LADY   There are two lodg'd together.
MACBETH   One cried 'God bless us,' and 'Amen'
   the other,
  As they had seen me with these Hangman's Hands.   25
  List'ning their Fear, I could not say 'Amen'
  When they did say 'God bless us.'
LADY   Consider it not so deeply.
MACBETH   But wherefore could not I pronounce
   'Amen'?
  I had most need of Blessing, and 'Amen'
  Stuck in my Throat.
LADY   These Deeds must not be thought   30
  After these ways: so, it will make us Mad.
MACBETH   Me thought I heard a Voice cry 'Sleep
   no more:
  Macbeth does murther Sleep,' the innocent Sleep,
  Sleep that knits up the ravell'd Sleeve of Care,
  The Death of each Day's Life, sore Labour's
   Bath,   35
  Balm of hurt Minds, great Nature's second
   Course,
  Chief Nourisher in Life's Feast.

38 **still** unceasingly.

39 **murther'd Sleep** both (a) murdered a sleeping king, and (b) put an end to the murderer's own ability to sleep.

42 **unbend** permit to go slack. Macbeth's Lady means that the man who was earlier 'settled' (with his 'Courage' in 'the Sticking Place', I.vii.60–61, 79–80) has now lost his taut resolve; he is like a 'ravell'd Sleeve of Care' (line 34).

44 **this filthy Witness** The Lady refers to the blood of a king who was anything but 'filthy'. The idea that innocent blood can bear witness to a crime derives ultimately from Genesis 4:10, where the Lord tells Cain, the first murderer, that 'the voice of thy brother's blood crieth unto me from the ground'. 'Witness' was the original meaning for the Greek word *martyr*. Compare II.i.57. *Lie* (*lye* in the folio), line 46, recalls II.i.6.

49 **Infirm** ill; literally, lacking in firmness or manly resolution. Compare lines 34–35, 42, and II.iii.29–41, 140.

51 **but as Pictures** Macbeth's Lady means that (a) the dead look like people who are merely sleeping (compare lines 12–13, 34–35), and therefore (b) they are no more to be feared than 'painted' images. Again she is urging her husband to be satisfied with surface appearances. Unwittingly, by telling him that it is only 'the Eye of Childhood' that takes a 'painted Devil' for a real one, she is attempting to restore Macbeth to the childlike innocence she has prompted him to slay.

53 **guild** gild over; cover with gold. *Guilt* (line 54) plays on *gilt*, gold coating. Compare I.vii.70–72.

59 **incarnardine** turn as red as the blood on my hands.

LADY   What do you mean?

MACBETH   Still it cried 'Sleep no more' to all
  the House:
  'Glamis hath murther'd Sleep, and therefore
    Cawdor
  Shall sleep no more, Macbeth shall sleep no
    more.'   40

LADY   Who was it that thus cried? Why worthy
  Thane,
  You do unbend your Noble Strength, to think
  So Brain-sickly of things. Go get some Water,
  And wash this filthy Witness from your Hand.
  Why did you bring these Daggers from the place?   45
  They must lie there: go carry them, and smear
  The sleepy Grooms with Blood.

MACBETH   I'll go no more.
  I am afraid to think what I have done:
  Look on't again, I dare not.

LADY   Infirm of Purpose:
  Give me the Daggers. The Sleeping and the Dead   50
  Are but as Pictures: 'tis the Eye of Child-hood,
  That fears a painted Devil. If he do bleed,
  I'll guild the Faces of the Grooms withal,
  For it must seem their Guilt.   *Exit. Knock within.*

MACBETH   Whence is that Knocking?
  How is't with me, when every Noise appalls me?   55
  What Hands are here? Hah: they pluck out mine
    Eyes!
  Will all great Neptune's Ocean wash this Blood
  Clean from my Hand? No: this my Hand will rather
  The multitudinous Seas incarnardine,
  Making the Green one, Red.   60

Enter Lady.

LADY   My Hands are of your Colour, but I shame

62 **White** pale, bloodless; 'infirm' (line 49). White was associated with cowardice because a pale complexion supposedly indicated that the blood had retreated from its colours in fear.

65 **A . . . Deed** Clears recalls I.vii.1–20 and II.i.27, and it serves as a reminder that no amount of hand-washing can make the Lady and her husband 'clear' in the way that Duncan was. 'Water' recalls Pontius Pilate's attempt to evade responsibility for the Crucifixion (Matthew 27:24).

66 **Constancy** Macbeth's Lady means 'firmness of purpose'. But her words also apply to another sense of *Constancy* (loyal obedience) that has 'left [Macbeth] unattended'.

69 **Night-Gown** dressing gown (not sleepwear).

70 **Watchers** people who are awake when they should be asleep. The Lady's phrasing recalls 1 Thessalonians 5:1–24 (also echoed in II.iii.88–89) and Mark 13:34–37, where Jesus says 'Watch ye therefore: for ye know not when the master of the house cometh.' Meanwhile the banging at the gate echoes I.iii.132–35 and alludes to Revelation 3:20, where Jesus says 'Behold, I stand at the door and knock: if any man hear my voice, and open the door, I will come in to him, and will sup with him, and he with me.'

II.iii. This scene takes us to the gate of the castle.

2 **old** an abundance of.

4 **Belzebub** Beelzebub, a name for the Devil (Matthew 12:24).

4–6 **Here's . . . Plenty** The Porter alludes to a farmer who hoarded his grain to reap profits when crops were scarce; when crops proved plentiful, he hanged himself. See I.vii.1–28.

6 **Come in time** you've come at just the right time.
Napkins enow handkerchiefs enough [to wipe your brows in the heat of the 'Hell' whose gate I'm about to open].

9 **Equivocator** one whose words are designed to have multiple meanings.

11 **Treason** treachery; infidelity to his oaths of allegiance.

15–16 **for . . . Hose** for taking for himself some of the cloth for a pair of French breeches (which could be either loose- or tight-fitting). The phrasing could also mean (a) stealing while wearing French hose, and (b) sneaking out of French hose.

To wear a Heart so White.   *Knock*.
I hear a Knocking at the South Entry:
Retire we to our Chamber.
A little Water clears us of this Deed: 65
How easy is it then? Your Constancy
Hath left you unattended.   *Knock*.
Hark, more Knocking.
Get on your Night-Gown, least Occasion call us
And shew us to be Watchers. Be not lost   70
So poorly in your Thoughts.
MACBETH   To know my Deed, *Knock*.
'Twere best not know my Self.
Wake Duncan with thy Knocking: I would thou
   couldst.   *Exeunt*.

Scene 3

Enter a Porter. Knocking within.

PORTER   Here's a Knocking indeed: if a Man were
Porter of Hell Gate, he should have old turning
the Key. *Knock*. – Knock, knock, knock. Who's
there, i' th' name of Belzebub? – Here's a
Farmer, that hang'd himself on th' Expectation   5
of Plenty. – Come in time, have Napkins enow
about you, here you'll sweat for't. *Knock*.
– Knock, knock. Who's there, in th' other
Devil's name? – Faith, here's an Equivocator,
that could swear in both the Scales against   10
either Scale, who committed Treason enough for
God's sake, yet could not equivocate to Heaven.
– O come in, Equivocator. *Knock*. – Knock, knock,
knock. Who's there? – 'Faith, here's an
English Tailor come hither, for stealing out   15

17   **rost your Goose**   both (a) roost (rest), and (b) roast (heat) your
      smoothing iron. *Goose* could also refer to (a) flesh (and hence
      here imply 'cook your goose' in Hell-fire), (b) a stupid person,
      (c) a swelling in the groin caused by venereal disease, and (d)
      a whore. *Rost* echoes *rest* in I.iv.44, I.vi.20.

19   **Devil-Porter**   pretend to be the keeper of Hell-gate. Compare
      Othello, IV.ii.88–90.

21–22 **that . . . Bonfire**   that take 'the Primrose Path of Dalliance'
      (*Hamlet*, I.iii.50) and earn an eternity in Hell.

23   **remember**   both (a) be kind to (give a tip, or a round of
      applause, to), and (b) pay heed to the words of.

25   **lye**   lie, sleep in. The Porter will proceed to play on other senses
      of both *lye* and *lie*. Compare I.vii.68, as well as the other
      passages where the Folio uses *y*-spellings for *lie* and its
      derivatives: I.iv.50, I.vii.68, II.i.6, II.ii.46, IV.ii.78,
      V.vii.10–11.

27   **Second Cock**   the crowing that occurred at three in the
      morning.

31   **Nose-painting**   both (a) inflaming the nose, and (b) the use of
      cosmetics.

32–33 **provokes and unprovokes**   urges on and then discourages. The
      Porter's words about 'Lechery' will also prove applicable to
      the equivocating of the three Witches. Meanwhile they remind
      us of what his Lady's 'Drink' has just provoked and
      unprovoked in Macbeth. Compare I.v.27–32, 56–72,
      I.vii.59–80, II.i.30–55, II.ii.10–11, 41–43, 49–50.

36   **mars**   unmakes, 'dis-hardens' (see the pun in line 38). Compare
      I.vii.46–54.

40   **giving . . . Lye**   Here the word *Lye* itself is an equivocator. The
      Porter's phrase can mean (a) lying to him, (b) causing his
      'corporal Agent' (I.vii.80) to lie down rather than 'stand to',
      (c) making him lie down and sleep rather than 'lying' with a
      woman, and (d) leaving him with a discharge of urine ('Lye')
      rather than semen. *Sleep* echoes II.i.11, 28, II.ii.32–40.

44   **i' . . . Throat**   The Porter gives a literal sense (pouring drink
      down one's gullet) to the most emphatic way of calling a
      person a liar: 'That's a Lie in thy Throat' (*Henry V*,
      IV.viii.17).

of a French Hose. – Come in, Tailor, here you
may rost your Goose. *Knock.* – Knock, knock!
Never at quiet. What are you? – But this
place is too cold for Hell: I'll Devil-Porter
it no further. I had thought to have let in   20
some of all Professions that go the Primrose
Way to th' everlasting Bonfire. *Knock.* Anon,
anon, I pray you remember the Porter.

Enter Macduff, and Lenox.

MACDUFF   Was it so late, Friend, ere you went
      to Bed,
That you do lye so late?   25
PORTER   Faith, Sir, we were carousing till the
   Second Cock. And Drink, Sir, is a great
   Provoker of three things.
MACDUFF   What three things does Drink especially
   provoke?   30
PORTER   Marry, Sir, Nose-painting, Sleep, and
   Urine. Lechery, Sir, it provokes and
   unprovokes: it provokes the Desire, but it
   takes away the Performance. Therefore much
   Drink may be said to be an Equivocator with   35
   Lechery: it makes him, and it mars him; it sets
   him on, and it takes him off; it persuades
   him, and dis-heartens him; makes him stand to,
   and not stand to; in conclusion, equivocates
   him in a Sleep and, giving him the Lye,   40
   leaves him.
MACDUFF   I believe Drink gave thee the Lye last
   Night.
PORTER   That it did, Sir, i' th' very Throat on
   me; but I requited him for his Lye, and (I   45

46–48 **though . . . him**   both (a) though he grabbed my leg like a wrestler, I devised a way to throw him, and (b) though he made me lift my leg like a dog, yet I managed to discharge him (by urinating). Compare the wordplay on *casting* in *Othello*, II.iii.277 and V.ii.320–21. The Porter's phrasing is a reminder that the Macbeths have just 'made a Shift [contrived] to cast' their Lord and will in due course be cast themselves. See Matthew 5:27–30, Mark 9:42–48.

49   **stirring**   up and about. Compare I.iii.141–42.

53   **timely**   betimes; early. Macduff's phrasing echoes line 6.

55   **a . . . you**   the kind of inconvenience a gracious host is happy to bear. Compare I.vi.11–14.

57   **Physics**   heals; treats medically. Macbeth's words keep us aware that the 'Labour' he thought he would 'delight in' has now given him the kind of 'Pain' that only one Physician can heal. Compare II.ii.32–37, and see Luke 5:31 and 4:23–24.

58   **my limited Service**   (a) my special assignment, and (b) my humble duty.

62   **strange Schreams**   extraordinary cries, manifestations.

64   **dire Combustion**   terrifying destruction by fire. Lenox is probably referring to bolts of lightning; but his phrasing echoes the imagery of Hell-fire in the Porter's remarks (lines 1–22).
     confus'd Events   chaotic happenings (such as insurrections and other forms of tumult). *Confusion* in line 72 means 'devastation'. It derives from the same Latin word as *confounds*; see II.ii.10–11.

65   **obscure Bird**   bird of shadows (the screech owl). Compare II.ii.3, 15.

67   **fevorous**   feverous; trembling with the chills of ague (high fever).
     shake   This verb recalls I.iii.137–40 and I.v.47–49 and anticipates lines 82 and 136.

68–69 **parallel . . . it**   recall anything to equal it.

think) being too strong for him, though he
took up my Legs sometime, yet I made a Shift
to cast him.

Enter Macbeth.

MACDUFF   Is thy Master stirring?
Our Knocking has awak'd him: here he comes.   50
LENOX   Good morrow, Noble Sir.
MACBETH   Good morrow, both.
MACDUFF   Is the King stirring, worthy Thane?
MACBETH   Not yet.
MACDUFF   He did command me to call timely on him:
I have almost slipp'd the Hour.
MACBETH   I'll bring you to him.
MACDUFF   I know this is a joyful Trouble to you,   55
But yet 'tis one.
MACBETH   The Labour we delight in
Physics Pain. This is the Door.
MACDUFF   I'll make
So bold to call, for 'tis my limited Service.   *Exit.*
LENOX   Goes the King hence to day?
MACBETH   He does: he did
Appoint so.
LENOX   The Night has been unruly. Where   60
We lay, our Chimneys were blown down. And, as
They say, Lamentings heard i' th' Air: strange
   Schreams
Of Death, and Prophesying, with Accents terrible,
Of dire Combustion and confus'd Events
New hatch'd to th' Woeful Time. The obscure Bird   65
Clamour'd the live-long Night. Some say the Earth
Was fevorous and did shake.
MACBETH   'Twas a rough Night.
LENOX   My young Remembrance cannot parallel
A Fellow to it.

62

70 **Tongue ... conceive** neither Tongue nor Heart can
comprehend. Compare 1 Corinthians 2:9, and Bottom's
garbled version of it in *A Midsummer Night's Dream*,
IV.i.213–17.

73 **sacrilegious** impious, blasphemous, ungodly.

74 **The ... Temple** the body of the divinely anointed King. See 1
Corinthians 3:16, 6:19, Matthew 12:6, 27:45–52, and John
2:19–21.

78 **Gorgon** the Medusa, a monster whose gaze turned a person to
stone.

82 **this Downy Sleep** this peaceful slumber on beds of down (the
softest and whitest of feathers).
Death's Counterfeit the image of death. See II.ii.50–51.

84 **The ... Image** a preview of Doomsday.

85 **As ... up** rouse yourselves like ghosts ('Sprights' or sprites)
from the grave. Macduff's imagery hints at the Resurrection,
but its purpose is to invoke Duncan's kin to take on the roles
of ghosts demanding vengeance.

86 **countenance** both (a) look upon, and (b) accord with (by
assuming countenances that mirror 'this Horror'). Macduff
may be speaking with verbal irony, telling Duncan's loved
ones to (c) tolerate this outrage the way a wrathful ghost
would.

87 **Business** matter. The Lady's words echo I.iii.72, 126–27;
I.v.69–70; I.vi.14–18; I.vii.31; and II.ii.22, 47–48.

88 **That ... Parley** Macbeth's Lady refers to the kind of trumpet
call that signals a cessation of hostilities. But her words also
suggest 'the last Trump' (1 Corinthians 15:51–52), an image
with ominous implications for the Macbeths.

91–93 **'Tis ... fell** This woman is anything but the 'weaker vessel' (1
Peter 3:7) Macduff assumes. But in a sense he is right;
Macbeth's Lady will in time prove unable to withstand the
'Repetition' of what she and her husband have done.

Enter Macduff.

MACDUFF   O Horror, Horror, Horror,
  Tongue nor Heart cannot conceive nor name thee!   70
MACBETH AND LENOX   What's the matter?
MACDUFF   Confusion now hath made his Masterpiece!
  Most sacrilegious Murther hath broke ope
  The Lord's anointed Temple and stole thence
  The Life o' th' Building.
MACBETH   What is't you say, the Life?   75
LENOX   Mean you his Majesty?
MACDUFF   Approach the Chamber, and destroy your
      Sight
  With a new Gorgon. Do not bid me speak:
  See, and then speak your selves. – Awake,
      awake!   *Exeunt Macbeth and Lenox.*
  Ring the Alarum Bell: Murther and Treason!   80
  – Banquo and Donalbain! Malcolm, awake!
  Shake off this Downy Sleep, Death's Counterfeit,
  And look on Death it self. Up, up, and see
  The great Doom's Image! Malcolm, Banquo,
  As from your Graves rise up, and walk like
      Sprights   85
  To countenance this Horror! – Ring the Bell.

Bell rings. Enter Lady.

LADY   What's the Business,
  That such a hideous Trumpet calls to Parley
  The Sleepers of the House? Speak, speak!
MACDUFF   O gentle Lady,   90
  'Tis not for you to hear what I can speak:
  The Repetition in a Woman's Ear
  Would murther as it fell.

96   **contradict**   literally, counter-speak or un-say; give the lie to what you have uttered.

98–99 **Had . . . Time**   Macbeth implies that he is so shocked by what he has witnessed that he wishes he had died before learning of it. In fact his words are profoundly true. *Chance* (unlucky moment) recalls Macbeth's words in I.iii.141–42.

99–   **For . . . Toys**   For from this point on there is nothing in this
101   earthly life worth caring about. In reality, the 'Instant' Macbeth's Lady looked forward to in I.v.60 has now destroyed any 'Future' that matters. *Toys* recalls I.iii.120–24.

101   **Renown**   honour; fame. For the Macbeths, 'Grace *is* dead'.

102   **the mere Lees**   the dregs alone. See the note to I.iv.10–11.

103   **Vault**   (a) the wine vault or cellar, with wordplay on (b) the Heavens over-arching the earth.

105   **Spring, Head, Fountain**   all synonymous with 'Source'. *Stopp'd* (line 106) echoes I.iii.73–76, I.v.45–56, and I.vii.60–61.

109   **badg'd with Blood**   wearing blood as their insignia (like the crest or coat of arms of a servant's household).

111   **star'd**   looked crazed; astonished (terrified) when they awoke.
      distracted   in a state of mental agitation; distraught.

Enter Banquo.

          O Banquo, Banquo,
Our royal Master's murther'd.
LADY   Woe, alas!
What, in our House?
BANQUO   Too Cruel any where.   95
— Dear Duff, I prythee contradict thy self
And say it is not so.

Enter Macbeth, Lenox, and Rosse.

MACBETH   Had I but di'd an Hour before this Chance,
I had liv'd a Blessed Time. For from this Instant
There's nothing serious in Mortality: 100
All is but Toys. Renown and Grace is dead;
The Wine of Life is drawn, and the mere Lees
Is left this Vault to brag of.

Enter Malcolm and Donalbain.

DONALBAIN   What is amiss?
MACBETH   You are, and do not know't:
The Spring, the Head, the Fountain of your Blood   105
Is stopp'd; the very Source of it is stopp'd.
MACDUFF   Your Royal Father's murther'd.
MALCOLM   Oh, by whom?
LENOX   Those of his Chamber, as it seem'd, had
    done't:
Their Hands and Faces were all badg'd with Blood,
So were their Daggers, which unwip'd we found   110
Upon their Pillows. They star'd and were
    distracted:

114 **Wherefore** why; for what reason.

116 **in a Moment** both (a) all at once, and (b) immediately.

117–
18 **Th' . . . Reason** Macbeth suggests that the impulsiveness prompted by his love for Duncan outpaced the restraint that would have made him delay before executing the assassins. But Macbeth's own 'violent Love' of the crown and of his wife's approbation also outran 'the Pauser, Reason'. See I.iv.16–18, I.vi.21–24, I.vii.31–80.

119 **lac'd . . . Blood** streaked with a pattern of blood that looked gold by contrast. Compare I.vii.32–35 and II.ii.53–54.

121 **For . . . Entrance** for Devastation to enter and lay the body waste. Macbeth's reference to a 'Breach' recalls the Greeks' use of the Trojan Horse to penetrate the walls of Troy. Compare lines 72–75.

123 **breech'd** so 'Steep'd' in 'Gore' as to resemble blood-coloured breeches. Compare *cleave* in I.iii.142–44, II.i.24.

127 **That . . . ours** who are most affected by this matter, most endangered by (if not seemingly implicated in) the 'Argument' (plot, design) that led to our father's assassination.

128–
29 **What . . . us?** What should we gain by speaking here when the fate that has been plotted for us, lying hidden in an ominous hole small enough to have been made by an auger, may seize us at any moment? Compare I.v.64–68.

133–
34 **And . . . Exposure** and when we have put away our exposed weakness (our unmanly tears), which shame us by being so openly displayed here. Compare I.iv.33–34, IV.ii.27–29.

136 **Scruples** doubts, apprehensions.

137–
39 **In . . . Malice** Despite my terror, I place myself in God's care, and I am resolved to fight against the hidden intents of treacherous hate. *Stand* echoes I.iii.71–73 and II.iii.38–39; it thus defines a Luther-like spiritual assertion quite different from the kind of standing up the Macbeths have just displayed.

No man's Life was to be trusted with them.
MACBETH   O, yet I do repent me of my Fury,
  That I did kill them.
MACDUFF   Wherefore did you so?
MACBETH   Who can be Wise, Amaz'd, Temp'rate, and
    Furious,   115
  Loyal, and Neutral, in a Moment? No Man:
  Th' Expedition of my violent Love
  Outrun the Pauser, Reason. Here lay Duncan,
  His Silver Skin lac'd with his Golden Blood,
  And his gash'd Stabs look'd like a Breach in
    Nature   120
  For Ruin's wasteful Entrance; there the Murtherers,
  Steep'd in the Colours of their Trade, their Daggers
  Unmannerly breech'd with Gore. Who could refrain
  That had a Heart to love; and in that Heart,
  Courage to make's Love known?
LADY   Help me hence, ho!   125
MACDUFF   Look to the Lady.
MALCOLM   – Why do we hold our Tongues,
  That most may claim this Argument for ours?
DONALBAIN   What should be spoken here, where our
    Fate, hid
  In an Augur-hole, may rush and seize us? Let's
  Away, our Tears are not yet brew'd.
MALCOLM   Nor our   130
  Strong Sorrow upon the Foot of Motion.
BANQUO   – Look
  To the Lady.
  And when we have our naked Frailties hid,
  That suffer in Exposure, let us meet
  And question this most bloody Piece of Work,   135
  To know it further. Fears and Scruples shake us:
  In the great Hand of God I stand, and thence
  Against the undivulg'd Pretence I fight
  Of Treasonous Malice.

140 **briefly** quickly.
put ... Readiness cover over our 'naked Frailties' and arm ourselves like brave soldiers. Compare I.vii.46–54, 60–61, 79–80.

141 **Well contented** We are very content with that proposal.

142 **consort** join; literally, sort together. Compare I.vii.33.

143 **Office** task, function. Compare I.vii.18, II.i.13.

147 **There's ... Smiles** Compare *Hamlet*, I.v.105–7.

147– **The ... Bloody** The closer one's blood relationship to the
48 royal line of descent, the more quickly one is likely to be bloodied by those daggers. *Near* echoes I.iv.36 and I.v.19–20.

148 **Shaft** arrow. Compare I.vii.60–61.

149 **lighted** found its final resting place (ultimate target). Compare I.iii.118–20. *Way* recalls II.i.41, II.ii.30–31, and II.iii.20–22.

151 **dainty of** unduly fastidious (polite) about. Compare III.iv.116–18.

152 **There's ... Theft** there is justification in that stealing [away]. *Shift* echoes line 47. *Steals* puns on *steels* (hardens) and recalls lines 14–16. Compare I.vii.72–74, 79–80.

II.iv This scene takes place outside Macbeth's castle in Inverness.

3 **sore** dire, fearful. Compare II.i.55 and II.ii.18, 35.

4 **trifled former Knowings** made all I've seen before seem trifling. *Trifled* recalls I.iv.10–11, and II.iii.98–103.

5 **Heavens** skies. But in keeping with his use of the theatrical terms 'Act' and 'Stage' (lines 5–6), Rosse is also playing on another sense of *Heavens*: the roof that covered the boards on which the actor portraying Rosse first spoke these lines.

MACDUFF And so do I.

ALL   So all.

MACBETH Let's briefly put on Manly Readiness   140
And meet i' th' Hall together.

ALL   Well contented.

    Exeunt [leaving only Malcolm and Donalbain].

MALCOLM What will you do? Let's not consort
with them.
To shew an unfelt Sorrow is an Office
Which the False Man does easy. I'll to England.

DONALBAIN To Ireland, I. Our separated Fortune   145
Shall keep us both the Safer. Where we are
There's Daggers in Men's Smiles. The Near in
Blood,
The nearer Bloody.

MALCOLM   This murtherous Shaft that's shot
Hath not yet lighted: and our Safest Way
Is to avoid the Aim. Therefore to Horse,   150
And let us not be dainty of Leave-taking,
But shift away. There's Warrant in that Theft
Which steals it self when there's no Mercy
left.   *Exeunt.*

Scene 4

Enter Rosse with an Old Man.

OLD MAN Threescore and Ten I can remember well,
Within the Volume of which Time I have seen
Hours Dreadful and Things Strange; but this
sore Night
Hath trifled former Knowings.

ROSSE   Ha, good Father,
Thou seest the Heavens, as troubled with Man's Act,   5

7   **travailing Lamp**   the Sun, here depicted as a lonely
         overburdened traveller who has been assaulted and strangled
         by 'dark Night' (see *Othello*, V.i.64). Lines 6–10 recall the
         Gospels' account of the Crucifixion. According to Matthew
         27:45–52, 'from the sixth hour there was darkness over all
         the land unto the ninth hour'. After Jesus 'yielded up the
         ghost, . . . behold, the veil of the temple was rent in twain
         from the top to the bottom; and the earth did quake, and the
         rocks rent; And the graves were opened, and many bodies of
         the saints which slept arose.' This passage would also have
         been called to mind by Macbeth's reference to the breach of
         'the Lord's anointed Temple' in II.iii.72–75.

12   **tow'ring . . . Place**   circling in the heights to which only noble
         falcons normally attain. A falcon that was occupying its
         ordained position in the hierarchy was attacked by an owl
         with a 'Vaulting Ambition' (I.vii.27) no less unnatural than
         Macbeth's. Compare I.ii.34–36.

16   **Wild in Nature**   unruly, as opposed to the 'Minions' (darlings)
         of their breed who had been so obedient to their masters
         before. Lines 14–18 recall II.iii.150–53.
         flong   flung; threw themselves.

18   **eat**   ate.

24   **What . . . pretend?**   what could they gain by it?
         suborned   incited to it, or hired, by someone else.

27   **'Gainst Nature still**   More unnatural behaviour!

28   **Thriftless**   unprofitable, wasteful; self-destructive.
         raven up   ravenously devour. The Folio spelling suggests
         wordplay on the name of a bird proverbially associated with
         murder; compare I.v.40–42.

Threatens his bloody Stage. By th' Clock 'tis Day,
And yet dark Night strangles the travailing Lamp.
Is't Night's Predominance or the Day's Shame
That Darkness does the Face of Earth entomb
When living Light should kiss it?

OLD MAN   'Tis unnatural,   10
Even like the Deed that's done. On Tuesday last
A Falcon tow'ring in her Pride of Place
Was by a Mousing Owl hawk'd at and kill'd.

ROSSE   And Duncan's Horses (a thing most strange
       and certain),
Beauteous and Swift, the Minions of their Race,   15
Turn'd Wild in Nature, broke their Stalls,
       flong out,
Contending 'gainst Obedience, as they would
Make War with Mankind.

OLD MAN   'Tis said they eat each other.

ROSSE   They did so: to th' Amazement of mine Eyes
That look'd upon't.

Enter Macduff.

                        Here comes the good Macduff.   20
– How goes the World, Sir, now?

MACDUFF   Why see you not?

ROSSE   Is't known who did this more than bloody
       Deed?

MACDUFF   Those that Macbeth hath slain.

ROSSE   Alas, the Day,
What Good could they pretend?

MACDUFF   They were suborned.
Malcolm and Donalbain, the King's two Sons,   25
Are stol'n away and fled, which puts upon them
Suspicion of the Deed.

ROSSE   'Gainst Nature still:
Thriftless Ambition, that will raven up

29 **Thine ... Means** both (a) the source of your own life, and (b) your means of sustaining yourself. See II.iii.105–6.
like likely.

31 **Scone** the ancient capital of Scotland, just north of Perth. Scottish kings were crowned and 'invested' (clothed in the robes of royalty, line 32) on the 'Stone of Scone' (also known as the Stone of Destiny). They were buried at Colmekill (Iona) in the Hebrides, home of the monastery of Saint Columba (AD 521–97), who converted Scotland to Christianity.

36 **Fife** the site ('Seat', I.vi.1) of the Thane of Fife.

37 **adieu** to God (and His protection). Macduff's farewell is more than perfunctory; he means what he says.

38 **Least ... New** lest we find ourselves uncomfortable in the new livery we will be wearing as servants of the man who will himself be clothed in new robes at Scone (line 31).

40 **Benison** benediction; blessing.

41 **make ... Bad** transform these evil times into better ones. Compare I.i.9, I.iv.1–11, and *Othello*, IV.iii.104–5.

S.D. **Exeunt omnes** All depart.

Thine own Live's Means. Then 'tis most like
The Sovereignty will fall upon Macbeth.   30

MACDUFF   He is already nam'd, and gone to Scone
To be invested.

ROSSE   Where is Duncan's Body?

MACDUFF   Carried to Colmekill,
The sacred Store-house of his Predecessors,
And Guardian of their Bones.

ROSSE   Will you to Scone?   35

MACDUFF   No, Cousin, I'll to Fife.

ROSSE   Well, I will thither.

MACDUFF   Well may you see things well done there:
adieu,
Least our Old Robes fit easier than our New.

ROSSE   Farewell, Father.

OLD MAN   God's Benison go with you, and with those   40
That would make Good of Bad, and Friends of
Foes.   *Exeunt omnes.*

III.1   This scene takes place in the royal palace at Forres.

2   **weyard Women**   the 'weyward Sisters'. See the note to I.iii.30.

3   **playdst most foully**   Banquo's verb is yet another theatrical
         metaphor (compare II.iv.5–6); and *foully* echoes I.i.9.

4   **It . . . Posterity**   the Crown should not stay (a word that
         derives, like *stand*, from the Latin *stare*) in your line of
         descent. Banquo's verb plays on the procreative sense of *stand*
         (see the note to I.iii.72, and compare II.iii.26–39, 137–39).

5   **Root**   source. Compare I.iii.82–83 and II.iv.29. *Root* is
         sometimes phallic in significance: see *The Merry Wives of
         Windsor*, IV.i.56. Here it also suggests a family tree. It thus
         relates to the imagery of planting and growing in I.iii.56–57,
         I.iv.28–29, 32–33, I.v.59–60, I.vi.6–9, and II.ii.36–37. *Father*
         echoes II.iv.39.

6   **If . . . them**   if their prophecies are accurate.

8   **Verities**   truths.

10   **set . . . Hope**   Banquo's phrasing plays on the kind of standing
         hinted at in line 4. Compare the Porter's wordplay in
         II.iii.32–41, where 'it sets him on, and it takes him off' can
         refer both to Lechery and to the kind of 'Hope' that expresses
         itself in the 'Pride of Place' (II.iv.21) that fosters 'tow'ring'
         ambition. See I.iii.52–55 and I.vii.35–36 for previous
         references to *Hope*. Lines 1–10 recall II.i.7–9. For similar
         treatments of analogies between two types of hope and
         overreaching desire, see *2 Henry IV*, I.iii.41–62 and
         II.iv.283–84, *Measure for Measure*, I.iii.39–47 and
         II.iv.89–99, and *Troilus and Cressida*, II.ii.1–212.

S.D.   **Sennet**   a trumpet fanfare to indicate a ceremonial entrance.

11   **If . . . forgotten**   either (a) if we had neglected to invite him, or
         (b) if he had forgotten himself and failed to appear.

12   **great Feast**   the evening's 'solemn Supper'. Compare
         II.ii.36–37.

13   **all-thing unbecoming**   everything in disarray. Compare I.vii.46.

16   **Command upon me**   order me to do whatever pleases you.

18   **knit**   interwoven. This word echoes II.ii.34.

ACT III

Scene 1

Enter Banquo.

BANQUO   Thou hast it now: King, Cawdor, Glamis,
    all,
  As the weyard Women promis'd. And I fear
  Thou playdst most foully for't. Yet it was
    said
  It should not stand in thy Posterity,
  But that my self should be the Root and Father   5
  Of many Kings. If there come Truth from them
  (As upon thee, Macbeth, their Speeches shine),
  Why, by the Verities on thee made good,
  May they not be my Oracles as well,
  And set me up in Hope? But hush, no more.   10

Sennet sounded. Enter Macbeth as King, Lady, Lenox,
Rosse, Lords, and Attendants.

MACBETH   Here's our chief Guest.
LADY   If he had been forgotten,
  It had been as a Gap in our great Feast,
  And all-thing unbecoming.
MACBETH   To night we hold a solemn Supper, Sir,
  And I'll request your Presence.
BANQUO   Let your Highness   15
  Command upon me, to the which my Duties
  Are with a most indissoluble Tie
  For ever knit.

76

19   I both 'I [do]' and 'Ay'. Compare II.ii.16.

20   **still** always.
         Grave wise; sober, trustworthy. This phrasing will prove
         ominous.

21   **Prosperous** valuable; promoting our welfare. Compare I.iii.71.

22   **take to morrow** take advantage of tomorrow for that purpose.

24   **this** now; this time.
         Go . . . better if my horse does not go faster than usual.

26   **a . . . twain** an hour or two of darkness after sunset. Compare
         II.iv.6–7.
         Fail not be sure that you don't return too late for. Lines 26–27
         will prove ironic.

28   **bestow'd** now residing.

31   **strange Invention** wild tales of their own devising.

32–33 **Cause . . . jointly** affairs of state begging for our joint
         attention. *Hie* recalls I.v.22, 27. *Adieu* echoes II.iv.37.

35   **our . . . upon's** our business requires that we leave right away.

36   **wish your Horses** pray that your horses will be.

39   **Master . . . Time** free to use his time as he wishes. Compare
         I.v.69–72.

40–41 **Society . . . welcome** the company of others more enjoyable.

42   **While then** meanwhile.

43   **Sirrha** a mode of address for a social inferior.

44   **Attend . . . Pleasure?** Are the men I spoke about with you
         ready to be of service to me? *Without* (line 45) means
         'outside'. *Attend* recalls I.v.22, 39, 43.

MACBETH   Ride you this Afternoon?

BANQUO   I, my good Lord.

MACBETH   We should have else desir'd
   Your good Advice (which still hath been both Grave   20
   And Prosperous) in this Day's Council; but
   We'll take to morrow. Is't far you ride?

BANQUO   As far, my Lord, as will fill up the Time
   'Twixt this and Supper. Go not my Horse the
     better,
   I must become a Borrower of the Night   25
   For a dark Hour or twain.

MACBETH   Fail not our Feast.

BANQUO   My Lord, I will not.

MACBETH   We hear our bloody Cousins are bestow'd
   In England and in Ireland, not confessing
   Their cruel Parricide, filling their Hearers   30
   With strange Invention. But of that to morrow,
   When therewithal we shall have Cause of State
   Craving us jointly. Hie you to Horse. Adieu,
   Till you return at Night. Goes Fleance with
     you?

BANQUO   Ay, my good Lord: our Time does call
   upon's.   35

MACBETH   I wish your Horses swift and sure of
   Foot,
   And so I do commend you to their Backs.
   Farewell.   *Exit Banquo.*
   – Let every man be Master of his Time
   Till Seven at Night, to make Society   40
   The sweeter welcome: we will keep our self
   Till Supper-time alone. While then, God
   Be with you.   *Exeunt Lords.*
        – Sirrha, a Word with you:
   Attend those Men our Pleasure?

SERVANT   They are, my Lord,
   Without the Palace Gate.

47 **safely thus** securely enthroned. Compare lines 50–52,
I.iv.24–27, and III.ii.33–36.

48 **Stick deep** are deeply embedded (like a thorn). Compare
I.vii.60–61.

50 **to** in addition to; accompanying.
dauntless Temper fearless resolve. *Temper* is a complex word,
one that could refer to both (a) the temper (hardness and
durability) of a sword that has been subjected to extremes of
heat and cold, and (b) the self-governance of a mind in which
Reason assures that the humours are well tempered (properly
mixed and duly subordinated).

54 **My . . . rebuk'd** my guardian inner spirit is beaten back (held
in check, reprimanded). Compare V.vii.46–47, and see
Antony and Cleopatra, II.iii.15–20.

59 **fruitless** 'barren' (line 60), non-bearing. See the note to line 5.

60 **barren Sceptre** staff of office, here likened to the trunk of a tree
that has been blighted before maturing.
Gripe grasp, grip.

61 **Thence . . . Hand** from which it is to be seized by someone
who is not in my line of descent. Compare I.vii.7–12.

63 **fil'd** defiled; fouled (made foul); 'clipt' (line 92).

65 **Rancours** rank malice; bitter rancidity ('Gall', I.v.50).
the . . . Peace Macbeth refers to the communion cup used in
the Eucharist; for him it is now a 'poison'd Chalice' (I.vii.11).

66 **Onely** only. Compare I.v.73 and I.vii.25–27.
mine eternal Jewel the soul that might otherwise have spent an
eternity in Heaven. Macbeth may be thinking of Revelation
3:10–4:11. Compare I.iv.8–11 and *Othello*, V.ii.340–42.

67 **the . . . Man** the Devil.

69 **the List** the enclosed field where knights engage in combat.

70 **to th' Utterance** both (a) to the uttermost (*à l'outrance*, a
French chivalric term) and (b) to the proclaiming of my
victory.

MACBETH   Bring them before us.   45
                                        Exit Servant.
                    — To be thus is nothing,
But to be safely thus. Our Fears in Banquo
Stick deep, and in his Royalty of Nature
Reigns that which would be fear'd. 'Tis much he
    dares,
And to that dauntless Temper of his Mind   50
He hath a Wisdom that doth guide his Valour
To act in Safety. There is none but he
Whose being I do fear; and under him
My Genius is rebuk'd, as it is said
Mark Antony's was by Caesar. He chid the
    Sisters   55
When first they put the Name of King upon me,
And bad them speak to him. Then Prophet-like
They hail'd him Father to a Line of Kings.
Upon my Head they plac'd a fruitless Crown,
And put a barren Sceptre in my Gripe,   60
Thence to be wrench'd with an unlineal Hand,
No Son of mine succeeding. If't be so,
For Banquo's Issue have I fil'd my Mind,
For them the gracious Duncan have I murther'd,
Put Rancours in the Vessel of my Peace,   65
Onely for them, and mine eternal Jewel
Given to the common Enemy of Man,
To make them Kings, the Seeds of Banquo Kings.
— Rather than so, come Fate into the List,
And champion me to th' Utterance. — Who's
    there?   70

          Enter Servant and two Murtherers.

— Now go to the Door, and stay there till we
    call.   *Exit Servant.*
— Was it not yesterday we spoke together?

78 **pass'd ... you** reviewed with you (to prove my assertions to be true).

79 **borne in hand** misled; 'cross'd' (thwarted).
the Instruments those who were the tools of his deceit. Compare I.iii.122.

80 **wrought with them** manipulated them to do what they did.

81 **To ... Soul** to even a half-spirited man. Compare *Othello*, I.i.53.
a Notion craz'd even a defective (literally, cracked) intellect.

84–86 **Do ... go?** Are you men of such forbearance (turning the other cheek) that you can permit this mistreatment?

86 **Gospell'd** instructed in the Gospels. See Matthew 5:44.

88 **heavy Hand** oppressive tyranny; a play on 'borne in hand' (line 79). *Grave* echoes lines 20–21.

89 **beggar'd yours** subjected your own 'Issue' to poverty forever.

90 **Catalogue** listing of Earth's creatures.
go for Men are counted as men. Compare I.vii.46–54, 72, and II.iii.140. *Ay* is *I* in the Folio; so also in line 34.

92 **Shoughs** shaggy lap-dogs from Iceland.
Water-rugs rough-haired water dogs.
clipt clept; called (perhaps with wordplay on the clipped tails of low-bred 'Curs').

93 **valued File** the exclusive list of special dogs. Compare lines 63 and 100.

97 **clos'd** enclosed, deposited.

98–99 **Particular ... alike** an individual designation (such as 'Housekeeper', watchdog) to sort him from the catalogue that lumps them all together. *Addition* recalls I.iii.103–5.

100 **Station** standing. See the note to line 4.

MURTHERERS   It was, so please your Highness.
MACBETH   Well then, now
  Have you consider'd of my Speeches: know
  That it was he in the Times past which held you   75
  So under Fortune, which you thought had been
  Our innocent self. This I made good to you
  In our last Conference, past in Probation
    with you,
  How you were borne in hand, how cross'd; the
    Instruments;
  Who wrought with them; and all things else that
    might   80
  To half a Soul, and to a Notion craz'd,
  Say 'Thus did Banquo.'
1 MURTHERER   You made it known to us.
MACBETH   I did so, and went further, which is now
  Our point of second Meeting. Do you find
  Your Patience so predominant in your Nature   85
  That you can let this go? Are you so Gospell'd
  To pray for this good Man, and for his Issue,
  Whose heavy Hand hath bow'd you to the Grave,
  And beggar'd yours for ever?
1 MURTHERER   We are Men, my Liege.
MACBETH   Ay, in the Catalogue ye go for Men,   90
  As Hounds and Greyhounds, Mungrels, Spaniels,
    Curs,
  Shoughs, Water-rugs, and Demi-wolves are clipt
  All by the name of Dogs. The valued File
  Distinguishes the Swift, the Slow, the Subtle,
  The House-keeper, the Hunter, every one   95
  According to the Gift which bounteous Nature
  Hath in him clos'd: whereby he does receive
  Particular Addition from the Bill
  That writes them all alike. And so of Men.
  Now if you have a Station in the File,   100
  Not i' th' worst Rank of Manhood, say't,

108 **incens'd** enflamed. Compare *Othello*, I.i.68.
   reckless care-less; unreckoning (unthinking). Macbeth has now
   'wrought' (line 80) the Second Murtherer to the point where
   he is insensible to moral considerations; compare *Othello*,
   V.ii.316–17, 339–40.

110 **Disasters** literally, star-crossings; misfortunes.
   tugg'd with pulled about by Fortune. Compare II.iii.42–48.

111 **set . . . Chance** stake my life on any wager. *Set* echoes lines
   6–10.

114– **in . . . Life** at such a dangerously close range that every minute
 16 he lives he threatens my heart with the thrust of his sword.
   Compare Iago's phrasing in *Othello*, II.iii.54–57, 184–87.

118 **bid . . . it** bring my will and conscience to justify it.

119 **For** because of.

120 **but wail** but [instead I] must [pretend to] weep over.

122 **make love** woo (with the implication that your 'love' will be
   rewarded).

127 **plant** place, with ironic echoes of the other senses that *plant*
   has acquired in previous passages (see the note to line 5, and
   compare I.iv.28–29).

128 **Acqaint . . . Time** familiarize yourselves with the best
   intelligence (espial) the time affords, and the best vantage
   point for the ambush.

130 **something from** somewhat away from (at some 'bloody
   Distance', line 114).

And I will put that Business in your Bosoms
Whose Execution takes your Enemy off,
Grapples you to the Heart and Love of us,
Who wear our Health but sickly in his Life,   105
Which in his Death were perfect.

2 MURTHERER   I am one, my Liege,
Whom the vile Blows and Buffets of the World
Hath so incens'd that I am reckless what
I do to spight the World.

1 MURTHERER   And I another:
So weary with Disasters, tugg'd with Fortune,   110
That I would set my Life on any Chance
To mend it or be rid on't.

MACBETH   Both of you
Know Banquo was your Enemy.

MURTHERERS   True, my Lord.

MACBETH   So is he mine, and in such bloody Distance
That every Minute of his Being thrusts   115
Against my near'st of Life; and though I could
With bare-fac'd Power sweep him from my Sight
And bid my Will avouch it, yet I must not,
For certain Friends that are both his and mine,
Whose Loves I may not drop, but wail his Fall   120
Who I my self struck down. And thence it is
That I to your Assistance do make love,
Masking the Business from the common Eye
For sundry weighty Reasons.

2 MURTHERER   We shall, my Lord,
Perform what you command us.

1 MURTHERER   Though our Lives —   125

MACBETH   Your Spirits shine through you. Within
     this Hour, at most,
I will advise you where to plant your selves,
Acquaint you with the perfect Spy o' th' Time,
The Moment on't, for't must be done to Night,
And something from the Palace; always thought   130

130–31 **always ... Clearness** bear in mind at all times that I must be kept clear of any association with your deed. The 'Clearness' Macbeth has in mind is freedom from suspicion, not from actual guilt. Compare I.vii.17–18, II.iii.64.

132 **Rubs** imperfections, rough spots, 'Botches'.

134 **Absence** removal from my presence.
material something that matters.

135–36 **embrace ... Hour** share his father's fate. Macbeth's verb echoes 'make love' (line 122), and is thus another reminder of what he and his Lady have done to pervert the normal forms of human intercourse (linguistic as well as social and sexual). *Dark Hour* recalls line 26 and I.iii.145 (where it alludes to an hourglass); also see II.i.21, II.iii.54, 98.

136 **Resolve ... apart** step aside to put yourselves into 'Manly Readiness' (II.iii.140).

138 **straight** right away [now that you've stiffened your resolve].
abide wait.

139 **concluded** arranged; literally, 'closed together', as in an embrace. Macbeth probably speaks to himself as the Murderers exit.

III.ii This scene takes place in another room of the palace.

3 **I ... Words** I would like to speak with him for a moment if he is at leisure to see me. Compare I.iii.146.

4–5 **Nought's ... Content** We possess nothing, and have spent everything, when we get what we want but are not satisfied. Compare III.i.46–47. The Lady's comments illustrate the applicability of such New Testament passages as Matthew 5:19–34, 1 John 2:15–17, and 1 Timothy 6:1–19.

8 **sorriest Fancies** most melancholy reveries. *Sorriest* recalls II.ii.18.

11–12 **Things ... Regard** Things that cannot be mended should go unthought about. Compare II.ii.41–71. Lines 10–11 will be echoed in V.v.17.

That I require a Clearness; and with him,
To leave no Rubs nor Botches in the Work,
Fleance his Son, that keeps him Company,
Whose Absence is no less material to me
Than is his Father's, must embrace the Fate   135
Of that dark Hour. Resolve your selves apart,
I'll come to you anon.
MURTHERERS   We are resolv'd, my Lord.
MACBETH   I'll call upon you straight: abide within,
It is concluded. — Banquo, thy Soul's Flight,
If it find Heaven, must find it out to Night.   140

                                    Exeunt.

Scene 2

Enter Macbeth's Lady, and a Servant.

LADY   Is Banquo gone from Court?
SERVANT   Ay, Madam, but
Returns again to Night.
LADY   Say to the King,
I would attend his Leisure for a few Words.
SERVANT   Madame, I will.   *Exit.*
LADY   Nought's had, all's spent,
Where our Desire is got without Content.   5
'Tis safer to be that which we destroy,
Then by Destruction dwell in doubtful Joy.

Enter Macbeth

— How now, my Lord? Why do you keep alone,
Of sorriest Fancies your Companions making,
Using those Thoughts which should indeed have
   died   10
With them they think on? Things without all
   Remedy
Should be without Regard: what's done is done.

13 **scorch'd** scored, slashed (here in a way that cuts the snake in two).

14 **close** rejoin her severed parts. It was believed that the only way to kill a snake was to crush its head (see Genesis 3:15); even a snake that had been cut in half was thought capable of reuniting. *Close* echoes III.i.97.
    poor Malice inadequate ability to do it harm.

16 **But . . . dis-joint** but allow the structure that holds the cosmos together to be 'scorch'd' itself. Most editors unite what the Folio sets asunder as disjointed part-lines (16–17).

17 **Both . . . suffer** [let] both this world and the next (eternity) be tortured by the severance. Compare I.vii.1–12 and V.v.48–49.

21 **Whom . . . Peace** whom we, to gain rest for our 'fitful' souls (line 25), have sent to their eternal rest. Compare II.ii.32–40, III.i.64–65, and I.vi.18–20.

23 **restless Ecstasy** the madness induced by unceasing pain (as from the rack). Compare I.v.6 and II.i.11.

27 **Malice . . . Levy** civil insurrection, invasion from abroad.

29 **Jovial** both (a) merry, and (b) Jove-like (majestic and 'Sleek', smooth). Lines 29–30 recall I.v.64–68 and I.vii.81–82.

31–32 **Let . . . Banquo** remember to be especially attentive to Banquo. Compare II.iii.23, 68.

32 **present him Eminence** bestow royal favour on him.

33–36 **Unsafe . . . are** [We must bear in mind that we are] insecure, so we must still 'lave' (wash) our 'Honours' (eminence) in these 'flattering Streams' (cajoling gestures).

35 **Vizards** masks. Compare I.v.64–68 and I.vii.81–82.

39 **But . . . eterne** But Nature has not given them an eternal copyhold (lease) on life. Macbeth's Lady may also be thinking of another sense of *Copy*: something reproduced from a pattern or mould. But a third sense is also applicable – 'abundance' or 'fruitfulness' (from the Latin *copia*) – and it casts an ironic light on her remarks.

41 **jocund** jocular, cheerful.

MACBETH   We have scorch'd the Snake, not kill'd it:
  She'll close and be her self whilst our poor
      Malice
  Remains in Danger of her former Tooth.   15
  But let the Frame of things dis-joint,
  Both the Worlds suffer,
  Ere we will eat our Meal in Fear, and sleep
  In the Affliction of these terrible Dreams
  That shake us Nightly. Better be with the Dead,   20
  Whom we, to gain our Peace, have sent to Peace,
  Than on the Torture of the Mind to lie
  In restless Ecstasy.
  Duncane is in his Grave;
  After Life's fitful Fever, he sleeps well,   25
  Treason has done his worst; nor Steel, nor Poison,
  Malice Domestic, Foreign Levy, nothing,
  Can touch him further.
LADY   Come on: gentle my Lord,
  Sleek o'er your rugged Looks, be Bright and
      Jovial
  Among your Guests to Night.
MACBETH   So shall I, Love,   30
  And so I pray be you. Let your Remembrance
  Apply to Banquo: present him Eminence, both
  With Eye and Tongue. Unsafe the while, that we
  Must lave our Honours in these flattering
      Streams,
  And make our Faces Vizards to our Hearts,   35
  Disguising what they are.
LADY   You must leave this.
MACBETH   O, full of Scorpions is my Mind, dear
      Wife:
  Thou know'st that Banquo and his Fleance lives.
LADY   But in them Nature's Copy's not eterne.
MACBETH   There's Comfort yet, they are assailable: 40
  Then be thou jocund. Ere the Bat hath flown

43   **Shard-borne**   both (a) bred (born) out of dung, and (b) borne on scaly wings.

46   **Chuck**   a term of affection (like *Chick*). Compare *Othello*, III.iv.50.

47   **seeling**   sealing over, either (a) by seeling (sewing shut, as with the eyelids of a falcon being tamed), or by covering with a 'Scarf' (line 48). Compare *Othello*, III.iii.204–5.

50   **Bond**   the pale-coloured lease on life ('Copy') that makes Banquo dangerous. Macbeth shreds his own ties with Heaven.

52   **Rooky**   both (a) filled with rooks (crows), and (b) gloomy, thick. *Pale* recalls II.i.51, 55, and II.ii.61–62.

54   **Night's black Agents**   Macbeth associates Night with Hecat (line 42) and her ministers; see the notes to II.i.51, 54. Compare I.vii.79–80.

55   **still**   both (a) quiet, and (b) constant.

56   **make strong themselves**   both (a) strengthen themselves, and (b) safeguard themselves (by fortifying themselves behind a stronghold). Macbeth will eventually learn that piling ill on ill to build a wall of security (a) promotes a false sense of invulnerability, and (b) hardens one's heart to the influence of conscience – a process that accompanies the closing of one's eyes (lines 47–51, echoing I.iv.50–53, I.v.42–56, II.ii.71–72), ears, and other means of 'Regard' (lines 11–12).
      Ill   evil. Compare I.iii.128–29, I.v.20–22, III.i.102–6.

III.iii   This scene takes place a short distance from the palace.

2   **He ... Mistrust**   there is no reason for us to mistrust him (the Third Murderer).

2–4   **since ... just**   since he outlines our duties correctly. See I.i.126–39.

His cloister'd Flight, ere to black Hecat's
   Summons
The Shard-borne Beetle, with his drowsy Hums,
Hath rung Night's yawning Peal, there shall be
   done
A Deed of dreadful Note.

LADY   What's to be done?   45

MACBETH   Be innocent of the Knowledge, dearest
   Chuck,
Till thou applaud the Deed. – Come, seeling
   Night,
Scarf up the tender Eye of pitiful Day,
And with thy bloody and invisible Hand
Cancel and tear to Pieces that great Bond   50
Which keeps me pale. – Light thickens, and the
   Crow
Makes Wing to th' Rooky Wood:
Good things of Day begin to droop and drowse,
Whiles Night's black Agents to their Preys do
   rouse.
Thou marvell'st at my Words: but hold thee still,   55
Things bad begun make strong themselves by Ill.
So prythee go with me.   *Exeunt.*

Scene 3

Enter three Murtherers.

FIRST   But who did bid thee join with us?

THIRD   Macbeth.

SECOND   He needs not our Mistrust, since he
   delivers
 Our Offices, and what we have to do,
 To the Direction just.

4   **stand** wait. Compare III.i.100, and see the notes to III.i.4, 100.

6   **lated** belated. Compare II.iv.6–7. *Spurs* echoes I.vi.22–24 and I.vii.25–28.

7   **end** Most editors emend to *and*; but *end*, a variant spelling of *and*, plays on both (a) 'Inn' and (b) the 'end' that 'approaches' for the 'Subject' of this 'Watch'. *Watch* recalls II.ii.68.

10   **Note of Expectation** list informing us whom to expect.

11   **go about** take a roundabout route.

14   **Make . . . Walk** walk rather than ride. Shakespeare had a practical reason for imparting this piece of information: to avoid a scene that called for horses on the Globe stage.

15   **Stand to't** Be firm in your resolve; hold your positions.

16   **Let . . . down** The First Murderer plays on what Banquo says; his meaning is 'let it rain down blows upon you'. *Rayne*, the Folio spelling, refers primarily to *rain*, of course, but it also hints at two other words with the same sound: (a) *reign* (alluding to Macbeth's doomed effort to secure his reign against the reign prophesied for Banquo's heirs), and (b) *rein* (alluding to Macbeth's attempt to rein in Banquo and Fleance). See III.i.18–37, 69–70.

17   **fly** flee.

19   **Who . . . Light?** This line reverberates with the play's many other references to striking at 'the Light'. In doing so, it reminds us of the ethical, political, and theological significance of the Macbeths' efforts to deny or destroy virtually every manifestation of the order of Grace. See John 1:1–5 and *Othello*, V.ii.7–15. And compare such passages in *Macbeth* as I.i.9; I.iii.120–24; I.iv.50–53; I.v.52–60, 69–72; II.i.48–59; II.ii.32–35; II.iv.5–10; III.ii.41–54; IV.iii.4–8, 21–24; 38–39; V.i.28–29; V.v.19–28, 48–49.

       Was't . . . way? Was that not according to plan? The First Murderer is probably thinking of what Macbeth has said in III.i.130–31. *Way* echoes I.iii.75–76, I.iv.48–50, I.v.19–20, II.i.41, II.ii.30–31, II.iii.20–22, 149–50.

21   **Best . . . Affair** the more important half of our job. *Half* recalls II.i.48–49 and III.i.80–82.

22   **say . . . done** report what has been accomplished.

FIRST   Then stand with us.
  The West yet glimmers with some Streaks of Day: 5
  Now spurs the lated Traveller apace,
  To gain the timely Inn, end near approaches
  The Subject of our Watch.
THIRD   Heark, I hear Horses.
BANQUO *within*   Give us a Light there, ho!
SECOND   Then 'tis he.
  The rest that are within the Note of Expectation   10
  Already are i' th' Court.
FIRST   His Horses go about.
THIRD   Almost a Mile: but he does usually,
  So all men do, from hence to th' Palace Gate
  Make it their Walk.

Enter Banquo and Fleance, with a Torch.

SECOND   A Light, a Light.
THIRD   'Tis he.
FIRST   Stand to't.   15
BANQUO   It will be Rayne to night.
FIRST   Let it come down.
               [*They set upon Banquo.*]
BANQUO   O, Treachery! – Fly, good Fleance: fly,
  fly, fly,   [*Fleance escapes.*]
  Thou may'st revenge. – O Slave!   [*Banquo dies.*]
THIRD   Who did strike out the Light?
FIRST   Was't not the way?
THIRD   There's but one down: the Son is fled.
SECOND   We have lost   20
  Best Half of our Affair.
FIRST   Well, let's away,
  And say how much is done.   *Exeunt.*

III.iv This scene takes place at the banqueting hall of Macbeth's palace.

1 **Degrees** ranks (and thus your designated positions at the table).

3 **Our . . . Society** I will not seat myself according to rank (at the head of the table), but will instead 'humble' myself (line 4) in the 'Midst' of this company (line 9). One of the ironies of the situation is that if Macbeth had remained where he belonged in degree (if he were still Thane of Cawdor), he would in fact be able to 'mingle with Society' (compare III.i.40–42) now rather than remaining 'alone' in a 'keep' (III.ii.8), a fortress of his own making. He has traded 'Golden Opinions from all sorts of People' (I.vii.33) for a 'Golden Round' (I.v.30) that confines him to a 'doubtful Joy' (III.ii.7).

5 **Her State** either (a) the place at the table designated for the Queen, or (b) her private chamber (if she has yet to emerge officially).

5–6 **but . . . Welcome** but at the proper time I will ask her to bestow her welcome on you (telling you that you are 'well come,' pleasing your hosts with your presence).

8 **encounter thee** return your greeting. Macbeth plays on the chivalric sense of a meeting of knights in noble combat.
   Harts' Hearts'; but Shakespeare frequently associates harts (male deer) with noblemen and princes. See *Julius Caesar*, III.i.205–10, and *Hamlet*, II.ii.620.

9 **Both . . . Even** Our guests are our equals [with 'Thanks' that weigh evenly with our 'Welcome'].

10 **large in Mirth** unrestrained in your merrymaking.

12 **– There's . . . Face** Macbeth has walked to where the Murderer beckoned.

13 **'Tis . . . within** Macbeth means 'It's better to have his blood on your exterior than on his interior.' But here as in III.ii.7 the Folio spelling and pointing provide an ambiguity that modernizing would obscure. Soon 'then he within' will prove ironically apt.

Scene 4

Banquet prepar'd. Enter Macbeth, Lady, Rosse, Lenox, Lords,
and Attendants.

MACBETH   You know your own Degrees, sit down.
   At first
And last, the hearty Welcome.
LORDS   Thanks to your Maiesty.
MACBETH   Our self will mingle with Society
And play the humble Host. Our Hostess keeps
Her State, but in best Time we will require   5
Her Welcome.
LADY   Pronounce it for me, Sir, to all
Our Friends: for my Heart speaks, they are
   Welcome.

Enter First Murtherer.

MACBETH   See they encounter thee with their
   Harts' Thanks:
Both Sides are Even: here I'll sit i' th' Midst.
Be large in Mirth; anon we'll drink a Measure   10
The Table round.
 — There's Blood upon thy Face.
MURTHERER   'Tis Banquo's then.
MACBETH   'Tis better thee without, then he within.
Is he dispatch'd?
MURTHERER   My Lord, his Throat is cut;
That I did for him.

17 **the Non-pareil**   the Cut-throat without a parallel (equal).
Macbeth's phrasing recalls 'peerless Kinsman' (I.iv.58).

19 **Fit**   fever, 'restless Ecstasy' (III.ii.23).
Perfect   complete, 'Whole' (see the note to I.iii.46). Compare
III.i.105–6. *Perfect* recalls I.iii.68, and it reinforces the idea
that Macbeth, forced out of the part he'd hoped to settle into,
is again required to improvise. Compare lines 3–4 and
I.iii.125–27, I.iv.23–24, I.v.64–68, I.vii.35–41, II.i.16–18,
II.iii.32–48.

20 **Whole . . . Marble**   Macbeth is probably thinking of a piece of
solid, unblemished marble. Compare *Othello*, V.ii.3–5,
137–40.
founded   built on a firm foundation. Macbeth's image echoes
Matthew 7:21–27, the parable about the wise (godly) man
who 'built his house upon a rock', as opposed to the 'foolish
man, which built his house upon the sand'. Macbeth's
ill-founded house will succumb to the 'rain' (as hinted in
III.iii.16).

21 **As . . . Air**   as unconstrained and free as the enveloping air.

23 **saucy**   unruly, uncontrollable.

27 **Worm**   young snake. Compare III.ii.13–15.

31 **give the Cheer**   provide the hospitality a host should.

31–33 **The . . . Welcome**   A feast that is not 'Given' (generously
bestowed) to its guests with frequent assurances (vouchings)
of welcome is no better than the kind of meal that is 'Sold'
(charged for) in an inn. Compare lines 1–7, especially lines
5–6, which now take on an unintended pertinence.

33–35 **To . . . it**   If one were merely eating to 'Feed' (provide for the
body's basic needs), it would be better to do so at home;
when one is away from home ('from thence'), one expects
one's 'Meat' (food) to be served with a special 'Sauce': the
'Ceremony' (festivity) that transforms a meal into a 'Meeting',
a gracious coming-together of like-minded people.

35 **Remembrancer**   reminder. Compare III.ii.31–32.

36 **wait on**   attend, follow after. Compare I.v.52 and I.vii.44.

MACBETH   Thou art the best o' th' Cut-throats,   15
  Yet he's good that did the like for Fleance:
  If thou didst it, thou art the Non-pareil.
MURTHERER   Most Royal Sir, Fleance is scap'd.
MACBETH   Then comes
  My Fit again. I had else been Perfect:
  Whole as the Marble, founded as the Rock,   20
  As broad and general as the casing Air.
  But now I am cabin'd, cribb'd, confin'd, bound in
  To saucy Doubts and Fears. But Banquo's safe?
MURTHERER   Ay, my good Lord: safe in a Ditch he
      bides,
  With twenty trenched Gashes on his Head,   25
  The least a Death to Nature.
MACBETH   Thanks for that:
  There the grown Serpent lies. The Worm that's
      fled
  Hath Nature that in Time will Venom breed,
  No Teeth for th' Present. Get thee gone.
      To morrow
  We'll hear our selves again.   *Exit Murtherer.*
LADY   My Royal Lord,   30
  You do not give the Cheer. The Feast is Sold
  That is not often Vouch'd while 'tis a making;
  'Tis Given with Welcome. To Feed were best at
      Home;
  From thence, the Sauce to Meat is Ceremony;
  Meeting were bare without it.

Enter the Ghost of Banquo, and sits in Macbeth's place.

MACBETH   Sweet Remembrancer.   35
  – Now good Digestion wait on Appetite,
  And Health on both.
LENOX   May't please your Highness sit.

38   **our . . . roof'd**   all the nobility of our nation under one roof.

40   **challenge for Unkindness**   accuse of a lapse of kindness (the
      courtesy to be expected from the kind of courtier he is). Lines
      40–43 echo I.v.18–20 and III.i.26–27. For other references to
      kind behaviour, see I.iii.12, 148; II.i.15, 23; III.iv.119; and
      IV.i.130.

41   **pity for Mischance**   be forced to pity him for some misfortune.

46   **done this**   played this trick on me.

48   **gory Locks**   bloody hair. See lines 24–26, where the Murderer
      says he put twenty trench-like gashes in Banquo's head. As
      Macbeth addresses the Ghost, it becomes clear that Banquo is
      not as 'safe' as the Murderer had thought. Compare
      III.i.11–13, 46–47, 49–52.

50   **often thus**   often seized by this kind of hallucinatory 'Fit' (line
      52). As she takes control of the situation, Macbeth's Lady
      again shows herself to be a quick-witted, resourceful partner.

52   **upon a Thought**   as quickly as one can have a thought.
      Macbeth's Lady is hoping that a collected 'Thought' will draw
      Macbeth out of his 'rapt' state (compare I.iii.55, 140).
      Thought echoes I.iii.137–40, I.v.42–45, and II.ii.19, 30–31.

54   **offend . . . Passion**   disturb him and prolong his suffering.

55   **Feed**   eat. The Lady's verb is an ironic reminder of lines 30–35.
      Are . . . Man?   The Lady's implication is that the frightened
      Macbeth is acting more like a silly child or a weak woman
      than a resolute, self-possessed man. Lines 55 and 57–65 echo
      her remarks in I.vii.35–54 and II.ii.49–54, 61–62. They
      anticipate lines 97–106. *I* means both 'I [am]' and 'Ay'.

57   **proper Stuff**   handsome nonsense; stuff well becoming a brave
      man. *Air-drawn* (line 59) hints at 'Heir-drawn'. See the note
      to III.v.29.

60   **Flaws**   both (a) outbursts of passion (like gusts of wind), and
      (b) cracks in your composure (see the note to line 20).

63   **Authoriz'd**   authored; as told by, or on the authority of.

MACBETH   Here had we now our Country's Honour
   roof'd
  Were the Grac'd Person of our Banquo present:
  Who may I rather challenge for Unkindness   40
  Than pity for Mischance.
ROSSE   His Absence, Sir,
  Lays Blame upon his Promise. Please't your
   Highness
  To grace us with your Royal Company?
MACBETH   The Table's full.
LENOX   Here is a Place reserv'd, Sir.
MACBETH   Where?
LENOX   Here, my good Lord. What is't that moves
  your Highness?   45
MACBETH   Which of you have done this?
LORDS   What, my good Lord?
MACBETH   – Thou canst not say I did it: Never shake
  Thy gory Locks at me.
ROSSE   Gentlemen, rise: his Highness is not well.
LADY   Sit, worthy Friends: my Lord is often thus,   50
  And hath been from his Youth. Pray you keep
   Seat,
  The Fit is momentary; upon a Thought
  He will again be well. If much you note him,
  You shall offend him and extend his Passion:
  Feed, and regard him not. – Are you a Man?   55
MACBETH   I, and a bold one, that dares look on
  that
  Which might appall the Divel.
LADY   O proper Stuff:
  This is the very Painting of your Fear;
  This is the Air-drawn Dagger which you said
  Led you to Duncan. O these Flaws and Starts   60
  (Impostors to true Fear) would well become
  A Woman's Story, at a Winter's Fire
  Authoriz'd by her Grandam. Shame it self,

64 **When all's done** in the final analysis. Compare III.ii.12.

68 **Charnel-houses** storehouses for unearthed bones.

69 **Monuments** tombs.

70 **Shall . . . Kites** will be the stomachs of birds of prey.

74 **Ere . . . Weal** before humane laws [based on Christian precepts] purified the realm of the inhuman revenge codes that once prevailed. *Humane* recalls I.v.9.

76 **has** Modern usage would call for *have*; in Shakespeare's time the rules of grammar were less rigid than they are now.

78 **they** slain men. *End* echoes III.iii.7.

79 **twenty . . . Crowns** Macbeth paraphrases what the First Murderer has told him in lines 24–26. The phrase 'their Crowns' (tops of their heads) is a reminder that Macbeth's assassins have not been able to inflict 'mortal Murthers' on Banquo's progeny (or on the crowns they will wear in due course). See the note to I.v.73.

80 **push . . . Stools** shove us out of our seats at the table. Macbeth is also thinking about the other 'stool' he hopes to make 'safe' from Banquo and his line; compare III.i.46–70. Macbeth's phrasing echoes line 65 and anticipates line 107.

82 **lack you** suffer for lack of your company as their host.

83 **muse** wonder.

84 **strange Infirmity** unusual illness. See the notes to I.iii.46, 82; I.v.6, 22; II.ii.36, 48–50; III.i.50; and III.iv.3.

Why do you make such Faces? When all's done,
You look but on a Stool.

MACBETH   Prythee see there: 65
Behold, look, lo! How say you?
— Why what care I, if thou canst nod, speak
    too.
If Charnel-houses and our Graves must send
Those that we bury back, our Monuments
Shall be the Maws of Kites.   [*Exit Ghost.*]   70

LADY   What? Quite unmann'd in Folly.

MACBETH   If I stand here, I saw him.

LADY   Fie, for Shame.

MACBETH   Blood hath been shed ere now, i' th'
    Olden Time
Ere humane Statute purg'd the gentle Weal;
Ay, and since too, Murthers have been perform'd   75
Too terrible for the Ear. The Times has been
That when the Brains were out the Man would
    die,
And there an End. But now they rise again
With twenty mortal Murthers on their Crowns,
And push us from our Stools. This is more
    Strange   80
Than such a Murther is.

LADY   My worthy Lord,
Your Noble Friends do lack you.

MACBETH   I do forget.
— Do not muse at me, my most worthy Friends:
I have a strange Infirmity, which is nothing
To those that know me. Come, Love and Health
    to all,   85
Then I'll sit down. — Give me some Wine, fill
    full.

                Enter Ghost.

89   **him we thirst**   the guest we thirst for ('miss') and drink to now.
      Would . . . here recalls II.ii.73.

90   **the Pledge**   that which our King has pledged (proposed) as a
      toast.

91   **Avaunt**   begone. Macbeth has just noticed Banquo again.
      quit   leave.

93   **Speculation**   vision, perception. Macbeth's noun provides an
      aptly haunting reminder that he is addressing a spectre.

95   **a . . . Custom**   something he has long been prone to do.

98   **rugged**   rough. Russian bears were imported for baiting.

99   **arm'd**   armour-plated.
      Hyrcan   Hyrcanian; fierce tigers from an area near the Caspian
      Sea.

102 **dare . . . Desart**   challenge me to some deserted locale.

103 **inhabit**   wear, exhibit.
      protest   pronounce, attest; proclaim, swear.

105 **Mock'ry**   both (a) illusion, counterfeit, and (b) mocker of my
      manhood.

107 **displac'd the Mirth**   replaced the merriment with another mood
      (compare line 10). The Lady's verb suggests usurpation; it is
      thus a reminder that Macbeth has 'displac'd the Mirth' in a
      way that 'broke the good Meeting' of all Scotland. In line 108
      admir'd means 'astonishing, wondered at'. *Meeting* echoes
      line 35.

110– **You . . . owe**   you make me feel like a stranger even to my own
  11 courageous temperament. Compare I.ii.16.

114 **blanch'd**   made white. Compare II.ii.61–62 and III.ii.50–51.

— I drink to th' general Joy o' th' whole Table,
And to our dear Friend Banquo, whom we miss.
Would he were here. To all, and him we thirst,
And all to all.

LORDS   Our Duties, and the Pledge.   90

MACBETH   — Avaunt, and quit my Sight; let the
     Earth hide thee!
Thy Bones are Marrowless, thy Blood is cold;
Thou hast no Speculation in those Eyes
Which thou dost glare with.

LADY   Think of this, good Peers,
But as a thing of Custom: 'tis no other,   95
Onely it spoils the Pleasure of the Time.

MACBETH   — What Man dare, I dare.
Approach thou like the rugged Russian Bear,
The arm'd Rhinoceros, or th' Hyrcan Tiger;
Take any Shape but that, and my firm Nerves   100
Shall never tremble. Or be alive again,
And dare me to the Desart with thy Sword;
If trembling I inhabit then, protest me
The Baby of a Girl. Hence, horrible Shadow;
Unreal Mock'ry, hence!   [*Exit Ghost.*]
                    — Why so: being gone,   105
I am a Man again. Pray you sit still.

LADY   You have displac'd the Mirth, broke the
     good Meeting
With most admir'd Disorder.

MACBETH   Can such things be,
And overcome us like a Summer's Cloud,
Without our special Wonder? You make me Strange   110
Even to the Disposition that I owe,
When now I think you can behold such Sights,
And keep the natural Ruby of your Cheeks,
When mine is blanch'd with Fear.

ROSSE   What Sights, my Lord?

116 **enrages him** drives him mad. Compare line 54.

117 **Stand . . . Going** don't stand on ceremony (feel obliged to adhere to the decorum that would normally have you depart ceremoniously, in accord with your rank); compare line 1 and II.iii.150–51. *Stand* echoes III.i.4 and III.iii.15.

120 **Blood . . . Blood** The blood that is shed will demand blood in return. Compare I.vii.2–12 and Genesis 4:10 (echoed in II.i.53–59 and II.ii.44) and 9:6.

121 **Stones . . . move** Macbeth is probably thinking of the tombstones over the graves of murdered men. Compare line 20 and II.i.57.
Trees to speak According to Virgil, one of the portents of Caesar's assassination was that trees uttered warnings.

122 **Augures** auguries; omens. Compare II.iii.128–29.
understood Relations comprehensible accounts.

123 **Maggot Pies** magpies.
Choughs jackdaws, like rooks members of the crow family.

123– **brought . . . Blood.** disclosed the most secretive murderer.
24 Compare II.i.55–59, II.ii.43–44.

125 **at Odds with** in competition with. See the note to line 107.

130 **Feed** on a retainer's fee, to feed me information. *Feed* echoes line 55.

131 **betimes** very early.

132 **bent** resolved. Compare I.vii.79–80, II.ii.42–43.

136 **Returning . . . o'er** it would be as wearisome to 'wade' back as to continue to the other side. Compare I.vii.4–7.

137– **Strange . . . scann'd** I have secret thoughts that demand to be
38 acted on before they are examined too closely.

LADY   I pray you speak not: he grows worse and
    worse.   115
  Question enrages him. At once Goodnight.
  Stand not upon the Order of your Going,
  But go at once.
LENOX   Good night, and better Health
  Attend his Maiesty.
LADY   A kind Goodnight to all.
                               Exeunt Lords.
MACBETH   It will have Blood, they say: Blood
    will have Blood.   120
  Stones have been known to move, and Trees to
    speak;
  Augures and understood Relations have
  By Maggot Pies and Choughs and Rooks brought
    forth
  The secret'st Man of Blood. What is the Night?
LADY   Almost at Odds with Morning, which is which.   125
MACBETH   How say'st thou that Macduff denies his
    person
  At our great Bidding?
LADY   Did you send to him, Sir?
MACBETH   I hear it by the way; but I will send.
  There's not a one of them but in his House
  I keep a Servant Feed. I will to morrow   130
  (And betimes I will) to the weyard Sisters;
  More shall they speak. For now I am bent to
    know,
  By the worst Means, the Worst; for mine own
    Good,
  All Causes shall give way. I am in Blood
  Stepp'd in so far that should I wade no more   135
  Returning were as tedious as go o'er.
  Strange things I have in Head, that will to
    Hand,
  Which must be acted ere they may be scann'd.

139   **the . . . Natures** that which seasons (nourishes and preserves) all living things. Compare II.ii.3–8, 32–37.

140   **My . . . Abuse** the strange way in which I am abusing myself. Macbeth believes that he has allowed himself to be cowed by hallucinations: deceptions induced by the 'initiate Fear' (line 141) of a youthful beginner. He seeks the self-possession of a seasoned criminal whose conscience has become callow, or calloused, from 'hard Use'. See the note to III.ii.56.

141   **wants hard Use** is lacking in the experience that toughens a novice's tender sensibilities. Compare *Hamlet*, V.i.73–74.

142   **indeed** both (a) in fact, and (b) in deed.

III.v   This scene probably takes place on the heath. Many scholars believe it to be an interpolation, but there is no proof that it was not written by Shakespeare.

1   **angerly** angrily; literally, 'anger-like'.

2   **Beldams** hideous old women, hags (literally, 'beautiful matrons').

7   **close** both (a) secret, and (d) closely observant and controlling. Compare III.ii.14.

11   **wayward** disloyal, disobedient; perverse. *Wayward* echoes *weyward/weyard* (see the note to I.iii.30), a word that means both (a) evil, and (b) 'fateful'.

13   **Loves . . . Ends** loves you only for what he can gain from you. Hecat is right, of course; that kind of self-love is precisely what makes Macbeth 'wayward' in a spiritual sense. Compare III.iv.132–34.

15   **Acheron** one of the rivers of Hades (Hell).

21   **Unto . . . End** to accomplish something sinister and fatal. *Dismal* (from the Latin for 'evil days') recalls I.ii.52–54.

22   **Great Business** important matters. Compare I.v.69–72.
      wrought accomplished (literally, shaped or worked). Compare I.iii.147, II.i.18, III.i.80.

24   **vap'rous Drop profound** a drop of water, condensed from vapour, that is just about ready to fall.

LADY   You lack the Season of all Natures, Sleep.
MACBETH   Come, we'll to sleep. My strange and
 self Abuse   140
Is the initiate Fear that wants hard Use.
We are yet but young indeed.   *Exeunt.*

Scene 5

Thunder. Enter the three Witches, meeting Hecat.

I WITCH   Why how now, Hecat? You look angerly.
HECAT   Have I not Reason, Beldams, as you are?
 Saucy and over-bold, how did you dare
 To trade and traffic with Macbeth
 In Riddles and Affairs of Death?   5
 And I, the Mistress of your Charms,
 The close Contriver of all Harms,
 Was never call'd to bear my Part
 Or shew the Glory of our Art?
 And which is worse, all you have done   10
 Hath been but for a wayward Son,
 Spightful and wrathful, who, as others do,
 Loves for his own Ends, not for you.
 But makes Amends now: get you gone,
 And at the Pit of Acheron   15
 Meet me i' th' Morning. Thither he
 Will come to know his Destiny.
 Your Vessels and your Spells provide,
 Your Charms, and every thing beside.
 I am for th' Air; this Night I'll spend   20
 Unto a Dismal and a Fatal End.
 Great Business must be wrought ere Noon.
 Upon the Corner of the Moon
 There hangs a vap'rous Drop profound;

26   **Slights**   sleights, devices (designed to make Macbeth 'slight').

29   **draw him on**   attract him, seduce him. Compare the punning phrase 'Air-drawn Dagger' (III.iv.59), which depicts the air as an artist, and the 'Fatal Vision' it alludes to (II.i.33–46). *Draw* can also mean 'drain, empty' (I.iii.17–22). See the note to III.iv.57.
      Confusion   both (a) bewilderment, and (b) destruction. Compare II.iii.64, 72.

30   **spurn Fate**   kick at (disregard) the operations of Destiny.
      scorn Death   treat Death with audacious contempt, not fear.

30–31 **bear . . . Fear**   allow his hopes to be carried higher than what prudence, respect for the workings of Providence, and fear of God would dictate. Compare I.vii.25–28 and II.iii.4–6 (where the Porter describes a 'Farmer' who 'hang'd himself' in a way that parallels the crime and punishment of Macbeth), 34–41.
      Hopes   This word recalls I.iii.53–54, I.vii.35–36, and III.i.9–10.

32   **Security**   unwarranted self-assurance. Compare *Julius Caesar*, II.iii.9. *Mortals'* recalls I.v.3, 33.

S.D.   **Come away**   What may be a version of this song appears in Thomas Middleton's *The Witch* (circa 1609); it was included in an operatic adaptation of *Macbeth* by William Davenant in 1674.

III.vi   This scene takes place at an unspecified location in Scotland.

1   **My former Speeches**   what I have said before. Compare III.i.73–84.
      hit your Thoughts   touched on (coincided with) what you yourself have been thinking. Lenox is taking care to speak with prudent indirection; the consequence is that virtually everything he says is couched in verbal irony. *Hit* recalls I.v.48–49; *Thoughts* echoes III.iv.52.

3   **strangely borne**   carried (conducted) in an unusual manner. Compare II.iv.20–41, III.i.28–31.
      gracious   grace-filled; pious, godly.

4   **marry . . . Dead**   but of course Duncan was dead.

5   **walk'd too late**   was out walking beyond the time when he should have been. Compare III.iii.6, 14–15.

8   **cannot . . . Thought**   is unable to avoid thinking.
      monstrous   without precedent.

10   **Fact**   deed.

11   **straight**   immediately.

I'll catch it ere it come to Ground.   25
And that distill'd by Magic Slights
Shall raise such Artificial Sprights
As by the strength of their Illusion
Shall draw him on to his Confusion.
He shall spurn Fate, scorn Death, and bear   30
His Hopes 'bove Wisdom, Grace, and Fear.
And you all know, Security
Is Mortals chiefest Enemy.

                                                   Music, and a Song.

Hark, I am call'd: my little Spirit, see,
Sits in a foggy Cloud and stays for me.   [*Exit.*]   35

          Sing within: 'Come away, come away', etc.

1 WITCH   Come, let's make haste; she'll soon be
    back again.   *Exeunt.*

Scene 6

Enter Lenox, and another Lord.

LENOX   My former Speeches have but hit your
    Thoughts,
Which can interpret further; onely I say
Things have been strangely borne. The gracious
    Duncan
Was pitied of Macbeth: marry he was dead.
And the right valiant Banquo walk'd too late,   5
Whom you may say (if't please you) Fleance
    kill'd,
For Fleance fled: Men must not walk too late.
Who cannot want the Thought, how monstrous
It was for Malcolm and for Donalbain
To kill their gracious Father? Damned Fact,   10
How it did grieve Macbeth? Did he not straight

12 **Delinquents** criminals.

13 **Thralls** captives. *Ay* (line 14) is *I* in the Folio text. So also in
II.i.35; II.ii.16; III.ii.1; III.iv24, 75; IV.i.124, 142; IV.ii.44;
IV.iii.141; V.vii.76. Compare III.i.19, V.i.29, and especially
V.vii.73 (where *I* means 'Ay' but plays on the same masculine
sense noted for the number *1* in I.v.73).

17 **borne . . . well** carried off everything prudently. Compare line
3, and III.i.79.

18 **under his Key** in his custody [and in his prison].

20 **What . . . Father** what happens to parricides.

21–22 **for . . . Feast** for, because he has spoken too openly, and
because he failed to appear at the new King's royal feast.
Compare III.i.26 and III.iv.126–30. *Cause* means "cause'
(because).

23 **Disgrace** disfavour with Macbeth.

25 **holds . . . Birth** holds in his grasp what should properly have
fallen to Malcolm as his 'due' (birthright, inheritance).
Compare I.iv.18–27.

27 **Pious Edward** saintly Edward the Confessor (King of England,
1042–66).
such Grace both (a) unrestrained hospitality, and (b) all the
holiness a pious king bestows upon a worthy fellow prince.

29 **Takes . . . Respect** steals from the honours (and obedience) he
should be receiving from the people of Scotland.

30 **upon his Aid** on behalf of Malcolm (line 24).

31 **Northumberland** the county in northern England of which
Seyward was Earl. Modern editions normally spell the Earl's
surname 'Siward'.

36 **Do faithful Homage** dutifully obey our ruler [because he is
legitimate]. Compare I.vi.25–28.

38 **exasperate their King** infuriated either (a) Edward, or (b)
Macbeth. Most editors emend *their* to *the*.

In pious Rage the two Delinquents tear
That were the Slaves of Drink and Thralls of
   Sleep?
Was not that Nobly done? Ay, and Wisely too:
For 'twould have anger'd any Heart alive   15
To hear the Men deny't. So that I say
He has borne all things well, and I do think
That had he Duncan's Sons under his Key
(As and't please Heaven, he shall not) they
   should find
What 'twere to kill a Father; so should Fleance.   20
But peace: for from broad Words, and cause he
   fail'd
His Presence at the Tyrant's Feast, I hear
Macduff lives in Disgrace. Sir, can you tell
Where he bestows himself?
LORD   The Son of Duncan
(From whom this Tyrant holds the Due of Birth) 25
Lives in the English Court, and is receiv'd
Of the most Pious Edward with such Grace
That the Malevolence of Fortune nothing
Takes from his high Respect. Thither Macduff
Is gone to pray the Holy King upon his Aid   30
To wake Northumberland and warlike Seyward,
That by the help of these (with Him above
To ratify the Work) we may again
Give to our Tables Meat, Sleep to our Nights;
Free from our Feasts and Banquets bloody
   Knives;   35
Do faithful Homage and receive free Honours,
All which we pine for now. And this Report
Hath so exasperate their King that he
Prepares for some Attempt of War.
LENOX   Sent he to Macduff?
LORD   He did: and with an absolute 'Sir, not I!'   40

41–43 **The . . . Answer** His unsunny (scowling) messenger (a) sent
Macbeth's emissary back, or (b) turned his back on Macbeth
with a 'humph', as if to say, 'You'll regret the time that has
encumbered me long enough for this reply.' *Cloudy* recalls
III.iv.109.

44 **Advise . . . Caution** be a signal to him that he should take
precautions to protect himself. Lenox implies that Macduff is
so incensed against Macbeth that he fails to exercise
prudence. Macduff thus sets himself up for the affliction that
awaits those with an unwarranted sense of 'Security'
(III.v.30–33). The classical Greek term for such complacency
was *pleonexia*. In the *Iliad* and in Greek tragedy, smug
overconfidence often leads on to *atê*, a 'cloudy' blindness to
danger (line 41) that prompts a person to commit an act of
hubris (an outrageous, defiant manifestation of arrogance that
calls down retribution from the heavens). In biblical terms the
moral is much the same: 'Pride goeth before destruction, and
a haughty spirit before a fall' (Proverbs 16:18). Compare
III.v.30–34, IV.i.89–93, V.iv.8–10, and V.vii.48–51.
hold what Distance put whatever distance between himself and
Macbeth. Compare III.i.114–16.

45 **Some** may some.

46 **unfold** disclose, reveal.

47 **Blessing** From this point on, virtually every reference to
England associates her and her holy King with a God who
delivers His people from unmerited afflictions. It is also clear
that Macbeth is now to be regarded as a tyrant: a usurper
with no claim on the loyalties of those who are subject to his
cruelty.

48 **suffering** both (a) abused, and (b) passively (because helplessly)
enduring.

49 **a Hand Accurs'd** the hand of a man who is damned. Compare
II.ii.44, 56–60, II.iii.137, III.i.60–61, 77–79, 86–89, and
III.iv.137–38, for previous references to the hand.

The cloudy Messenger turns me his Back
And hums: as who should say, 'You'll rue the
   Time
That clogs me with this Answer.'
LENOX   And that well might
  Advise him to a Caution, t' hold what Distance
  His Wisdom can provide. Some holy Angel   45
  Fly to the Court of England, and unfold
  His Message ere he come, that a swift Blessing
  May soon return to this our suffering Country,
  Under a Hand Accurs'd.
LORD   I'll send my Prayers with him.
                             Exeunt.

IV.i   This scene takes place at 'the Pit of Acheron' (III,v.15), with a cauldron encircled by the Witches.

1   **brinded**   branded; that is, brindled or streaked (a tabby cat). The First Witch's familiar spirit is a cat (I.i.8).

2   **Hedge-pig**   hedgehog; probably the Second Witch's familiar spirit in this scene (though in I.i the only other familiar mentioned was a 'Padock', a toad).

3   **Harpier**   probably another familiar, named after the Harpies who pursued the guilty in classical myth. It is not clear whether (a) ''tis Time' because Harpier calls, or (b) Harpier calls ''Tis time'.

4   **Cauldron**   a large pot for use in boiling; probably one of the 'Vessels' ordered by Hecat in III.v.18.

8   **Swelt'red . . . got**   sweat-exuded poisons conceived (begotten). *Venom* probably refers to infant toads, each carrying its own venom.

9   **charmed Pot**   pot that has been placed under a magic spell.

10   **Double, double**   Fittingly, the Witches refer twice to their doubling-back movements. The imagery they use is central to their role in an action where almost everything can be perceived 'in a Double Sense' (V.viii.49). Compare I.i.9; I.ii.25–28, 38–39; I.iii.128–31; I.iv.11–12; I.v.64–68; I.vi.14–18; I.vii.12–14, 60–61; II.iii.9–41, 143–44; III.ii.4–7, 33–36; IV.iv.124–25.
    Trouble   This word recalls I.vii.11–14, II.iii.55–57.

11   **Fire**   here as frequently elsewhere, a two-syllable word.

12   **Fillet . . . Snake**   slice of a swamp-inhabiting snake.

14   **Newt**   small salamander-like amphibian.

16   **Adder's Fork**   the forked tongue of a venomous snake.
    Blind-worm's Sting   venom of a small, snake-like lizard.

17   **Howlet**   owlet.

18   **powreful**   both (a) powerful, and (b) pour-full. Compare I.v.28 and I.iii.98.

ACT IV

Scene 1

Thunder. Enter the three Witches.

1 WITCH	Thrice the brinded Cat hath mew'd.
2 WITCH	Thrice, and once the Hedge-pig whin'd.
3 WITCH	Harpier cries, 'tis Time, 'tis Time.
1 WITCH	Round about the Cauldron go;

In the poison'd Entrails throw   5
Toad, that under cold Stone,
Days and Nights, has thirty-one
Swelt'red Venom sleeping got;
Boil thou first i' th' charmed Pot.

ALL   Double, double, Toil and Trouble;   10
Fire burn, and Cauldron bubble.

2 WITCH   Fillet of a Fenny Snake,
In the Cauldron boil and bake;
Eye of Newt, and Toe of Frog,
Wool of Bat, and Tongue of Dog;   15
Adder's Fork, and Blind-worm's Sting,
Lizard's Leg, and Howlet's Wing;
For a Charm of powreful Trouble,
Like a Hell-broth, boil and bubble.

ALL   Double, double, Toil and Trouble;   20

23   **Witches' Mummy** the mummified remains of one or more witches.
      Maw and Gulf throat and stomach.

24   **ravin'd** ravenous; literally, stuffed with prey.
      salt both (a) salt-saturated, and (b) lustful (as in *Othello*, II.ii.247–48).

25   **Hemlock** highly poisonous plant of the parsley and carrot family.
      i' th' Dark Hemlock was thought to be most potent at night.

26   **blaspheming Jew** Like the 'Turk' and the 'Tartar' (line 29), the Jew represented a rejection of the Christian faith. His 'Liver' is thus a key ingredient in a formula to assure that Macbeth will keep denying Christ.

27   **Yew** a tree traditionally planted in graveyards, to deter cattle, with highly poisonous leaves and berries.

31   **Ditch-deliver'd by a Drab** delivered in a ditch by a whore.

32   **slab** sticky, dense.

33   **Chawdron** entrails. *Cawdron* (line 34) means 'cauldron'.

34   **Ingredience** ingredients.

38   **firm and good** fixed and effectual.

43   **Inchanting** placing a charm on (literally, 'singing in').

44   **By ... Thumbs** I can tell by the pricking sensation in my thumbs. *Open Locks* may mean 'Open, Locks'.

48   **A ... Name** A deed so terrible it can't be spoken. Compare Macbeth's initial reaction to his own crime: II.ii.48, 69–70.

Fire burn, and Cauldron bubble.
3 WITCH   Scale of Dragon, Tooth of Wolf,
  Witches Mummy, Maw and Gulf
  Of the ravin'd salt Sea Shark;
  Root of Hemlock, digg'd i' th' Dark,   25
  Liver of blaspheming Jew,
  Gall of Goat, and Slips of Yew,
  Sliver'd in the Moon's Eclipse;
  Nose of Turk, and Tartar's Lips,
  Finger of Birth-strangled Babe,   30
  Ditch-deliver'd by a Drab,
  Make the Gruel thick and slab;
  Add thereto a Tiger's Chawdron
  For th' Ingredience of our Cawdron.
ALL   Double, double, Toil and Trouble,   35
  Fire burn, and Cauldron bubble.
2 WITCH   Cool it with a Baboon's Blood,
  Then the Charm is firm and good.

  Enter Hecat, and the other three Witches.

HECAT   O well done: I commend your Pains,
  And every one shall share i' th' Gains;   40
  And now about the Cauldron sing
  Like Elves and Fairies in a Ring.
  Inchanting all that you put in.
                  Music and a Song. 'Black Spirits', etc.
2 WITCH   By the pricking of my Thumbs,
  Something Wicked this way comes: 45
  Open Locks, who ever knocks.

                  Enter Macbeth.

MACBETH   How now, you secret, black, and
  midnight Hags?
  What is't you do?

49   **that ... profess**   the art you profess to know; the prophetic powers you claim to possess.

51   **untie**   release, set free to wreak havoc. Compare *Othello*, IV.ii.76–78. *Ere* can mean both (a) before, and (b) ever.

51–52 **fight ... Churches**   oppose themselves against the steeples of churches. Macbeth's imagery suggests that he wishes to enlist the Witches in his own 'fight / Against the Churches'. See the note to III.vi.47.

52   **yesty**   yeasty, frothing, with play on *iesty* (jesty, scornful).

53   **Confound ... up**   wreck and devour ships.

54   **bladed ... lodg'd**   ripe grain be beaten down by wind, rain, and hail.

55   **Warders'**   keepers', guards'. Compare I.vii.65–67. *Pyramids* can refer to any large gabled or obelisk-shaped structure.

56   **slope**   bend down, permit to decline.

58   **Germain**   germen; germs or seeds from which all living things are generated (germinated). Compare I.iii.56–57.
      altogether   both (a) all together (into a single lump), and (b) all at once.

59   **Even ... sicken**   even to the point where Destruction itself is sickened from satiation.

62   **Masters**   either (a) Masters' or (b) Masters.

63   **Powre**   pour. But see the note to line 18, and compare line 79.

64   **nine Farrow**   litter of nine infant pigs.
      sweaten   sweated. Compare line 8.

65   **Gibbet**   the scaffold from which the bodies of executed criminals were hung to rot.

66   **high or low**   from the heights or the depths.

S.D.   **an Armed Head**   a helmeted head (a prophetic image both of the avenging Macduff and of Macbeth's own decapitation).

67   **deaftly**   deftly, with play on *deaf*. See lines 76–77, and compare *2 Henry IV*, I.ii.75.

68   **He ... Thought**   he can read your mind [so there is no reason for you to express your thoughts].

69   **nought**   naught, nothing.

ALL   A Deed without a Name.
MACBETH   I conjure you, by that which you
    profess
  (How ere you come to know it), answer me: 50
  Though you untie the Winds, and let them fight
  Against the Churches, though the yesty Waves
  Confound and swallow Navigation up,
  Though bladed Corn be lodg'd, and Trees blown
    down,
  Though Castles topple on their Warders' Heads,   55
  Though Palaces and Pyramids do slope
  Their Heads to their Foundations, though the
    Treasure
  Of Nature's Germain tumble altogether,
  Even till Destruction sicken, answer me
  To what I ask you.
1 WITCH   Speak.
2 WITCH   Demand.
3 WITCH   We'll answer.   60
1 WITCH   Say if th' hadst rather hear it from
    our Mouths
  Or from our Masters.
MACBETH   Call 'em: let me see 'em.
1 WITCH   Powre in Sow's Blood, that hath eaten
  Her nine Farrow; Grease that's sweaten
  From the Murderer's Gibbet, throw   65
  Into the Flame.
ALL   Come high or low,
  Thy Self and Office deaftly show.   *Thunder.*
                First Apparition, an Armed Head.
MACBETH   Tell me, thou unknown Power –
1 WITCH   He knows thy Thought:
  Hear his Speech, but say thou nought.
1 APPARITION   Macbeth, Macbeth, Macbeth: beware
  Macduff,   70
  Beware the Thane of Fife. Dismiss me. Enough.

S.D. **He descends** This stage direction suggests that the apparitions appeared and disappeared through the trap door in the floor of the Globe stage.

73 **harp'd** Macbeth's verb can refer to a note on the musical harp or to the voice of a harpy. Compare line 3.

S.D. **a Bloody Child** This apparition is a 'potent' symbol (line 75) of much that happens in the play. It is a reminder of what Macbeth's Lady has said in I.vii.54–59, when she describes what she would have done with 'the Babe' that milked her if she had proven so unmanly as Macbeth. It turns out to be a prophecy of what Macbeth's henchmen do to Macduff's child. And it alludes to the infancy of Macduff himself, who will tell Macbeth that he was 'from his Mother's Womb / Untimely ripp'd' (V.vii.44–45).

82 **Assurance double sure** This phrase echoes III.v.32–33. See the notes to line 10 and III.vi.44.

83 **take . . . Fate** take out a bond (contract) with Fate [to deal Macduff a fatal wound]. Compare III.ii.49–51.

84 **That . . . lies** so I may scorn the 'Caution' (line 72) commended by 'pale-hearted Fear'. Compare I.vii.37–38 and II.ii.61–62.

85 **sleep . . . Thunder** sleep in peace despite the rumblings of thunder (as in *Othello*, V.ii.227–28). *Issue* recalls III.i.59–68.

S.D. **a Child Crowned** This apparition echoes the Witches' prophecy in I.iii.65. The 'Tree in his Hand' recalls the growth and fertility earlier associated with Duncan.

87–88 **Round . . . Sovereignty** Crown. Compare I.v.30–32.

89 **Lion-mettled** as metal-hearted (brave) as the lion, proverbial for its mettle (spirit). Compare I.vii.72–74. *Mettle* and *metal* are interchangeable in Shakespeare.
Proud arrogant. The apparition is counselling Macbeth to give himself over to the hubris that precipitates a fall.
take no Care throw caution to the winds.

92 **Byrnam** This is the Folio's only use of the final *m* for this name. In Holinshed's *Chronicles* Shakespeare would have found both *Bernane* and *Birnane*. This edition preserves the Folio's spelling variations.

He descends.

MACBETH   What ere thou art, for thy good
   Caution, thanks.
  Thou hast harp'd my Fear aright. But one Word
   more.
1 WITCH   He will not be commanded: here's
   another
  More potent than the first.   *Thunder.*   75
               Second Apparition, a Bloody Child.
2 APPARITION   Macbeth, Macbeth, Macbeth.
MACBETH   Had I three Ears, I'd hear thee.
2 APPARITION   Be bloody, bold, and resolute:
   laugh to Scorn
  The Powre of Man: for none of Woman borne
  Shall harm Macbeth.   *Descends.*   80
MACBETH   Then live Macduff: what need I fear
   of thee?
  But yet I'll make Assurance double sure,
  And take a Bond of Fate: thou shalt not live,
  That I may tell pale-hearted Fear it lies,
  And sleep in spight of Thunder.   *Thunder.*
          Third Apparition, a Child Crowned,
             with a Tree in his Hand.
           – What is this,   85
  That rises like the Issue of a King,
  And wears upon his Baby-brow the Round
  And Top of Sovereignty?
ALL   Listen, but speak not to't.
3 APPARITION   Be Lion-mettled, Proud, and take no
   Care
  Who chafes, who frets, or where Conspirers are: 90
  Macbeth shall never vanquish'd be until
  Great Byrnam Wood to high Dunsinane Hill
  Shall come against him.   *Descend.*
MACBETH   That will never be.

94   **impress**   press (force) into military service.

95   **Unfix ... Root**   Macbeth's phrasing echoes I.iii.132–33 and III.i.5–6.
       Sweet Bodements   welcome (delicious) prophecies.

98   **Shall ... Nature**   shall live out the full lease (allotted time) that Nature gives human beings in accord with 'mortal Custom' (line 99) – the 'threescore years and ten' noted as a norm in Psalm 90:10.

104   **And ... you**   Macbeth thinks it in his power to curse the very embodiments of the power to carry out a curse.

S.D.   **Shew**   show, pageant; also in lines 106–8.
       Glass   mirror (here one that reflects the future). See line 118.

113   **the First**   the first descendant of Banquo. Macbeth addresses the second. *Hair* (with play on both *heir* and *air*) recalls I.iii.132–35, III.iv.59.

115   **Start**   be astonished. Compare I.iii.49 and III.iv.60–62.

116   **Crack of Doom**   dawning of the Day of Judgement.

118   **Eight**   eighth (either Banquo or the eighth king in his line).

120   **two-fold Balls**   double orbs (a part of the King's regalia, symbolizing the Earth). This image is probably an allusion to the double crowning of the descendant of Banquo who occupied the throne when *Macbeth* was first performed: James VI of Scotland, who also became James I of England after the death of Elizabeth in 1603. Eight Stuart monarchs preceded James.
       treble Sceptres   the sceptre used in the Scottish coronation, plus the two used in the English. Since James's official title was 'King of Great Britain, France, and Ireland', however, the 'treble Sceptres' may refer as well to the three realms he claimed to rule.

Who can impress the Forest, bid the Tree
Unfix his Earth-bound Root? Sweet Bodements,
   good.   95
– Rebellious Dead, rise never till the Wood
Of Byrnan rise, and our high plac'd Macbeth
Shall live the Lease of Nature, pay his Breath
To Time and mortal Custom. – Yet my Heart
Throbs to know one thing: tell me, if your Art   100
Can tell so much, shall Banquo's Issue ever
Reign in this Kingdom?

ALL   Seek to know no more.

MACBETH   I will be satisfi'd. Deny me this,
And an eternal Curse fall on you. Let me know.
Why sinks that Cauldron? And what Noise is
   this?   *Hoboys.* 105

1 WITCH   Shew.

2 WITCH   Shew.

3 WITCH   Shew.

ALL   Shew his Eyes, and grieve his Heart;
Come like Shadows, so depart.   110

          A Shew of eight Kings, and Banquo last,
                  with a Glass in his Hand.

MACBETH   Thou art too like the Spirit of Banquo:
   down.
Thy Crown does sear mine Eyeballs. And thy
   Hair,
Thou other Gold-bound Brow, is like the First.
A Third is like the former. – Filthy Hags,
Why do you shew me this? – A Fourth?
   Start, Eyes!   115
What, will the Line stretch out to th' Crack of
   Doom?
Another yet? A Seventh? I'll see no more.
And yet the Eight appears, who bears a Glass,
Which shews me many more; and some I see
That two-fold Balls and treble Sceptres carry.   120

122 **Blood-bolter'd** his hair caked with blood.

125 **amazedly** frozen in bewilderment. Compare II.iii.115–16.

126 **Sprights** spirits. Compare III.v.27.

129 **Antique** both (a) ancient, accustomed, and (b) antic (wild and intricate dance). *Round* can be either an adverb (meaning 'around') or a noun (referring to a circular movement. The Folio capitalizes *Antique*, but lowercases *round*.

131 **Our . . . pay** our tributes repaid him for the welcome he gave us.

132 **pernicious** fatal, deadly.

133 **aye** forever.

134 **without there** you who stand outside there.

137 **Infected** death-dealing. *Air* echoes lines 112–13.

138 **damn'd . . . them** Ironically, Macbeth curses himself to damnation.

143 **thou anticipat'st** you prevent, forestall.

144–
45 **The . . . it** The fleeting purpose we set our hearts on (the intention we resolve to carry out) can never be seized unless we send along a deed to execute our resolve immediately. Compare II.i.59–60 and III.iv.134–38.

Horrible Sight: now I see 'tis true,
For the Blood-bolter'd Banquo smiles upon me,
And points at them for his. What? Is this so?

1 WITCH   Ay Sir, all this is so. But why
Stands Macbeth thus amazedly?   125
– Come, Sisters, cheer we up his Sprights,
And shew the best of our Delights.
I'll charm the Air to give a Sound,
While you perform your Antique round:
That this great King may kindly say   130
Our Duties did his welcome pay.   *Music.*
                    The Witches dance, and vanish.

MACBETH   Where are they? Gone? Let this
    pernicious Hour
Stand aye accursed in the Calendar.
– Come in, without there.

                    Enter Lenox.

LENOX   What's your Grace's Will?
MACBETH   Saw you the Weyard Sisters?
LENOX   No, my Lord.   135
MACBETH   Came they not by you?
LENOX   No indeed, my Lord.
MACBETH   Infected be the Air whereon they ride,
    And damn'd all those that trust them. I did
    hear
    The Galloping of Horse. Who was't came by?
LENOX   'Tis two or three, my Lord, that bring
    you Word: 140
    Macduff is fled to England.
MACBETH   Fled to England?
LENOX   Ay, my good Lord.
MACBETH   – Time, thou anticipat'st my dread
    Exploits:
    The flighty Purpose never is o'ertook

145–   **From ... Hand** From now on, the first impulse that comes to
47   my heart shall be the one that activates my hand.

148   **crown ... Acts** It took Macbeth considerably longer to 'crown'
        his first 'Thoughts' with 'Acts'. Compare I.iii.125–27;
        I.v.42–45, 68–73; I.vii.39–41; IV.i.82–88.
        be ... done let the thinking and the acting be so close in time
        as to seem simultaneous. *Hand* echoes III.vi.49.

149   **surprise** take by surprise; 'seize upon', line 150.

150   **Fife** 'The Castle of Macduff', the Thane of Fife.

152   **trace ... Line** follow him as his descendants.
        No ... Fool let me not stand around foolishly boasting about
        what I'm going to do. Compare II.i.59–60.

153   **This ... cool** I'll strike while the iron is hot. Compare
        III.iv.137–38, and *Hamlet*, III.ii.210–25 (a passage that
        echoes III.i.80–85, III.vi.39–45, IV.iv.62–63, and
        IV.vii.107–20 of the same play).

154   **But ... Sights** But let me subject myself to no more visions
        [like the 'Shew' the Witches have just displayed].

IV.ii   This scene takes place at Macduff's castle in Fife.

1   **What ... Land?** What had he done to make him flee the
        country like someone who had committed a capital crime?

3–4   **When ... Traitors** Macduff's Wife probably means that when
        we do nothing treasonous, the fears that prompt us to flee
        make us appear nevertheless to be traitors. Compare lines
        17–19, and see II.iii.148–53, II.iv.22–29, III.i.28–31.

5   **Wisdom** prudence; 'Caution' (III.vi.44).

9   **wants ... Touch** lacks a sense of natural bonding. In I.v.19–20
        Macbeth's Lady has criticized her husband for having too
        much 'o' th' Milk of Humane Kindness / To catch the Nearest
        Way' (I.v.19–20). According to Macduff's Wife, the unkind
        Thane of Fife has acted on the 'Firstlings' of his unfeeling
        'Heart' (IV.i.146).

10   **diminitive** diminutive; tiny and weak. The references to birds
        recall I.vi.4–8, II.iv.10–13, III.ii.51–52, III.iv.68–70, 120–24.

Unless the Deed go with it. From this Moment   145
The very Firstlings of my Heart shall be
The Firstlings of my Hand. And even now
To crown my Thoughts with Acts, be it thought
   and done.
The Castle of Macduff I will surprise,
Seize upon Fife, give to th' edge o' th' Sword   150
His Wife, his Babes, and all unfortunate Souls
That trace him in his Line. No Boasting like a
   Fool,
This Deed I'll do before this Purpose cool.
But no more Sights. — Where are these
   Gentlemen?
Come bring me where they are.   *Exeunt.* 155

Scene 2

Enter Macduff's Wife, her Son, and Rosse.

WIFE   What had he done, to make him fly the Land?
ROSSE   You must have Patience, Madam.
WIFE   He had none:
  His Flight was Madness. When our Actions do
   not,
  Our Fears do make us Traitors.
ROSSE   You know not
  Whether it was his Wisdom or his Fear.   5
WIFE   Wisdom? To leave his Wife, to leave his
   Babes,
  His Mansion, and his Titles, in a place
  From whence himself does fly? He loves us not,
  He wants the Natural Touch. For the poor Wren
  (The most diminitive of Birds) will fight,   10
  Her Young Ones in her Nest, against the Owl.

14 **Cooz** Cousin.

15 **school your self** subject yourself to the discipline of wisdom
  and obedience (trusting your husband to know what is best
  for his wife and children). Rosse's verb echoes I.vii.5–10.

17 **The . . . Season** what fits the present time. *Fits* can mean both
  (a) fashions (compare II.iv.38) and (b) fevers, seizures
  (compare III.ii.25, III.iv.19, 52); it also echoes I.vii.53–54.
  Season recalls III.iv.139.

18–20 **But . . . fear** It is not clear whether Rosse is (a) agreeing with
  what Macduff's Wife has said about her husband, or (b)
  suggesting that she doesn't really know herself if she suspects
  him of betraying her, or (c) saying that everyone now lives in
  fear and self-doubt. Lines 18–22 echo *Antony and Cleopatra*,
  I.iv.44–47, III.ii.47–50.

24 **climb upward** ascend on the Wheel of Fortune. Compare *King
  Lear*, IV.i.1–6.

27 **I . . . Fool** Rosse says that he is about to make a fool of himself
  and cry. Compare II.iii.131–41, and *Hamlet*, IV.vii.181–87.

32–33 **As . . . they** These lines allude to such passages as Luke 9:58
  ('Foxes have holes, and the birds of the air have nests; but the
  Son of man hath not where to lay his head'), Matthew 6:26
  ('Behold the fowls of the air: for they sow not, neither do they
  reap, nor gather into barns; yet your heavenly Father feedeth
  them. Are ye not much better than they?'), and Matthew
  10:29 ('Are not two sparrows sold for a farthing? and one of
  them shall not fall on the ground without your Father').

32 **with** both (a) by eating, and (b) alongside.

34 **Lime** birdlime; the sticky substance used to capture woodcocks
  and other birds.

35 **Pitfall** covered pit; trap.
  Gin snare.

36 **Poor** worthless, unwanted. The boy gives a twist to his
  mother's use of *Poor* (line 34) to mean 'impotent' or 'pitiful'.
  Compare I.vi.14–18, I.vii.44–45, II.ii.68–69, and III.ii.13–15.

All is the Fear, and nothing is the Love;
As little is the Wisdom, where the Flight
So runs against all Reason.

ROSSE   My dearest Cooz,
  I pray you school your self. But for your
    Husband,   15
He is Noble, Wise, Judicious, and best knows
The Fits o' th' Season. I dare not speak much
    further,
But Cruel are the Times when we are Traitors
And do not know our selves; when we hold Rumour
From what we fear, yet know not what we fear,   20
But float upon a wild and violent Sea
Each way, and move. I take my leave of you:
Shall not be long but I'll be here again.
Things at the Worst will cease, or else climb
    upward
To what they were before. My pretty Cousin,   25
Blessing upon you.

WIFE   Father'd he is, and yet
  He's Father-less.

ROSSE   I am so much a Fool,
  Should I stay longer it would be my Disgrace
  And your Discomfort. I take my Leave at once.   *Exit.*

WIFE   Sirrah, your Father's dead,   30
  And what will you do now? How will you live?

SON   As Birds do, Mother.

WIFE   What, with Worms and Flies?

SON   With what I get, I mean, and so do they.

WIFE   Poor Bird, thou'dst never fear the Net, nor
    Lime,
  The Pitfall, nor the Gin.

SON   Why should I, Mother?   35
  Poor Birds they are not set for. My Father is
  Not dead, for all your Saying.

WIFE   Yes, he is dead:

41   **withal**   both (a) with all, and (b) withal (here, notwithstanding).

42   **I' ... thee**   indeed, with enough intelligence for one of your tender years.

45   **swears**   Macduff's Wife is probably thinking about her husband's wedding vows, among them the promise to remain with his spouse 'till death us depart [part]'. Compare *Hamlet*, III.ii.275-76.

51   **Then ... Fools**   The boy's remarks appear precociously wise, at least in the kind of world now dominated by Macbeth (compare lines 69-72); in time, though, what looks like worldly success is normally frustrated in Shakespeare's plays, and 'Liars and Swearers' turn out to be 'Fools' too.

52   **enow**   enough.

57   **would not**   refused to weep.

58   **quickly ... Father**   Macduff's son probably means 'soon have my father back again.' His words, however, will prove unintentionally ironic: he will shortly 'have a new Father' in Heaven. See the note to lines 32-33. Here *quickly* hints at a secondary sense, one that relates to *quick* as a word for 'alive', living (as in *Hamlet*, V.i.124-37). Compare IV.iii.176-79.

60   **I ... known**   you have never met me.

61   **Though ... perfect**   though I am fully knowledgeable about what an honourable woman you are. Here *perfect* means 'well rehearsed' (see the notes to I.iii.68 and III.iv.19), 'complete', or 'whole'; it carries ominous echoes of Macbeth's use of the word in III.i.106 and III.iv.19.

How wilt thou do for a Father?
SON   Nay, how will
You do for a Husband?
WIFE   Why I can buy me twenty
At any Market.
SON   Then you'll buy 'em to sell   40
Again.
WIFE   Thou speak'st withal thy Wit, and yet
I' faith with Wit enough for thee.
SON   Was my Father a Traitor, Mother?
WIFE   Ay, that he was.
SON   What is a Traitor?
WIFE   Why one that swears, and lies.   45
SON   And be all Traitors that do so?
WIFE   Every one
That does so is a Traitor, and must be hang'd.
SON   And must they all be hang'd that swear and
lie?
WIFE   Every one.
SON   Who must hang them?
WIFE   Why, the Honest Men.   50
SON   Then the Liars and Swearers are Fools: for there
are Liars and Swearers enow to beat the Honest Men and
hang up them.
WIFE   Now God help thee, poor Monkey.
But how wilt thou do for a Father?   55
SON   If he were dead, you'd weep for him. If you
would not, it were a good Sign that I should
quickly have a new Father.
WIFE   Poor Prattler, how thou talk'st!

Enter a Messenger.

MESSENGER   Bless you, fair Dame. I am not to you
known,   60
Though in your state of Honour I am perfect.

62 **doubt** fear.

63 **Homely** humble (a yeoman rather than a gentleman).

66 **fell** dire, cruel. Compare I.v.47–48 and IV.iii.217–18.

68 **abide** stay.
Whether where, whither.

73 **womanly Defence** the 'Defence' of a 'weaker vessel' (1 Peter 3:7). Compare III.iv.55, 60–63, 71, 97, and IV.i.80.

76 **Unsanctified** both (a) unholy, and (b) unprotected (with allusion to the 'sanctuary' or asylum provided by churches and religious houses). Compare *Hamlet*, IV.vii.124.

78 **shag-ear'd** with hair so shaggy it covers the ruffian's ears.
Egg unhatched bird. Compare lines 32–33. *Li'st* (ly'st) echoes II.iii.45.

79 **Fry** spawn, offspring. Compare III.iv.27–29.

I doubt some Danger does approach you nearly.
If you will take a Homely Man's Advice,
Be not found here: hence with your Little Ones.
To fright you thus – Me thinks I am too Savage;   65
To do worse to you were fell Cruelty,
Which is too nigh your person. Heaven preserve
    you,
I dare abide no longer.   *Exit.*
WIFE   Whether should I fly?
I have done no Harm. But I remember now
I am in this earthly World, where to do Harm   70
Is often Laudable, to do Good sometime
Accounted dangerous Folly. Why then, alas,
Do I put up that womanly Defence
To say I have done no Harm?

                    Enter Murtherers.

                              What are these Faces?
MURTHERER   Where is your Husband?   75
WIFE   I hope in no Place so Unsanctified
Where such as thou mayst find him.
MURTHERER   He's a Traitor.
SON   Thou li'st, thou shag-ear'd Villain!
MURTHERER   What, you Egg?
Young Fry of Treachery?   [*He stabs the Boy.*]
SON   He has kill'd me, Mother:
Run away, I pray you!   *Exit* [*Wife,*] *crying 'Murther!'*   80
                    [*Exeunt Murtherers pursuing her.*]

IV.iii   This scene takes place in England, near the palace of King Edward.

2   **Weep . . . empty**   weep until our sad hearts are empty. Compare *Richard II*, III.ii.144–77, and *King Lear*, V.ii.1–11.

3   **Hold . . . Sword**   keep a firm grip on the deadly sword. *Mortal* recalls I.v.3, 43, and II.iii.98–100.

4   **Bestride . . . Birthdome**   stand over the downfallen form of our native land (like 'Good Men', courageous soldiers, protecting their wounded comrades in battle). *Birthdome* (birthdom) echoes *Masterdome* (I.v.72).

5   **New . . . cry**   Macduff doesn't realize how close to home his words strike.

6   **Strike . . . Face**   (a) display themselves to the sky, (b) defy Heaven and challenge God to avenge the injuries done to Him (compare IV.i.51–52), and (c) call the beneficence of Heaven itself into question (as in lines 222–23).
       resounds   reverberates, echoes. Compare IV.i.128–29.

7   **felt with Scotland**   suffered every pain that Scotland feels. Here *felt with* is an English transliteration of 'sympathized'.

8   **Like . . . Dolour**   the same cries of anguish.
       What . . . wail   Malcolm is reserving judgement and sympathy until he can be sure that the reports he hears from Macduff are true.

9   **redress**   correct, remedy; literally, 're-address' or 're-dress'. Compare I.vii.36.

10   **to Friend**   to be my friend; to be favourable to my cause.

12   **sole Name**   name alone. In his refusal to pronounce the name of 'this Tyrant', Malcolm anticipates the theatrical superstition that it is bad luck to utter the title of 'the Scottish play'.

14–17 **I . . . God**   I'm naive, but I suspect that you may perceive some way of winning him over (literally, of separating yourself from the wrath he directs at you) through me, and you may find it prudent to sacrifice an innocent Lamb [me] to appease an angry God [Macbeth]. Here *discern of* can mean 'discover on his behalf'. Most editors emend *discern* to *deserve*.

19–20 **A . . . Charge**   [And though you mean well now,] a good man may shrink back or turn against the virtues in his nature when commanded by a king to betray a trust.

Scene 3

Enter Malcolm and Macduff.

MALCOLM   Let us seek out some desolate Shade, and there
Weep our sad Bosoms empty.

MACDUFF   Let us rather
Hold fast the mortal Sword, and like good Men
Bestride our downfall Birthdome. Each new Morn
New Widows howl, new Orphans cry, new Sorrows   5
Strike Heaven on the Face, that it resounds
As if it felt with Scotland, and yell'd out
Like Syllable of Dolour.

MALCOLM   What I believe, I'll wail,
What know, believe; and what I can redress,
As I shall find the Time to Friend, I will.   10
What you have spoke, it may be so perchance.
This Tyrant, whose sole Name blisters our Tongues,
Was once thought Honest; you have lov'd him well,
He hath not touch'd you yet. I am Young, but something
You may discern of him through me, and Wisdom   15
To offer up a weak, poor, innocent Lamb
T'appease an angry God.

MACDUFF   I am not Treacherous.

MALCOLM   But Macbeth is.
A good and virtuous Nature may recoil

21   **transpose**   change, exchange; literally, move to that which you are not.

22   **Angels . . . fell**   There are still lustrous angels [and you may be one of them], though the one whose name means 'Brightest' fell (Isaiah 14:12–17 and Revelation 9:1); compare I.ii.16, 24, I.iv.50–58, and I.vii.25–28.

23   **Though . . . Grace**   Malcolm alludes to 2 Corinthians 11:14.

26   **in that Rawness**   unprotected in that bloody, savage realm. Compare III.iv.73–78.

27   **Those precious Motives**   those priceless motivations [to keep you in Scotland rather than allow you to flee to England].

29–30 **Let . . . Safeties**   don't allow my suspicions to be perceived as stains on your honour [because it is not to dishonour you that I express them]; think of them, rather, as deriving from my need to protect myself. Malcolm cannot help having 'Doubts' about the veracity of a man who claims to have abandoned his family to the mercy of a raw butcher. *Safeties* recalls III.i.47, 50–52, and III.v.32–33.

30   **rightly Just**   truly honourable.

32   **Basis sure**   foundation firm. Compare III.iv.20, IV.i.97.

33   **For . . . thee**   for the forces of Goodness are afraid to oppose you.

34   **The . . . affear'd**   both (a) the one who has a right to the title is afraid to proclaim that you 'wear' your regalia wrongly (compare lines 9–10), and thus (b) your title is *affeered* (confirmed legally). Compare I.vii.39–41; III.iv.58, 140–42; V.i.42. Most editions emend to *affeer'd*.

35–37 **I . . . boot**   I wouldn't be the villain you think I am for all of Scotland, even if the riches of the Orient were thrown in as well. Compare *Othello*, IV.iii.64–85.

38   **absolute Fear**   total distrust.

41   **withal**   in addition; along with all this. Compare IV.ii.41.

42   **Hands**   This word echoes IV.i.145–47 and III.vi.47–49.
       Uplifted   both (a) lifted up in prayer, and (b) raised in battle.

In an Imperial Charge. But I shall crave your
   Pardon;   20
That which you are, my Thoughts cannot
   transpose:
Angels are Bright still, though the Brightest
   fell.
Though all things Foul would wear the Brows of
   Grace,
Yet Grace must still look so.

MACDUFF   I have lost my Hopes.

MALCOLM   Perchance even there where I did find my
   Doubts.
Why in that Rawness left you Wife and Child,
Those precious Motives, those strong Knots of
   Love,
Without Leave-taking? I pray you,
Let not my Jealousies be your Dishonours,
But mine own Safeties: you may be rightly Just,
What ever I shall think.

MACDUFF   – Bleed, bleed, poor Country!
– Great Tyranny, lay thou thy Basis sure,
For Goodness dare not check thee: wear thou thy
   Wrongs,
The Title is affear'd. – Fare thee well, Lord:
I would not be the Villain that thou think'st
For the whole Space that's in the Tyrant's
   Grasp,
And the rich East to boot.

MALCOLM   Be not offended,
I speak not as in absolute Fear of you:
I think our Country sinks beneath the Yoke,
It weeps, it bleeds, and each new Day a Gash
Is added to her Wounds. I think withal,
There would be Hands uplifted in my Right;
And here from gracious England have I offer
Of goodly Thousands. But for all this,

50–52 It ... open'd   I refer to myself, knowing that in me all the individual manifestations of vice are so deeply implanted that when they are disclosed. Here *grafted* is a perverse variation on the plant images introduced earlier (see the note to III.i.5 and compare III.i.59, 127).

55   confineless Harms   unrestrained evils *Harms* echoes IV.ii. 70–71.
   Legions   Macduff alludes to the legion of devils that possessed a maniac exorcised by Jesus (see Mark 5:1–17).

58   Luxurious   lecherous.

59   Sudden   impulsively violent.

61   Voluptuousness   lust; love of sensual pleasure.

63   Cestern   cistern. Compare *Othello*, IV.ii.59–60.

64   continent   confining, restraining. Compare line 55.
   o'erbear   overwhelm ('bear' itself 'over' a woman).

65   Will   both (a) unbridled desire, and (b) genital 'Will'.

66   Boundless Intemperance   uncontrolled appetite. Compare line 55 and I.vii.25–28, and see the note to I.iii.82.

71–72 Convey ... Cold   steal your pleasures in wide abundance and yet seem chaste and passionless to the world at large.

72   The ... hoodwink   You may thus blindfold the times.

When I shall tread upon the Tyrant's Head,   45
Or wear it on my Sword, yet my poor Country
Shall have more Vices than it had before,
More suffer, and more sundry ways, than ever,
By him that shall succeed.
MACDUFF   What should he be?
MALCOLM   It is my self I mean: in whom I know   50
All the particulars of Vice so grafted
That when they shall be open'd, black Macbeth
Will seem as pure as Snow, and the poor State
Esteem him as a Lamb, being compar'd
With my confineless Harms.
MACDUFF   Not in the Legions   55
Of horrid Hell can come a Divel more damn'd
In Evils to top Macbeth.
MALCOLM   I grant him Bloody,
Luxurious, Avaricious, False, Deceitful,
Sudden, Malicious, smacking of every Sin
That has a Name. But there's no Bottom, none,   60
In my Voluptuousness. Your Wives, your
     Daughters,
Your Matrons, and your Maids could not fill up
The Cestern of my Lust; and my Desire
All continent Impediments would o'erbear
That did oppose my Will. Better Macbeth   65
Than such an one to reign.
MACDUFF   Boundless Intemperance
In Nature is a Tyranny: it hath been
Th' untimely Emptying of the happy Throne,
And Fall of many Kings. But fear not yet
To take upon you what is yours; you may   70
Convey your Pleasures in a spacious Plenty
And yet seem Cold. The Time you may so
     hoodwink.
We have willing Dames enough; there cannot be
That Vulture in you to devour so many

75–76 **As . . . inclin'd** as will give themselves over to a monarch, finding his 'Greatness' so 'inclin'd' (pointing in their direction). Compare *Pericles*, IV.iii.104–6, 155.

76–78 **With . . . Avarice** along with this vice, there grows in my most ill-assembled, ungoverned nature such an unstoppable covetousness. Malcolm's verb plays on the genital sense of 'Greatness' (compare I.v.69–70 and I.vii.25–28, 39–41, 50–54, 60–61); it is also a variation on the other growth and plant images in the play (compare lines 50–52 and 85). Meanwhile, *compos'd* (put together) recalls I.vii.72–74.

79 **cut . . . Lands** decapitate the nobility 'for Wealth' (line 84).

80 **his** this nobleman's. *Jewels* recalls III.i.62–68.

85 **Sticks deeper** (a) cuts more deeply (like a thorn or a stab), (b) is more deeply 'grafted' (line 51), and (c) penetrates further (compare I.vii.60).
grows . . . Root enlarges itself by means of a more poisonous root. *Root* echoes I.iii.82–83 and III.i.5–6.

86 **Summer-seeming Lust** the kind of lust one associates with teeming summer, when all of Nature is overflowing with fertility.

88–89 **Foisons . . . Own** enough bounty to satisfy your greed from that which you can claim as your own.

89 **portable** bearable, tolerable [when balanced by 'other Graces'].

96 **In . . . Crime** in all the varieties of each different vice.

98 **Concord** peace, harmony. *Milk* echoes I.v.19, 50, and I.vii.54–59. *Powre* (power) and *pour* (*poure* in the Folio) recall IV.i.63, 79.

99 **confound** cast into 'ill-compos'd' disunity (line 77), disorder. Compare III.iv.29 and IV.i.53.

104 **untitled** with no claim to the throne by birth or election.
bloody-Sceptred ruling with a murderous sword rather than a proper staff of office. Compare III.i.59–60.

As will to Greatness dedicate themselves,   75
Finding it so inclin'd.
MALCOLM   With this, there grows
In my most ill-compos'd Affection such
A stanchless Avarice that were I King
I should cut off the Nobles for their Lands,
Desire his Jewels, and this other's House,   80
And my more Having would be as a Sauce
To make me hunger more, that I should forge
Quarrels unjust against the Good and Loyal,
Destroying them for Wealth.
MACDUFF   This Avarice
Sticks deeper, grows with more pernicious Root,   85
Than Summer-seeming Lust; and it hath been
The Sword of our slain Kings. Yet do not fear:
Scotland hath Foisons to fill up your Will
Of your mere Own. All these are portable,
With other Graces weigh'd.   90
MALCOLM   But I have none. The King-becoming
    Graces,
As Justice, Verity, Temp'rance, Stableness,
Bounty, Perseverance, Mercy, Lowliness,
Devotion, Patience, Courage, Fortitude,
I have no Relish of them, but abound   95
In the Division of each several Crime,
Acting it many ways. Nay, had I Powre, I should
Pour the sweet Milk of Concord into
    Hell,
Uproar the universal Peace, confound
All Unity on Earth.
MACDUFF   — O Scotland, Scotland!   100
MALCOLM   If such a one be fit to govern, speak:
I am as I have spoken.
MACDUFF   Fit to govern?
No, not to live. — O Nation miserable!
With an untitled Tyrant, bloody-Sceptred,

105 **Wholesome** healthy, whole (unified), harmonious. See the note to I.iii.46.

107 **Interdiction** declaration against himself; self-disqualification.

108 **blaspheme his Breed** profane (speak evil against) his own parentage.

109 **Sainted** sanctified (set apart, dedicated to God); holy.

111 **Died ... liv'd** crucified her sinful self daily (see 1 Corinthians 15:31, Romans 14:7–8, and 2 Timothy 2:11–12).

112– **These ... Scotland** Evils such as those you say you too are
13   guilty of are what drove me away from my native land.

114 **Noble Passion** virtuous outburst. Compare III.iv.54.

116 **black Scruples** dark doubts about your veracity. Compare II.iii.136.

118 **these Trains** devices, stratagems of this sort.

119 **modest** self-possessed, well-controlled.

123 **abjure** 'unspeak', swear against.

125 **For ... Nature** as qualities foreign to my true self.

126 **Unknown to Woman** without sexual knowledge (experience) of women.
   forsworn guilty of lying or breaking an oath.

131 **upon** about.

133 **Whither** to which. The Folio prints *they*, not *thy*.

134 **Seyward** the Earl of Northumberland; see III.vi.31.

135 **at a Point** in 'Manly Readiness' (II.iii.140), 'Arm'd at Point' (*Hamlet*, I.ii.199), with weapons prepared for battle.
   foorth forth.

136– **Now ... Quarrel** Now we'll proceed together, and may our
37   chances of good fortune be equal to the warrant (justification) for our cause.

When shalt thou see thy Wholesome Days again?   105
Since that the truest Issue of thy Throne
By his own Interdiction stands accust
And does blaspheme his Breed? — Thy Royal Father
Was a most Sainted King; the Queen that bore
    thee,
Oft'ner upon her Knees, then on her Feet,   110
Died every Day she liv'd. Fare thee well:
These Evils thou repeat'st upon thy Self
Hath banish'd me from Scotland. — O my Breast,
Thy Hope end here.
MALCOLM   Macduff, this Noble Passion,
Child of Integrity, hath from my Soul   115
Wip'd the black Scruples, reconcil'd my
    Thoughts
To thy good Truth and Honour. Divelish Macbeth,
By many of these Trains, hath sought to win me
Into his Power; and modest Wisdom plucks me
From over-credulous Haste. But God above   120
Deal between thee and me: for even now
I put my self to thy Direction, and
Unspeak mine own Detraction; here abjure
The Taints and Blames I laid upon my Self
For Strangers to my Nature. I am yet   125
Unknown to Woman, never was forsworn,
Scarcely have coveted what was mine own,
At no time broke my Faith, would not betray
The Devil to his Fellow, and delight
No less in Truth than Life. My first False-
    speaking   130
Was this upon my Self. What I am truly
Is thine and my poor Country's to command:
Whither indeed, before thy here Approach
Old Seyward with ten thousand Warlike Men
Already at a Point was setting foorth.   135
Now we'll together, and the chance of Goodness

139   **reconcile** bring back together; literally, 'fit' (line 102) into a 'good Meeting' (III.iv.107).

140   **– Comes . . . you?** Is the King going to leave the privacy of his chambers today? This part-line is here indented to indicate a pause long enough for the Doctor to enter and get Malcolm's attention before Malcolm addresses him.

142   **stay his Cure** wait for him to apply his healing powers to their 'Malady' (illness).
      convinces vanquishes, conquers.

143   **great . . . Art** the greatest endeavours of medical art.
      his Touch the touch of his 'Hand' (compare lines 30, 42). Here *Touch* echoes line 14.

144   **Sanctity** holiness. Compare lines 108–9 and IV.ii.76–77.

148   **my here Remain** stay here began. Compare 'here Approach' (line 133).

150   **Strangely-visited People** people visited (afflicted) with strange maladies (illness of an especially horrible nature). Compare I.iii.74, 94–5.

151   **Ulcerous** festering and discharging. Malcolm is describing the symptoms of scrofula, referred to as the King's 'Evil' (line 146).

152   **The . . . Surgery** totally beyond anything that medical art can hope to do to treat it successfully. Compare V.i.83.

154   **spoken** said, reported [that].

155–   **To . . . Benediction** he leaves to his royal successors the healing
56   powers that will bestow blessings on the afflicted.

156   **strange** wondrous, miraculous. Up to now *strange* has usually referred to that which is extraordinarily evil. Compare line 150.

Be like our warranted Quarrel. Why are you
   Silent?
MACDUFF   Such Welcome and Unwelcome Things at
   once
'Tis hard to reconcile.
MALCOLM   Well, more anon.

                  Enter a Doctor.

                     – Comes the King forth, I
   pray you?   140
DOCTOR   Ay Sir: there are a Crew of wretched
   Souls
That stay his Cure. Their Malady convinces
The great Assay of Art; but at his Touch,
Such Sanctity hath Heaven given his Hand,
They presently amend.
MALCOLM   I thank you, Doctor.   145
                             Exit [Doctor].
MACDUFF   What's the Disease he means?
MALCOLM   'Tis call'd the Evil:
A most miraculous Work in this good King,
Which often since my here Remain in England
I have seen him do. How he solicits Heaven
Himself best knows; but Strangely-visited
   People,   150
All Swol'n and Ulcerous, Pitiful to the Eye,
The mere Despair of Surgery, he cures,
Hanging a golden Stamp about their Necks,
Put on with holy Prayers; and 'tis spoken
To the succeeding Royalty he leaves   155
The Healing Benediction. With this strange
   Virtue
He hath a Heavenly Gift of Prophecy,
And sundry Blessings hang about his Throne
That speak him full of Grace.

160   **My . . . not**   He's a Scotsman, but not someone I recognize yet.

162   **betimes**   as soon as possible. Compare III.iv.130–31. This line
can be rendered either (a) [may] good God betimes remove, or
(b) Good God, betimes remove.

163   **Means**   cause, reason (namely, Macbeth's usurpation of the
throne). *Means* may also refer to a disguise worn 'to beguile
the Time' (I.v.65). *Strangers* echoes line 156.

165   **Almost . . . self**   Macbeth's illness (II.ii.69–70) has infected the
whole country. See the notes to I.v.6, 22.

167   **who knows nothing**   one who is unaware of the situation.

168   **rent**   rend, tear. Compare lines 168–69 and I.vii.21–25,
II.iii.73–75, II.iv.7, and III.iii.19.

169   **not mark'd**   not noted as unusual. Compare III.iv.53–55.

170   **modern Ecstasy**   commonplace emotion. Compare III.ii.20–23.

173   **or ere**   before.
Relation   tale, narrative.

174   **Nice**   exquisitely (precisely) accurate.

175   **hiss the Speaker**   cause the teller to be hissed and scorned for
repeating old news.

176   **teems**   gives birth to.

177   **well**   In Shakespeare this word often refers to the state of those
who are now in Heaven, well off because removed from this
world's troubles. See *Romeo and Juliet*, V.i.14–19.

Enter Rosse.

MACDUFF   See who comes here.

MALCOLM   My Countryman: but yet I know him not.   160

MACDUFF   My ever gentle Cousin, welcome hither.

MALCOLM   I know him now. – Good God betimes
    remove

The Means that makes us Strangers!

ROSSE   Sir, Amen.

MACDUFF   Stands Scotland where it did?

ROSSE   Alas, poor Country,

Almost afraid to know it self. It cannot   165

Be call'd our Mother, but our Grave; where
    nothing

But who knows nothing is once seen to smile;

Where Sighs and Groans and Shrieks that rent
    the Air,

Are made, not mark'd; where violent Sorrow
    seems

A modern Ecstasy. The Dead Man's Knell   170

Is there scarce ask'd for who, and Good Men's
    Lives

Expire before the Flowers in their Caps,

Dying or ere they sicken.

MACDUFF   O Relation:

Too Nice and yet too True!

MALCOLM   What's the newest Grief?

ROSSE   That of an Hour's Age doth hiss the Speaker: 175

Each Minute teems a new one.

MACDUFF   How does my Wife?

ROSSE   Why well.

MACDUFF   And all my Children?

ROSSE   Well too.

MACDUFF   The Tyrant has not batter'd at their
    Peace?

183 **Of . . . out** of many worthy soldiers who were out in the field
(bearing arms). It is not clear whether Rosse uses 'worthy'
ironically (to refer to Macbeth's murderous 'Fellows') or
straightforwardly (to refer to men like the 'Messenger' in
IV.ii). *Borne* can mean both 'carried' and 'birthed'.

184 **Which . . . rather** either (a) which my own observations
confirmed all the sooner, or all the more, or (b) which my
own observations showed to be untrue [depending on how
line 183 is to be read].

188 **doff** put off (a new variation on the play's clothing imagery;
compare lines 9–10 and 33–34). Rosse's verb may involve
play on Macduff's name; and line 187 echoes what Macduff's
Wife has said in IV.ii.9–11, 73. By line 186, if not before,
Rosse may be addressing Malcolm as well as Macduff.

189 **Gracious England** the grace-filled King of England.

191– **none . . . out** [there is] none that the Christian nations can
92   boast of as their progeny.

193 **This . . . like** this comforting news with something equivalent.

194 **in . . . Air** in the air of a deserted place. *Air* echoes line 168.

195 **latch** latch onto; take hold of.

196– **Fee-grief . . . Breast** the kind of grief whose 'Fee' (complete
97   ownership) is exclusive to some individual heart.

198 **Main Part** both (a) chief portion, and (b) principal role.
Compare III.i.3 and III.v.6–9 for previous acting metaphors.
Singe (line 197) recalls I.vi.14–18.

202 **possess them** take possession of them. Rosse's phrasing
suggests an analogy with demon possession. Compare
Macduff's reference to 'the Legions / Of horrid Hell' in lines
55–56.

ROSSE   No, they were well at Peace when I did
    leave 'em.
MACDUFF   Be not a Niggard of your Speech: how
    goest?   180
ROSSE   When I came hither to transport the Tidings
    Which I have heavily borne, there ran a Rumour
    Of many worthy Fellows that were out,
    Which was to my Belief witness'd the rather,
    For that I saw the Tyrant's Power afoot.   185
    Now is the Time of Help: your Eye in Scotland
    Would create Soldiers, make our Women fight,
    To doff their dire Distresses.
MALCOLM   Be't their Comfort
    We are coming thither. Gracious England hath
    Lent us good Seyward and ten thousand Men: 190
    An older and a better Soldier, none
    That Christendom gives out.
ROSSE   Would I could answer
    This Comfort with the like. But I have Words
    That would be howl'd out in the Desert Air
    Where Hearing should not latch them.
MACDUFF   What concern they,   195
    The General Cause, or is it a Fee-grief
    Due to some Single Breast?
ROSSE   No Mind that's Honest
    But in it shares some Woe, though the Main Part
    Pertains to you alone.
MACDUFF   If it be mine
    Keep it not from me, quickly let me have it.   200
ROSSE   Let not your Ears despise my Tongue for
    ever,
    Which shall possess them with the heaviest
    Sound
    That ever yet they heard.
MACDUFF   Humh: I guess at it.

204   **surpris'd**   subjected to a surprise attack. Compare IV.i.149.

206   **Quarry**   a term referring to a heap of slaughtered corpses, either at the end of a hunt or at the conclusion of a battle. Rosse combines the two senses, to make it clear that what might have been construed as a military manoeuvre was more like the savage butchering of a herd of helpless deer. Compare I.ii.14–15.
    Deer   Rosse plays on 'dear ones'.

207   **To . . . you**   to throw your corpse on top of the pile.

210   **Whispers . . . Heart**   whispers to the over-freighted heart.

212   **I . . . thence**   I had to be away from there.

214– **Let's . . . Grief**   let us 'cure' our griefs by means of the
15   'Medicine' our hearts will derive from avenging Macbeth's crimes against our loved ones.

215   **He . . . Children**   It is not clear whether Macduff speaks this line to Rosse (meaning that Malcolm has no children, and thus cannot realize that no revenge can 'cure' such a 'deadly Grief' as Macduff has just suffered), or to Malcolm (meaning that Macbeth has no children whose loss he would feel if they were slaughtered).

218   **Dam**   mother. *Hell-kites* recalls III.iv.68–70.
    one fell Swoop   one dire swooping down from the sky.

219   **Dispute . . . Man**   Respond to it the way a man would. Malcolm's advice implies a concept of 'Man' similar to what Macbeth's Lady has proposed in I.vii.39–61 and III.iv.55.

220   **feel . . . Man**   Macduff's definition of humanity includes the emotions that men in Shakespeare's plays usually associate with 'weaker vessels'. Before he can 'put on Manly Readiness' (II.iii.140), Macduff says, he must first acknowledge that real men also have 'naked Frailties' (II.iii.133); they experience grief and guilt.

222   **Sinful Macduff**   Macduff's self-assessment recalls III.iv.216–28, III.vi.39–45, IV.i.140–52, IV.ii.1–58, and IV.iii.1–31.

224   **Naught**   naughty ('sinful') man.

ROSSE   Your Castle is surpris'd, your Wife and
 Babes
  Savagely slaughter'd; to relate the Manner   205
  Were on the Quarry of these murthered Deer
  To add the Death of you.
MALCOLM   Merciful Heaven!
  — What, Man, ne'er pull your Hat upon your
  Brows:
  Give Sorrow Words. The Grief that does not
   speak
  Whispers the o'er-fraught Heart and bids it
   break.   210
MACDUFF   My Children too?
ROSSE   Wife, Children, Servants, all
  That could be found.
MACDUFF   And I must be from thence?
  My Wife kill'd too?
ROSSE   I have said.
MALCOLM   Be comforted.
  Let's make us Med'cines of our great Revenge
  To cure this deadly Grief.
MACDUFF   He has no Children.   215
  — All my Pretty Ones? Did you say All?
  — O Hell-kite! — All? What, all my pretty
   Chickens
  And their Dam at one fell Swoop?
MALCOLM   Dispute it like a Man.
MACDUFF   I shall do so;
  But I must also feel it as a Man.   220
  I cannot but remember such things were
  That were most precious to me. Did Heaven look
   on,
  And would not take their Part? — Sinful
   Macduff,
  They were all strook for thee: Naught that I
   am,

225 **Demerits** deservings (here 'demerits' in the usual modern sense). Compare *Othello*, I.ii.22 and III.iii.182.

227 **Whetstone** an abrasive stone for the sharpening of blades.

228 **Blunt** dull (as opposed to sharpening on a whetstone). Macbeth's Lady has used similar 'keen Knife' imagery in I.v.54.

229 **play . . . Eyes** cry like a woman. Compare II.iii.90–93, 133–34, and IV.ii.27–29.

230 **Braggart . . . Tongue** This line echoes IV.i.152.

231 **Cut . . . Intermission** make the time short between now and when I enact my vengeance. Compare I.ii.16–23, II.iii.150–51, and IV.iv.117–18. *Intermission* literally means 'sending between', and it here suggests 'mediation' or 'measure', as well as 'delay'.
Front face; forehead. Compare *Othello*, I.iii.79.

234 **goes Manly** is conducive to 'Manly Readiness' (see line 220).

235 **King** King Edward the Confessor.
Power army (see lines 134–35).

236 **Our . . . Leave** the only thing our forces need is for us to give them the word to depart.

237 **ripe for Shaking** a tree whose ripe fruit is ready to be shaken down. *Shaking* echoes such previous passages as I.iii.135–40; I.v.45–48; II.iii.66–67, 82, 136; III.ii.16–20; and III.iv.48. *Powres* (powers) recalls lines 97–98.

238 **Put . . . Instruments** both (a) don their armaments, and (b) assume and urge on their ministers (those agents who work for 'the Powres above'). Compare line 188. *Instruments* recalls I.iii.122, II.i.41–42, III.i.77–79.

Not for their own Demerits but for mine   225
Fell Slaughter on their Souls. – Heaven rest
   them now.
MALCOLM   Be this the Whetstone of your Sword,
   let Grief
Convert to Anger: blunt not the Heart, enrage
   it.
MACDUFF   O I could play the Woman with mine
   Eyes,
And Braggart with my Tongue. – But gentle
   Heavens,   230
Cut short all Intermission. Front to Front
Bring thou this Fiend of Scotland and my Self;
Within my Sword's Length set him, if he scape
Heaven forgive him too.
MALCOLM   This Time goes Manly.
Come go we to the King: our Power is ready,   235
Our Lack is nothing but our Leave. Macbeth
Is ripe for Shaking, and the Powres above
Put on their Instruments. Receive what Cheer
   you may:
The Night is long that never finds the Day.   *Exeunt*.

V.i This scene appears to take place at Macbeth's castle in Dunsinane.

1 **watch'd** both (a) stayed awake when people are normally sleeping, and (b) observed. The Doctor's verb recalls II.ii.67–68 and III.iii.6–8.

3 **walk'd** sleepwalked. Compare III.vi.7.

5 **Field** field of battle. Apparently Macbeth is with 'the Tyrant's Power afoot' (IV.iii.185).

6 **Closet** either (a) a cabinet or desk, or (b) a private chamber containing valuables to be locked away.

7 **foorth** forth; out.

10 **Perturbation** disturbance; disruption of normal functions.

12 **the . . . watching** the things one does when awake. Compare line 1.

12–13 **slumbry Agitation** sleeping activity. The Doctor's oxymoronic phrasing (combining contradictory qualities in a single complex image) is in keeping with the violations that Macbeth's Lady has done her nature in I.v, when she invoked the powers of Hell to transform her into a manly woman.

14 **other Actual Performances** performing of other deeds. The Doctor's phrasing recalls such previous references to acting as those noted in I.iii.125–27; I.iv.23–24; I.v.64–68; I.vii.35–36, 39–41; II.iii.32–48; II.iv.5–6; III.iv.19; and IV.iii.197–99.

21 **confirm my Speech** corroborate my testimony.

ACT V

Scene 1

*Enter a Doctor of Physic, and a
Waiting Gentlewoman.*

DOCTOR   I have two Nights watch'd with you, but
can perceive no Truth in your Report. When was
it she last walk'd?

GENTLEWOMAN   Since his Majesty went into the
Field, I have seen her rise from her Bed, throw   5
her Night-Gown upon her, unlock her Closet, take
foorth Paper, fold it, write upon't, read it,
afterwards seal it, and again return to Bed;
yet all this while in a most fast Sleep.

DOCTOR   A great Perturbation in Nature, to   10
receive at once the Benefit of Sleep, and do
the Effects of Watching. In this slumbry
Agitation, besides her Walking and other
Actual Performances, what, at any time,
have you heard her say?   15

GENTLEWOMAN   That, Sir, which I will not report
after her.

DOCTOR   You may to me, and 'tis most meet you
should.

22   **her very Guise**   her accustomed dress and manner (compare
III.iv.50, 94–95). *Guise* suggests *disguise*; but the Lady we
will see in this scene discloses her true nature without any
subterfuge. Her 'naked Frailties' will not remain 'hid', but
'suffer in Exposure' (II.iii.133–34).

24   **stand close**   hide yourself from view. The Gentlewoman's
phrasing recalls an earlier scene in which eavesdroppers stand
close to await a 'lated Traveller' (III.iii.6); compare III.iii.4,
15, 117.

25   **How . . . Light?**   How did she get that taper (candle) she
carries? Compare III.iii.19.

29   **their . . . shut**   though they are open, they do not function as
organs of external perception (compare III.iv.93–94). The
situation and the Gentlewoman's words echo such previous
passages as I.iii.55, 140; I.v.45–60; I.vii.81–82; II.ii.27,
30–31, 50–52, 56; III.ii.11–12, 24–25, 47–51; III.iv.137–38;
IV.iii.72, 164–65.

33   **Washing her Hands**   Compare Macbeth and his Lady's remarks
in II.ii.56–65.

36   **Spot**   both (a) bloodstain, and (b) moral blemish. See *Othello*,
III.iii.424.

37   **set down**   transcribe. Compare *Hamlet*, I.v.106.

38   **satisfy my Remembrance**   assist and confirm my memory.
Compare II.iii.22–23, 68–69; II.iv.1; III.ii.31–32;
IV.ii.69–72; IV.iii.221–22.

40   **One, Two**   Macbeth's Lady is counting the chimes of a clock.
Affear'd (line 42) recalls IV.iii.34.

44   **call . . . accompt**   make us give an account of how we use our
unlimited royal power; summon us to a day of reckoning
(judgement). Compare I.vi.25–28, and see *Othello*,
IV.iii.79–82, V.ii.266–69. *Powre* (power) recalls IV.iii.237.

47   **mark**   take note of. Compare IV.iii.168–69.

49   **Hands**   See the note to IV.iii.42, and compare V.ii.16–17.

51   **mar . . . Starting**   undo everything with this involuntary
recoiling. *Mar* recalls II.iii.36; *Starting* echoes I.iii.49,
III.iv.60–62, and IV.i.115, and anticipates V.ii.22–25.

GENTLEWOMAN   Neither to you nor any one, having   20
no Witness to confirm my Speech.

Enter Lady, with a Taper.

Lo you, here she comes. This is her very Guise,
and upon my Life fast Asleep. Observe her,
stand close.

DOCTOR   How came she by that Light?   25

GENTLEWOMAN   Why it stood by her: she has Light
by her continually, 'tis her Command.

DOCTOR   You see her Eyes are open.

GENTLEWOMAN   I, but their Sense are shut.

DOCTOR   What is it she does now? Look how she   30
rubs her Hands.

GENTLEWOMAN   It is an accustom'd Action with
her, to seem thus Washing her Hands: I have
known her continue in this a Quarter of an
Hour.   35

LADY   Yet here's a Spot.

DOCTOR   Hark, she speaks; I will set down what
comes from her, to satisfy my Remembrance the more
strongly.

LADY   Out, damned Spot: out, I say! One, Two: why   40
then 'tis Time to do't. Hell is murky. Fie,
my Lord, fie: a Soldier, and affear'd? What
need we fear? Who knows it, when none can
call our Powre to accompt? Yet who would have
thought the Old Man to have had so much Blood in   45
him?

DOCTOR   Do you mark that?

LADY   The Thane of Fife had a Wife: where is she
now? What, will these Hands ne'er be clean? No
more o' that, my Lord, no more o' that: you   50
mar all with this Starting.

52   **Go to, go to** come now, for shame. The Doctor, now realizing
      what Macbeth's Lady is saying, may be suggesting that the
      Gentlewoman leave (compare II.iii.90–93); but lines 54–56
      suggest that he is addressing the sleepwalking Lady.

58   **sweeten** perfume, freshen.

60–61 **sorely charg'd** grievously burdened. Compare II.i.55, II.ii.35,
      II.iv.3.

63   **for . . . Body** even if it made the whole body regal. Compare
      Desdemona's remarks about what Aemilia calls 'a small Vice'
      in *Othello*, IV.iii.66–67.

65   **be** be well. Compare I.vii.1–2, II.iv.37, III.ii.25, III.iv.49–53,
      and IV.iii.176–79.

66   **This . . . Practice** this dis-ease is more than I am competent to
      cure. See the note to II.iii.57. The Doctor's remarks echo the
      discussion in IV.iii.141–59. Macbeth and his Lady have
      indeed 'murther'd Sleep' (II.ii.39).

74–75 **There's . . . Gate** These words recall the dramatic interruptions
      in II.ii.54–71. Once again the audience is reminded of
      Revelation 3:20, where Jesus says 'Behold, I stand at the door
      and knock.' The message implicit in that passage is the
      opposite of 'What's done cannot be undone' (line 76); but like
      her husband, Macbeth's Lady has so hardened her heart and
      sealed her ears (see the note to IV.i.67) that she is no longer
      capable of hearing the voice of Grace. For her, then, 'What's
      done is done' (III.ii.12): she will never be able to wash her
      hands with the cleansing waters of repentance.

76   **What's . . . undone** This sentence recalls II.ii.48, 69–70, and
      III.i.12.

81   **breed** beget, reproduce. Compare lines 80–81 to I.vii.7–12,
      60–61; III.i.4–46, 59–68; and IV.iii.104–8.
      infected Minds diseased consciences. Compare I.v.6, 20–22,
      II.i.35–38, and II.ii.36.

83   **the Divine** both (a) the priest, and (b) the ministrations of
      Divine Grace. See the note to II.iii.57, and compare V.i.66.

85   **Annoyance** injury to herself.

DOCTOR   Go to, go to: you have known what you
should not.

GENTLEWOMAN   She has spoke what she should not,
I am sure of that; Heaven knows what she has   55
known.

LADY   Here's the Smell of the Blood still. All
the Perfumes of Arabia will not sweeten this
little Hand. O, O, O!

DOCTOR   What a Sigh is there? The Heart is sorely   60
charg'd.

GENTLEWOMAN   I would not have such a Heart in my
Bosom for the Dignity of the whole Body.

DOCTOR   Well, well, well.

GENTLEWOMAN   Pray God it be, Sir.   65

DOCTOR   This Disease is beyond my Practice; yet
I have known those which have walk'd in their
Sleep who have died holily in their Beds.

LADY   Wash your Hands, put on your Night-Gown,
look not so Pale. I tell you yet again,   70
Banquo's buried: he cannot come out on's
Grave.

DOCTOR   Even so?

LADY   To Bed, to Bed. There's Knocking at the
Gate. Come, come, come, come, give me your   75
Hand. What's done cannot be undone. To Bed,
to Bed, to Bed.   *Exit.*

DOCTOR   Will she go now to Bed?

GENTLEWOMAN   Directly.

DOCTOR   Foul Whisp'rings are abroad. Unnatural
Deeds   80
Do breed unnatural Troubles; infected Minds
To their deaf Pillows will discharge their
Secrets.
More needs she the Divine than the Physician.
– God, God, forgive us all! – Look after her,
Remove from her the means of all Annoyance,   85

86 **still** constantly.

87 **mated** maddened, 'amaz'd'. Compare II.iii.115–16,
II.iv.19–20, and IV.i.124–25, and see *The Comedy of Errors*,
III.ii.54. Here *mated* can also mean 'checkmated',
confounded.

V.ii This scene takes place in the countryside near Dunsinane.

1 **Powre** power, army. Compare V.i.44.

3 **burn** with both (a) the wrath of God and the fire of Hell
(Revelation 19:20), and (b) a 'Valiant Fury' (line 14) or
feverish, desperate frenzy.
their dear Causes the causes (cases) of those dear to them.

4 **to ... Alarm** to the bloodletting and the grim call to arms.
Cathness is probably alluding to the medical practice of
'bleeding' patients afflicted with a fever; he implies that those
who shed Macbeth's blood will be ministering to an infected
Scotland. Compare V.i.66. 81–82.

5 **Excite ... Man** be enough to arouse a man who is either
moribund (on his deathbed) or dead (completely mortified).

6 **well** both (a) no doubt, (b) fittingly, and (c) healingly (as in
V.i.64).

8 **File** roll or list. This word recalls III.i.89–106.

10 **unruff** both (a) unrough (not yet bearded, and yet to be
initiated in the arts of military roughness), and (b) unruffed
(yet to flesh his 'sword' and earn the right to wear the ruff of
those who profess 'Manhood'; compare 2 *Henry IV*,
II.iv.144–45).

15 **distemper'd** diseased (bloated) and dis-eased (unruly).
Compare IV.iii.66–67.

And still keep Eyes upon her. So goodnight.
My Mind she has mated, and amaz'd my Sight:
I think, but dare not speak.
GENTLEWOMAN   Goodnight, good Doctor.
                                                          Exeunt.

Scene 2

Drum and Colours. Enter Menteth, Cathness,
Angus, Lenox, Soldiers.

MENTETH   The English Powre is near, led on by
    Malcolm,
    His Uncle Seyward, and the good Macduff.
    Revenges burn in them: for their dear Causes
    Would to the Bleeding and the grim Alarm
    Excite the mortified Man.
ANGUS   Near Byrnan Wood   5
    Shall we well meet them; that way are they
        coming.
CATHNESS   Who knows if Donalbain be with his
    Brother?
LENOX   For certain, Sir, he is not: I have a File
    Of all the Gentry. There is Seyward's Son
    And many unruff Youths, that even now   10
    Protest their first of Manhood.
MENTETH   What does the Tyrant?
CATHNESS   Great Dunsinane he strongly fortifies.
    Some say he's Mad; others, that lesser hate
        him,
    Do call it Valiant Fury; but for certain
    He cannot buckle his distemper'd Cause   15
    Within the Belt of Rule.

18   **minutely ... Faith-breach**   each minute new uprisings punish
      him for his breach of loyalty. Compare I.vii.7–12.

20–22 **Now ... Thief**   Like the clothing image in lines 15–16, this one
      recalls such previous passages as I.iii.140–44; I.vii.35–36;
      II.i.24–25, 58–59; II.ii.33–34; II.iii.133–34, 140; II.iv.31–32,
      38; and IV.iii.188, 236–38.

25   **Well, march**   both (a) well then, let us march, and (b) well
      march.

26   **truly ow'd**   legitimately (a) owned, and (b) owed, due. See the
      note to I.vi.26.

27   **Meet ... Weal**   let us join forces with the King (Malcolm), who
      is the medicine prescribed by the physician (Edward) to cure
      our sick commonwealth. Compare IV.iii.146–59, 164–70,
      188–90; V.i.80–84.

28   **pour we**   let us pour. Compare line 1, I.iii.96–98, and
      I.v.27–28.
      in ... Purge   as medicinal purgatives (cathartics) to prompt our
      country to void Macbeth. Compare lines 22–25, and the
      reference to the casting of 'Lye' in II.iii.34–48. Macduff's
      figure is a cruder version of 'Macbeth / Is ripe for Shaking'
      (IV.iii.236–37) – a casting-off that will prove mortal for him
      but cleansing for the country with 'the Evil' (IV.iii.146).

30   **dew ... Flower**   provide life-giving dew for the flower of true
      kingship. *Dew* plays on *endue* (clothe) and *due* (see *Richard
      III*, V.iii.46) and hints at the manna from Heaven that
      preserved the children of Israel (Exodus 16:4, 14–18).
      Compare I.iv.18–27.

V.iii   This scene returns us to Macbeth's castle in Dunsinane.

3   **taint**   be tainted; either stained (compare II.ii.58–60) or
      infected.

5   **All mortal Consequences**   all the causes and effects of mortal
      life. Compare I.v.3, 43; I.vii.1–12; III.v.32–33.
      pronounc'd me   spoken definitively (prophesied) to me.
      Compare I.ii.66.

ANGUS   Now does he feel
His secret Murthers sticking on his Hands;
Now minutely Revolts upbraid his Faith-breach;
Those he commands move onely in Command,
Nothing in Love. Now does he feel his Title   20
Hang loose about him, like a Giant's Robe
Upon a dwarfish Thief.

MENTETH   Who then shall blame
His pester'd Senses to recoil and start,
When all that is within him does condemn
It self for being there?

CATHNESS   Well, march we on,   25
To give Obedience where 'tis truly ow'd:
Meet we the Med'cine of the sickly Weal,
And with him pour we in our Country's Purge,
Each Drop of us.

LENOX   Or so much as it needs
To dew the Sovereign Flower, and drown the
    Weeds.   30
Make we our March towards Byrnane.   *Exeunt marching.*

Scene 3

Enter Macbeth, Doctor, and Attendants.

MACBETH   Bring me no more Reports, let them fly
    all:
Till Byrnane Wood remove to Dunsinane,
I cannot taint with Fear. What's the Boy
    Malcolm?
Was he not borne of Woman? The Spirits that
    know
All mortal Consequences have pronounc'd me
    thus: 5

8   **English Epicures**   overindulgent (and thus soft) English.

9   **The . . . by**   the mental disposition with which I rule the realm. But *sway* is equivocal: it can also mean something closer to 'sag' and 'shake' (line 10). Compare I.v.72, V.i.81–82, and IV.iii.236–37.

11   **cream-fac'd**   cowardly. Compare II.i.51, II.ii.58–62, III.ii.50–51, and III.iv.110–14.
       Loon   probably both (a) lown (low, base peasant, as in *Othello*, II.iii.92), and (b) loon (a bird that dives for fish and emits a weird cry). 'Goose-look' (line 12) also suggests a foolish, cowardly manner. Compare III.ii.17.

14   **over-red thy Fear**   restore blood to your cheeks.

15   **Lily-liver'd**   with a liver as soft, delicate, and white as the lily. A lack of red blood in the liver indicated cowardice.
       Patch   fool (referring to the particoloured uniform of the court clown).

17   **Whey-face**   with a face the colour of thin, watery milk.

20   **Push**   aggression, assault. Compare III.iv.78–80.

21   **cheer**   hearten, renew; with wordplay on *chair*, enthrone. Compare III.iv.31.
       dis-eat   uncheer; both (a) reject, vomit up (playing on *cheer* as a word for both 'hospitality' and 'food'), and (b) dis-seat, dethrone. Compare I.iii.134, III.iv.78–80.

23   **sear**   both (a) a seared (scorched) condition, and (b) the sere, the withered state associated with autumn leaves. Compare V.ii.3.

26   **steed**   stead (place), but with play on *steed* as a horse from which Macbeth will soon be unseated.

'Fear not, Macbeth; no Man that's borne of
   Woman
Shall ere have Power upon thee.' Then fly,
   false Thanes,
And mingle with the English Epicures;
The Mind I sway by, and the Heart I bear,
Shall never sag with Doubt, nor shake with
   Fear.   10

Enter a Servant.

– The Divel damn thee Black, thou cream-fac'd
   Loon:
Where got'st thou that Goose-look.
SERVANT   There is ten thousand –
MACBETH   Geese, Villain?
SERVANT   Soldiers, Sir.
MACBETH   Go prick thy Face, and over-red thy
   Fear,
Thou Lily-liver'd Boy. What Soldiers, Patch?   15
Death of thy Soul, those Linen Cheeks of thine
Are Counsellors to Fear. What Soldiers, Whey-
   face?
SERVANT   The English Force, so please you.
MACBETH   Take thy Face hence!   [*Exit Servant.*]

– Seyton! – I am
   Sick at Heart
When I behold – Seyton, I say, this Push   20
Will cheer me ever or dis-eat me now.
I have liv'd long enough: my Way of Life
Is fall'n into the Sear, the Yellow Leaf,
And that which should accompany Old Age,
As Honour, Love, Obedience, Troops of Friends,   25
I must not look to have, but in their steed
Curses not loud but deep, Mouth-honour, Breath

28   **poor** weak, worthless. Compare IV.ii.36.
    fain gladly. *Heart* echoes line 19.

35   **moe Horses** more cavalrymen.
    skirr scour, scurry. Compare *Henry V*, IV.vii.65–67.

37   **Sick** physically ill. Compare IV.i.59–60.

38   **thick-coming Fancies** hallucinations coming one right after
    another.

39   **Cure of that** Most editors add *her* after *Cure*. It may be,
    however, that Shakespeare wanted the actor playing Macbeth
    to swallow that word as he delivered this line.

40   **Mind diseas'd** both (a) a distempered (disturbed) mental state,
    and (b) a mind dis-eased (kept from its rest). Compare lines
    20–23 and V.ii.15. See the notes to I.v.6, 22.

41   **rooted Sorrow** a deeply planted grief. Compare the weed
    imagery in V.ii.29–30 and the withered leaf imagery in line
    23. For previous plant images see the notes to IV.i.95 and
    IV.iii.85.

42   **Raze out** both (a) raze (uproot), and (b) erase. See the note to
    V.i.28.
    written deeply written.

43   **Olivious** memory-obliterating.

44   **Cleanse** both (a) purge (compare line 21 and V.ii.28), and (b)
    wash (compare II.ii.64 and V.i.33). The word *stuff'd* is a
    reminder of the references to swelling in such passages as
    I.iii.126–27; I.v.42–56, 69–72; and I.vii.49–61.
    Perilous imperiling, overburdening.

46   **minister to himself** be his own physician. Compare II.iii.56–57,
    IV.iii.141–59, and V.i.66, 83.

47   **Throw Physic** discard medical science. Macbeth's phrasing is
    another variation on the imagery of casting off or trashing
    that recurs so frequently in both *Macbeth* (see lines 44,
    50–52, and I.iv.8–11, I.vii.35, and V.ii.28) and *Othello*
    (II.iii.272–73, 277, 372; III.iv.171; IV.i.180; V.i.80; and
    V.ii.321).

48   **Staff** probably the general's baton. The word also recalls
    III.i.60.

49   **send out** send someone to fetch my staff.

Which the poor Heart would fain deny and dare
 not.
Seyton?

Enter Seyton.

SEYTON   What's your Gracious Pleasure?
MACBETH   What News more?   30
SEYTON   All is confirm'd, my Lord, which was
 reported.
MACBETH   I'll fight till from my Bones my Flesh
 be hack'd.
Give me my Armour.
SEYTON   'Tis not needed yet.
MACBETH   I'll put it on.
Send out moe Horses; skirr the Country round;   35
Hang those that talk of Fear. Give me mine
 Armour.
– How does your Patient, Doctor?
DOCTOR   Not so Sick, my Lord,
As she is troubled with thick-coming Fancies
That keep her from her Rest.
MACBETH   Cure of that:
Canst thou not minister to a Mind diseas'd,   40
Pluck from the Memory a rooted Sorrow,
Raze out of the written Troubles of the Brain,
And with some sweet Oblivious Antidote
Cleanse the stuff'd Bosom of that Perilous Stuff
Which weighs upon the Heart?
DOCTOR   Therein the Patient   45
Must minister to himself.
MACBETH   Throw Physic to the Dogs, I'll none
 of it.
– Come, put mine Armour on: give me my Staff.
Seyton, send out. – Doctor, the Thanes fly
 from me.

50–51 **cast ... Land**   analyse the urine of Scotland.

51   **find her Disease**   diagnose her illness. Compare line 40.

52   **purge it**   remove it, either by bleeding or by an emetic to make it cast off the 'Stuff' (line 44) that imperils its health.

pristive   This word (*pristiue* in the Folio) is usually interpreted as a typographical error for *pristine* (unblemished in its original purity). But it may be a Shakespearean coinage to combine *pristine* and *pristly* (a variant of *priestly*). If so, it provides an ironic reminder that the 'Health' Macbeth seeks is the kind that only a 'Divine' (V.i.83) can minister.

54   **Pull't off**   Macbeth probably refers to a piece of armour.

55   **Cyme**   probably the top of a cynna (senna), a herb used as a purgative.

56   **scour**   cleanse, scrub, purge; scurry. Compare *skirr*, line 35.

59   **Bane**   curse, destruction.

61   **clear**   The Doctor's phrasing echoes I.vii.18, II.ii.64, and III.i.130–31.

V.iv   This scene takes place in the countryside near Byrnan Wood.

2   **Chambers**   bedrooms. Malcolm's phrasing is a reminder that his father's chamber was *not* 'safe', either for Duncan or for his two chamberlains.

5   **shadow**   disguise, cast in doubt.

6   **Host**   army.

Discovery   attempts to determine how many of us there are.

     — Come, Sir, dispatch. — If thou couldst,
       Doctor, cast   50
     The Water of my Land, find her Disease,
     And purge it to a sound and pristive Health,
     I would applaud thee to the very Echo
     That should applaud again. — Pull't off, I
       say!
     — What Rhubarb, Cyme, or what Purgative Drug   55
     Would scour these English hence? Hear'st thou
       of them?
DOCTOR   I, my good Lord: your Royal Preparation
     Makes us hear something.
MACBETH   — Bring it after me.
     — I will not be afraid of Death and Bane
     Till Birnane Forest come to Dunsinane.   60
DOCTOR   Were I from Dunsinane away, and clear,
     Profit again should hardly draw me here.   *Exeunt.*

Scene 4

Drum and Colours. Enter Malcolm, Seyward, Macduff,
Seyward's Son, Menteth, Cathness, Angus,
and Soldiers Marching.

MALCOLM   Cousins, I hope the Days are near at
     hand
     That Chambers will be safe.
MENTETH   We doubt it nothing.
SEYWARD   What Wood is this before us?
MENTETH   The Wood of Birnane.
MALCOLM   Let every Soldier hew him down a Bough
     And bear't before him: thereby shall we shadow   5
     The numbers of our Host and make Discovery
     Err in report of us.

168

8   **confident** overconfident, secure. Compare III.v.23–33, where Hecat describes a strategy for making Macbeth 'ripe for Shaking' (IV.iii.237). See the note to III.vi.44.

9–10 **will . . . 't** will permit us to lay siege to his castle, rather than heading us off before we get there.

11   **Advantage . . . given** an opportunity to take advantage of the situation (Macbeth's weakness).

12   **Both . . . Revolt** both the nobility and the common people have deserted him. Compare IV.i.66.

13   **Constrained Things** creatures who are forced to do so. Compare V.iii.24–28.

14   **Whose . . . too** whose hearts are just as alienated from Macbeth as the hearts of those in active 'Revolt'.

14–15 **Let . . . Event** both (a) let our just condemnation of Macbeth serve to effect an outcome ('Event') that is 'True' (good) and (b) let our assessment of the military situation await the outcome of battle. Macduff is warning against over-confidence. Compare lines 8–9.

15–16 **and . . . Soldiership** and [in the meantime] let us attire ourselves as hard-working soldiers. Macduff's phrasing echoes Ephesians 6:11–17. Compare V.ii.20–22.

17   **due Decision** a timely determination of the outcome. *Due* echoes *dew* (V.ii.30), and it suggests a 'Decision' that is 'due' in two other senses: (a) ready for harvesting (IV.iii.237), or prepared for 'Issue' (line 20) or birth (V.i.80–81), and (b) due for payment, as with a debt or inheritance (line 18). Compare I.iv.21, III.vi.24–26, IV.iii.196–97.

18   **owe** both (a) own (possess outright, rather than merely 'have' by lease, claim, or seizure), and (b) owe. See V.ii.25–26, and compare I.iii.74; I.iv.8–11, 22–23; I.vi.25–28; III.iv.110–11.

19   **Thoughts . . . relate** speculation may express its uncertain guesses about what the future holds. *Speculative* recalls III.iv.93–94; and *Unsure Hopes* echoes lines 1, 10, and I.iii.52–55, I.vii.35–36, III.i.6–10, III.v.30–31,S IV.III.113–14. *Issue* recalls III.i.46–70, IV.i.85–102.

20   **But . . . arbitrate** but certainty awaits the strokes of swords.

V.v   This scene returns us to Macbeth's castle in Dunsinane.

5   **forc'd** reinforced.

SOLDIERS   It shall be done.

SEYWARD   We learn no other but the confident
    Tyrant
    Keeps still in Dunsinane, and will endure
    Our setting down before't.

MALCOLM   'Tis his main Hope: 10
    For where there is Advantage to be given,
    Both More and Less have given him the Revolt,
    And none serve with him but Constrained Things,
    Whose Hearts are absent too.

MACDUFF   Let our just Censures
    Attend the true Event, and put we on   15
    Industrious Soldiership.

SEYWARD   The Time approaches
    That will with due Decision make us know
    What we shall we have, and what we owe:
    Thoughts Speculative their Unsure Hopes relate,
    But Certain Issue, Strokes must arbitrate,   20
    Towards which, advance the War.   *Exeunt marching.*

Scene 5

Enter Macbeth, Seyton, and Soldiers,
with Drum and Colours.

MACBETH   Hang out our Banners on the outward
    Walls:
    The Cry is still, they come. Our Castle's Strength
    Will laugh a Siege to scorn: here let them lie
    Till Famine and the Ague eat them up.
    Were they not forc'd with those that should be
    ours,   5
    We might have met them dareful, Beard to
    Beard,

10   **cool'd**   shivered with terror. Compare I.ii.50–51, II.iii.66–67, IV.i.152–53, and see the note to IV.ii.237.

11   **Night-shriek**   screech-owl's scream. Compare II.ii.3, 15, 32–33, and II.iii.60–67.
          Fell of Hair   hair-covered skin.

12   **a dismal Treatise**   ominous or frightening narrative.

13   **As . . . in't**   as if it were alive.
          supp'd . . . Horrors   sated myself (and dulled my 'Taste' and other senses) by all the 'Direness' I have consumed. Compare I.vii.29; III.i.14, 41–42; and V.iii.20–21, 43–45. See the note to II.ii.68.

15   **start**   startle, move. Compare V.ii.22–25 and V.i.51.

17   **She . . . hereafter**   either (a) she should have died later rather than now, or (b) she would have died sooner or later. Compare III.i.8–11.

22   **lighted**   provided torchlight (comparing the sun to a servant with a 'petty Pace': tiny, slow-moving steps). Compare I.iv.51, II.iii.148–49, III.ii.51–52. *Fools* recalls III.iv.51–53.

23   **dusty Death**   the dust we return to (Genesis 3:19). *Way* echoes III.iii.19; III.iv.128, 134; IV.i.45; IV.ii.22; V.ii.6; V.iii.22.
          brief Candle   both (a) our earthly life, and (b) the sun (as in line 48). Compare II.i.4–5, and *Othello*, V.ii.7–15.

24   **poor Player**   paltry, inept, impoverished, and short-lived actor. Compare V.i.14. *Poor* echoes V.iii.28.

27   **Fury**   Frenzy; uncontrolled agitation. Compare II.iii.113–14 and V.ii.13–14.

And beat them backward home.

A Cry within of Women.

What is that Noise?

SEYTON   It is the Cry of Women, my good Lord.

MACBETH   I have almost forgot the Taste of Fears.

The Time has been my Senses would have cool'd   10
To hear a Night-shriek, and my Fell of Hair
Would at a dismal Treatise rouse and stir
As Life were in't. I have supp'd full with
   Horrors:
Direness familiar to my slaughterous Thoughts
Cannot once start me. Wherefore was that Cry?   15

SEYTON   The Queen, my Lord, is dead.

MACBETH   She should have di'd hereafter;
There would have been a Time for such a Word:
To morrow, and to morrow, and to morrow,
Creeps in this petty Pace from Day to Day,   20
To the last Syllable of Recorded Time;
And all our Yesterdays have lighted Fools
The way to dusty Death. — Out, out, brief
   Candle.
Life's but a walking Shadow, a poor Player,
That struts and frets his Hour upon the Stage   25
And then is heard no more; it is a Tale
Told by an Idiot, full of Sound and Fury
Signifying nothing.

Enter a Messenger.

— Thou com'st to use
Thy Tongue: thy Story quickly.

MESSENGER   Gracious my Lord,
I should report that which I say I saw,   30
But know not how to do't.

MACBETH   Well, say, Sir.

MESSENGER   As I did stand my Watch upon the Hill,

36   **this three Mile**   three miles of this place.

38   **the next Tree**   Compare *The Tempest*, III.ii.40.

39   **Famine cling thee**   starvation grip you in its clutches.
     Sooth   [the] truth; truthful.

41   **pull in Resolution**   gather in some of the confident resolve that
has kept me feeling courageous. Compare III.i.136–37.

42   **doubt . . . Fiend**   fear that the Devil has been speaking to me
with duplicity. Compare I.i.9; I.iii.120–24; II.iii.9–13, 34–41;
III.ii.4–7, III.v.26–33; and IV.iii.20–24.

43   **lies like Truth**   tells lies while seeming to impart truths (what
Banquo has call'd 'honest Trifles', I.iii.123).

45   **out**   let us take to the field of battle.

46   **avouches does appear**   swears turns out to be true [and moving
woods do appear here].

48   **'gin**   begin.

49   **And . . . undone**   and wish the framework of the world would
be dismantled. Compare II.iii.83–84, 87–89, and *King Lear*,
V.iii.261–62, 294–95. In his world-weary despair, Macbeth
now longs for a disintegration of Creation itself. His verb
echoes all the play's previous references to doing, undoing,
and deeds; and it is yet another signal that Macbeth is now
'ripe for Shaking' (IV.iii.237), prepared for the 'even-handed
Justice', the 'Judgement here', that will foreshadow the
'End-all' awaiting him in 'the Life to come' (I.vii.4–10).

51   **Harness . . . Back**   Macbeth means 'armour on'; but his image
reminds us that he is now as constrained by circumstances as
a harnessed beast.

V.vi   This scene takes place in Dunsinane outside Macbeth's castle.

1   **Leavy**   leafy. Compare V.iii.22–23.

I look'd toward Byrnane and anon me thought
The Wood began to move.

MACBETH   Liar and Slave.

MESSENGER Let me endure your Wrath if't be
    not so.   35
Within this three Mile may you see it coming:
I say, a moving Grove.

MACBETH   If thou speak'st False,
Upon the next Tree shall thou hang alive
Till Famine cling thee; if thy Speech be Sooth,
I care not if thou dost for me as much.   40
— I pull in Resolution, and begin
To doubt th' Equivocation of the Fiend,
That lies like Truth. 'Fear not till Byrnane
    Wood
Do come to Dunsinane,' and now a Wood
Comes toward Dunsinane. Arm, arm, and out: 45
If this which he avouches does appear,
There is nor Flying hence nor Tarrying here.
I 'gin to be a-weary of the Sun,
And wish th' Estate o' th' World were now
    undone.
Ring the Alarum Bell, blow Wind, come
    Wrack,   50
At least we'll die with Harness on our Back.

                                       Exeunt.

Scene 6

Drum and Colours. Enter Malcolm, Seyward, Macduff,
and their Army, with Boughs.

MALCOLM Now near enough: your Leavy Screens
    throw down,

2   **shew**   show, appear. Compare V.v.46–47.
     Uncle   Seyward.

4   **Battell**   both (a) battalion, and (b) battle. Compare I.ii.4.
     we   I. The King employs the royal plural.

5   **take upon's**   assume as our responsibility. Malcolm's clothing
       image is a reminder that he is now beginning to don the
       mantle of rule. Compare V.v.15–16.

6   **our Order**   the ordered plan that will organize our attack.
       Compare III.iii.2–4.

7   **Do . . . Power**   if we can only discover (encounter) Macbeth's
       army. Compare lines 7–8 with IV.iii.231–34.

9   **speak**   utter their martial music.

10   **Harbingers**   forerunners, advance men. Compare I.iv.44–46,
       I.vi.20–24. Clamorous recalls I.vii.77–79.

V.vii   This scene takes place in another part of the battlefield before
        the castle.

1   **ti'd . . . Stake**   hemmed me in like baying dogs. Macbeth's
       image derives from bear-baiting. It is thus a reminder that
       amphitheatres similar to the Globe provided entertainments
       like the one Macbeth refers to, and did so only a short
       distance from where the actor who played Macbeth for the
       first time (probably Richard Burbage) would have spoken
       these lines. For other Shakespearean uses of the same
       metaphor, see *Twelfth Night*, III.i.127–29, *All's Well That
       Ends Well*, II.iii.156, *1 Henry VI*, V.iv.15, *2 Henry VI*,
       V.i.144–56, *Julius Caesar*, IV.i.48–51, *Hamlet*, IV.iv.50–53,
       and *King Lear*, II.i.63, III.vii.52. Line 2 echoes 1 Timothy
       6:12, 2 Timothy 4:7.

3   **borne of Woman**   This phrase can mean both (a) carried by a
       woman for the full term of her pregnancy, and (b) and given
       birth to by a woman (who must bear down to push the infant
       out of her womb).

6   **hoter**   both (a) haughtier, more arrogant, and (b) hotter, more
       associated with Hell-fire. Compare IV.iii.22.

And shew like those you are. – You, worthy
   Uncle,
Shall with my Cousin your right Noble Son
Lead our first Battell. Worthy Macduff and we
Shall take upon's what else remains to do,   5
According to our Order.
SEYWARD   Fare you well.
   Do we but find the Tyrant's Power to night,
   Let us be beaten if we cannot fight.
MACDUFF   Make all our Trumpets speak; give them
   all Breath,
   Those clamorous Harbingers of Blood and Death.   10
                              Exeunt. Alarums continued.

Scene 7

Enter Macbeth.

MACBETH   They have ti'd me to a Stake: I cannot
   fly,
   But Bear-like I must fight the Course. What's
   he
   That was not borne of Woman? Such a one
   Am I to fear, or none.

Enter Young Seyward.

YOUNG SEYWARD   What is thy Name?
MACBETH   Thou'lt be afraid to hear it.   5
YOUNG SEYWARD   No: though thou call'st thy self
   a hoter Name
   Than any is in Hell.
MACBETH   My name's Macbeth.

8   **Title**   both (a) designation, name, and (b) position.

11   **prove . . . speak'st**   demonstrate that what you say is false. *Lie*
      (spelled *Lye* in the Folio) recalls II.iii.24–47, IV.ii.78,
      V.iii.50–56, V.v.3, 43.

16   **still**   yet, forever.

17   **Kerns**   light-armoured Irish mercenaries. See I.ii.13.

18   **bear their Staves**   carry their spears. Macduff's verb suggests
      that 'hir'd' Kerns are more like beasts of burden than valiant
      soldiers. He regards it as beneath his dignity to fight against
      such base defenders of Macbeth.
      either thou   either I strike at you.

20   **undeeded**   without having accomplished any martial exploit.
      Macduff's verb recalls such passages as I.vii.12–25; II.ii.9–11,
      14, 64, 69–70; II.iv.10–11, 22, 25–27; III.ii.41–47;
      III.iv.140–42; IV.ii.48, 144–45, 152–53.

21   **by . . . Clatter**   [I would judge] by all the commotion I hear
      there.
      Greatest Note   highest rank.

22   **bruited**   proclaimed, rumoured. *Seems* recalls I.ii.2, 22, 27, 48;
      I.iii.55, 79; II.i.48–49; II.iii.108; IV.iii.168–70.

25   **on . . . fight**   are themselves divided about whose side they fight
      on. In lines 28–29 Malcolm says that those who should be
      'Foes' instead 'strike beside us' (wield their swords on our
      behalf, having joined us against Macbeth). *Sides* recalls II.i.54.

YOUNG SEYWARD   The Divel himself could not
   pronounce a Title
  More hateful to mine Ear.
MACBETH   No: nor more fearful.
YOUNG SEYWARD   Thou liest, abhorred Tyrant:
   with my Sword   10
  I'll prove the Lie thou speak'st.
               Fight, and Young Seyward slain.
MACBETH   Thou wast borne of Woman;
  But Swords I smile at, Weapons laugh to scorn,
  Brandish'd by Man that's of a Woman borne.   *Exit.*

        Alarums. Enter Macduff.

MACDUFF   That way the Noise is. – Tyrant, shew
   thy Face:
  If thou beest slain, and with no Stroke of
   mine,   15
  My Wife and Children's Ghosts will haunt me
   still.
  I cannot strike at wretched Kerns, whose Arms
  Are hir'd to bear their Staves: either thou,
   Macbeth,
  Or else my Sword with an unbattered Edge
  I sheathe again undeeded. There thou should'st
   be: 20
  By this great Clatter, one of Greatest Note
  Seems bruited. – Let me find him, Fortune,
  And more I beg not.   *Exit. Alarums.*

        Enter Malcolm and Seyward.

SEYWARD   This way, my Lord, the Castle's gently
   rend'red:
  The Tyrant's People on both Sides do fight,   25
  The Noble Thanes do bravely in the War,

27   **The . . . yours** the day itself almost seems to cast its lot with
you.

30   **play . . . Fool** commit suicide like a defeated Roman. This line
recalls other roles by the actor now playing Macbeth;
compare *Julius Caesar*, V.iii.44–45, and *Antony and
Cleopatra*, IV.xv.14–15. Though Macbeth is but a 'poor
Player' now, he will strut and fret until 'his Hour upon the
Stage' (V.v.24–25) is halted by a worthy successor. In most
modern editions this line begins a new scene; but the Folio
text treats the 'Alarum' after line 29 as a signal for the action
to continue uninterrupted. *Fool* recalls V.v.22.

34   **charg'd** both (a) burdened, weighted, and (b) guilty [as
charged]. Compare I.ii.38, IV.iii.18–20.

36–37 **thou . . . out** you villain too bloody for any terms that can be
devised to describe you. Compare lines 8–9.

37   **Thou loosest Labour** you waste your energy. *Loose* was the
normal spelling for both *lose* and *loose* (release, unbind,
throw off). Compare I.iii.109, I.v.14, II.i.25.

38   **intrenchant** untrenchable; impenetrable. Macbeth considers it
impossible for Macduff to put 'twenty trenched Gashes on his
Head' (III.iv.25).

39   **impress** (a) engrave, mark with an impression, and (b) press
into your service. Compare IV.i.94.

41   **bear . . . Life** carry a life that is magically exempt from danger.
Macbeth's verb combines a clothing metaphor with the other
senses of 'bearing' implied in *borne* (line 42).

42   **Despair** despair of; abandon all hope in. Compare IV.iii.152,
and see III.v.20–33.

43   **the . . . serv'd** the fallen angel (Lucifer) you have always served.
Compare I.vii.16–28 and IV.iii.22.

45   **Untimely ripp'd** torn from his mother's womb before the
completion of a nine-month term. Macbeth has interpreted
the Witches' prophecy to refer to any man born to an earthly
woman (see Matthew 11:11). But Macduff gives the prophecy
the more restricted sense of 'borne to full term', or given birth
to in the normal fashion (see the note to line 3).
Appropriately, the line in which he announces that the
Witches have equivocated yet again is a truncated one –
'ripp'd' short of the metrical norm.

The Day almost it self professes yours,
And little is to do.

MALCOLM   We have met with Foes
That strike beside us.

SEYWARD   Enter, Sir, the Castle.
                                        Exeunt. Alarum.

                Enter Macbeth.

MACBETH   Why should I play the Roman Fool, and
    die   30
On mine own Sword? Whiles I see Lives, the
    Gashes
Do better upon them.

                Enter Macduff.

MACDUFF   Turn, Hell-hound, turn!
MACBETH   Of all Men else I have avoided thee:
But get thee back, my Soul is too much charg'd
With Blood of thine already.

MACDUFF   I have no Words,   35
My Voice is in my Sword, thou bloodier Villain
Than Terms can give thee out.   *Fight. Alarum.*

MACBETH   Thou loosest Labour:
As easy may'st thou the intrenchant Air
With thy keen Sword impress as make me bleed.
Let fall thy Blade on vulnerable Crests: 40
I bear a charmed Life, which must not yield
To one of Woman borne.

MACDUFF   Despair thy Charm,
And let the Angel whom thou still hast serv'd
Tell thee Macduff was from his Mother's Womb
Untimely ripp'd.   45

MACBETH   Accursed be that Tongue that tells me
    so:

47 **Cow'd . . . Man** turned my courage cow-like. See line 52 and III.i.52–55.

48 **Juggling** deceiving, cheating. Lines 46–51 echo II.iii.34–41, and prompt us to 'remember the Porter' (II.iii.23).

49 **palter** equivocate, speak 'in a Double Sense' (ambiguously).

51 **Hope** expectations. For previous passages referring to hope, see the note to V.iv.19.

53 **the . . . Time** the display that everyone in our time will gaze upon. Here *Shew* hints at *eschew*: fear, shun, abhor.

55 **Painted . . . Pole** your picture painted on a canvas and uplifted on a pole. Macduff's image also hints at what will happen to Macbeth if he does *not* 'yield' himself as a coward: his head will be impaled upon a blood-soaked pole.
Under-writ subscribed with a painted proclamation.

58 **baited** mocked (literally, barked at and bitten, as by baying dogs). See lines 1–2.

60 **oppos'd** opposing me.

61 **try the last** make trial of Fate to the 'End-all' here (I.vii.5).

65 **Some . . . off** it is ordained that some must die. Seyward's phrasing suggests that those who have not 'safe arriv'd' have taken a different 'way' (compare V.v.22–23), one that leads to Heaven.

70 **Prowess confirm'd** bravery ratified (made firm). Compare II.ii.49, III.iv.84.

For it hath Cow'd my better part of Man.
And be these Juggling Fiends no more believ'd,
That palter with us in a Double Sense,
That keep the Word of Promise to our Ear   50
And break it to our Hope.
I'll not fight with thee.

MACDUFF   Then yield thee Coward,
And live to be the Shew and Gaze o' th' Time.
We'll have thee, as our rarer Monsters are,
Painted upon a Pole, and under-writ   55
'Here may you see the Tyrant.'

MACBETH   I will not yield
To kiss the Ground before young Malcolm's Feet,
And to be baited with the Rabble's Curse.
Though Byrnane Wood be come to Dunsinane,
And thou oppos'd, being of no Woman borne,   60
Yet I will try the last. Before my Body
I throw my Warlike Shield. Lay on, Macduff,
And damn'd be him that first cries 'Hold,
    enough!'   *Exeunt fighting. Alarums.*

Enter Fighting, and Macbeth slain.

*Retreat and Flourish. Enter, with Drum and Colours,
Malcolm, Seyward, Rosse, Thanes, and Soldiers.*

MALCOLM   I would the Friends we miss were safe
    arriv'd.
SEYWARD   Some must go off; and yet by these I
    see,   65
So great a Day as this is cheaply bought.
MALCOLM   Macduff is missing, and your Noble Son.
ROSSE   Your Son, my Lord, has paid a Soldier's
    Debt:
He onely liv'd but till he was a Man,
The which no sooner had his Prowess confirm'd   70

71 **unshrinking Station** uncowering standing-up in his assigned
post. Rosse's imagery implies an analogy between two kinds
of initiation. As in I.v.73 and I.vii.26, *onely* (line 69) suggests
the erect 'I' (as the Folio renders the 'Ay' of lines 73, 76) the
'keen Knife' (I.v.54), of a soldier whose 'Prow' is
'unshrinking' in its 'Station' (lines 70–71). Young Seyward
has earned the 'Addition' (I.iii.104) of a true 'Man'. He thus
provides an instructive instance of the kind of manly assertion
that is prompted by the Spirit rather than by the flesh; see the
comment on I.v.70. See the notes to III.i.4, 100, and compare
1 Henry VI, IV.vi.35–36, and *All's Well That Ends Well*,
IV.iii.19–20.

74 **be measur'd by** have its extent determined by. Rosse plays on
another sense of *measur'd*: moderated in accordance with the
kind of 'measure' defined by the Aristotelian mean (the
median between two extremes). His phrasing echoes III.iv.10
(where *Measure* refers to a drink from a large cup) and
anticipates line 102 (where it refers to orderly decorum). Lines
73–75 recall IV.iii.265–67.

77 **Hairs** Seyward puns on *heirs*; compare I.iii.132–33.

79 **Knell is knoll'd** death knell is toll'd (by the figurative bells of
those who have recounted his merits). See II.i.61–63, II.ii.3,
IV.iii.170–73.

81 **paid his Score** made good on his debts. *Score* is another word
that hints at more than one kind of male prowess; see
Othello, IV.i.128.

83 **stands** Macduff's verb suggests that Macbeth's head is held
aloft on a pole. 'Th' Usurper's' fate is altogether in keeping
with the manner in which he himself has stood up in defiance
of every form of order; it also echoes what Macbeth did to an
earlier rebel (I.ii.15–23). See the notes to line 71 and III.iii.15,
III.iv.117, and V.i.24.

84 **Free** liberated from tyranny.

85 **compass'd . . . Pearl** surrounded by the pearls (the loyal
nobility) who constitute the most precious jewels of your
kingdom. Compare I.iv.39–42, III.i.59–68.

86 **That . . . Minds** who all hail you mentally. Compare I.iii.46,
I.v.1–16.

90 **reckon . . . Loves** take into account the love that each of you
have shown us.

In the unshrinking Station where he fought,
But like a Man he di'd.

SEYWARD   Then he is dead?

ROSSE Ay, and brought off the Field. Your cause
    of Sorrow
Must not be measur'd by his Worth, for then
It hath no End.

SEYWARD   Hath he his Hurts before?   75

ROSSE Ay, on the Front.

SEYWARD   Why then, God's Soldier be he.
Had I as many Sons as I have Hairs,
I would not wish them to a Fairer Death;
And so his Knell is knoll'd.

MALCOLM   He's worth more Sorrow,
And that I'll spend for him.

SEYWARD   He's worth no more: 80
They say he parted well, and paid his Score,
And so God be with him. Here comes newer
    Comfort.

Enter Macduff, with Macbeth's Head.

MACDUFF Hail, King, for so thou art. Behold
    where stands
Th' Usurper's cursed Head: the Time is Free.
I see thee compass'd with thy Kingdom's Pearl,   85
That speak my Salutation in their Minds,
Whose Voices I desire aloud with mine:
Hail King of Scotland.

ALL   Hail King of Scotland.

                                Flourish.

MALCOLM We shall not spend a large Expense of
    Time
Before we reckon with your several Loves   90

91   **even with you**   no longer in your debt. It is a sign of the
      stability that has finally been achieved that the word *even* now
      carries no implication of revenge. Compare III.iv.9.

92   **Earls**   The new titles (a promotion from thanes) symbolize the
      birth of a new social and political establishment. Shakespeare
      drew this detail from Holinshed's *Chronicles*.

94   **planted**   This verb echoes Duncan's wording in I.iv.28–29. See
      the note to V.iii.41.

96   **watchful**   spying and preying. Compare II.ii.67–68,
      III.iv.129–30, and V.i.1.

101   **Grace of Grace**   gracious (merciful) providence of a loving God.

And make us even with you. My Thanes and
   Kinsmen,
Henceforth be Earls, the first that ever
   Scotland
In such an Honour nam'd. What's more to do,
Which would be planted newly with the Time,
As calling home our exil'd Friends abroad   95
That fled the Snares of watchful Tyranny,
Producing forth the cruel Ministers
Of this dead Butcher and his Fiend-like Queen,
Who, as 'tis thought, by self and violent Hands
Took off her Life, this and what needful else   100
That calls upon us, by the Grace of Grace,
We will perform in Measure, Time, and Place.
So thanks to all at once, and to each one,
Whom we invite to see us Crown'd at Scone.

                    Flourish. Exeunt Omnes.

FINIS

PERSPECTIVES ON *MACBETH*

Anthologies of Shakespearean commentary usually commence with Samuel Johnson, the most eloquent and judicious critic of the eighteenth century. In the preface to his 1765 edition of the playwright's complete works, Dr Johnson said that

> Shakespeare is above all writers, at least above all modern writers, the poet of nature; the poet that holds up to his readers a faithful mirrour of Manners and of life. His characters are not modified by the customs of particular places, . . . by the peculiarities of studies or professions . . . or by the accidents of transient fashions or temporary opinions: they are the genuine progeny of common humanity, such as the world will always supply, and observation will always find. His persons act and speak by the influence of those general passions and principles by which all minds are agitated.

Although Johnson admired much about *Macbeth*, which he thought 'deservedly celebrated for the propriety of its fictions' and for the 'solemnity, grandeur, and variety of its actions', he nevertheless felt it necessary to make excuses for a playwright who would devote so much of his drama's plot to witchcraft.

> In order to make a true estimate of the abilities and merit of a writer, it is always necessary to examine the genius of his age and the opinions of his contemporaries. A poet who should now make the whole action of his tragedy depend upon enchantment and produce the chief events by the assistance of supernatural agents, would be censured as transgressing the bounds of probability, be banished from the theatre to the nursery, and condemned to write fairy tales instead of tragedies: but a survey of the notions that prevailed at the time when this play was written will prove that Shakespeare was in no danger of such censures, since he only turned the system that was then universally admitted to his advantage and was far from overburdening the credulity of his audience.

Johnson thought it regrettable that in *Macbeth*, as in so many of his other plays, Shakespeare was unable to resist the coarse punning that marred his best effects. Focusing on II.ii.52–54, where Macbeth's Lady says 'I'll guild the Grooms withal, / For it must seem their Guilt,' Johnson asked incredulously if the dramatist could 'possibly mean to play upon the similitude of *gild* and *guilt*'. Johnson expressed similar misgivings about the propriety of Shakespeare's language in II.iii.118–21, but in this instance he came up with an explanation for the passage's bad taste that would allow him to justify, and even commend, an effect he'd have otherwise found himself called upon to condemn.

> Mr Pope has endeavored to improve one of these lines by substituting *gory blood* for *golden blood*; but it may easily be admitted that he who could on such occasion talk of *lacing the silver skin* would lace it with *golden blood*. No amendment can be made to this line, of which every word is equally faulty, but by a general blot. It is not improbable that Shakespeare put these forced and unnatural metaphors into the mouth of Macbeth as a mark of artifice and dissimulation, to show the difference between the studied language of hypocrisy and the natural outcries of sudden passion. This whole speech so considered is a remarkable instance of judgement, as it consists entirely of antithesis and metaphor.

In general, Dr Johnson said of *Macbeth*,

> The danger of ambition is well described; and I know not whether it may not be said in defence of some parts which now seem improbable, that, in Shakespeare's time, it was necessary to warn credulity against vain and illusive predictions. The passions are directed to their true end. Lady Macbeth is merely detested; and though the courage of Macbeth preserves some esteem, yet every reader rejoices at his fall.

By the time William Hazlitt wrote *The Characters of Shakespeare's Plays* in 1817, qualities in *Macbeth* that had troubled Dr Johnson and his eighteenth-century contemporaries were being cited as evidence of the playwright's inspired brilliance.

> This tragedy is alike distinguished for the lofty imagination it displays, and for the tumultuous vehemence of the action; and the one is made the moving principle of the other. The overwhelming pressure of preternatural agency urges on the tide of human passion with redoubled force. Macbeth himself appears driven along by the violence of his fate like a vessel drifting before a storm: he reels to and fro like a drunken man; he staggers under the weight of his own purposes and the suggestions of others; he stands at bay with his situation; and from the superstitious awe and breathless suspense into which the com-

munications of the Weird Sisters have thrown him, is hurried on with daring impatience to verify their predictions, and with impious and bloody hand to tear aside the veil, which hides the uncertainty of the future. . . .

His speeches and soliloquies are dark riddles on human life, baffling solution, and entangling him in their labyrinths. . . . This part of his character is admirably set off by being brought in connexion with that of Lady Macbeth, whose obdurate strength of will and masculine firmness give her the ascendancy over her husband's faltering virtue. . . . The magnitude of her resolution almost covers the magnitude of her guilt. She is a great bad woman, whom we hate, but whom we fear more than we hate. . . . She is only wicked to gain a great end; and is perhaps more distinguished by her commanding presence of mind and inexorable self-will, which do not suffer her to be diverted from a bad purpose, when once formed, by weak and womanly regrets, than by the hardness of her heart or want of natural affections.

In Hazlitt's view,

Macbeth (generally speaking) is done upon a stronger and more systematic principle of contrast than any other of Shakespeare's plays. It moves upon the verge of an abyss, and is a constant struggle between life and death. The action is desperate and the reaction is dreadful. It is a huddling together of fierce extremes, a war of opposite natures which of them shall destroy the other.

Like Hazlitt, the poet and literary theorist Samuel Taylor Coleridge was moved by the psychological profundity of Shakespeare's characterization. Pondering Macbeth's wife, he observed that being a person 'of high rank, left alone, and feeding herself with daydreams of ambition', she 'mistakes the courage of fantasy for the power of bearing the consequences of the reality of guilt. Hers is the mock fortitude of a mind deluded by ambition.'

But of all the nineteenth century's commentators on *Macbeth*, the writer who has had the greatest influence on later interpreters was Thomas De Quincey, who in 1851 published a perceptive essay entitled 'The Knocking at the Gate'.

From my boyish days I had always felt a great perplexity on one point in *Macbeth*. It was this: the knocking at the gate, which succeeds to the murder of Duncan, produced to my feelings an effect for which I could never account. The effect was, that it reflected back upon the murder a peculiar awfulness and a depth of solemnity; yet, however obstinately I endeavoured with my understanding to comprehend this, for many years I never could see *why* it should produce such an effect.

What De Quincey finally concluded was that this dramatic moment in the play was part of Shakespeare's strategy for deflecting the audience's attention away from the murder of Duncan and fixing it instead on the heart of the murderer.

> Our sympathy must be with him; (of course, I mean a sympathy of comprehension, a sympathy by which we enter into his feelings, and are made to understand them – not a sympathy of pity or approbation.) In the murdered person, all strife of thought, all flux and reflux of passion and of purpose are crushed by one overwhelming panic; the fear of instant death smites him 'with its petrific mace.' But in the murderer, such a murderer as a poet will condescend to, there must be raging some great storm of passion, – jealousy, ambition, vengeance, hatred, – which will create a hell within him; and into this hell we are to look. . . .
>
> The murderers, and the murder, must be insulated, – cut off by an immeasurable gulf from the ordinary tide and succession of human affairs, – locked up and sequestered in some deep recess; we must be made sensible that the world of ordinary life is suddenly arrested – laid asleep, – tranced, – racked into a dread armistice; time must be annihilated; relation to things without abolished; and all must pass self-withdrawn into a deep syncope and suspension of earthly passion. Hence it is, that when the deed is done, when the work of darkness passes away like a pageantry in the clouds: the knocking at the gate is heard; and it makes known audibly that the reaction has commenced; the human has made its reflux upon the fiendish; the pulses of life are beginning to beat again; and the re-establishment of the goings-on of the world in which we live, first makes us profoundly sensible of the awful parenthesis that had suspended them.

One effect of De Quincey's exploration of the disturbance that ends the murder scene and introduces the Porter scene was to highlight *Macbeth* as a script that can tell us things about ourselves as we respond to it; another was to alert us to the dramaturgical techniques of the play's 'wright', the behind-the-scenes manipulator whose designs are ultimately responsible for the audience's reactions to a sequence of events.

Character analysis dominated most of the century that followed De Quincy's essay, and one of the more acute studies of the protagonist of the Scottish play appeared in Edward Dowden's *Shakspere: A Critical Study of His Mind and Art* (1875). According to Dowden, the soul of Macbeth never quite disappears into the blackness of darkness. He is a cloud without water, carried about of winds; a tree whose fruit withers, but not, even to the last, quite plucked up by the roots. For the dull ferocity of Macbeth is joyless. All his life has gone irretrievably astray, and he is aware of this. His suspicion becomes uncontrollable; his reign is a reign of terror; and as he drops deeper and deeper into the solitude and the gloom, his sense of error and misfortune, futile and unproductive as that sense is, increases. He moves under a dreary cloud, and all things look grey and cold. He has lived long enough, yet he clings to life; that which should accompany old age, 'as honor, love, obedience, troops of friends,' he may not look to have. Finally his sensibility has grown so dull that even the intelligence of his wife's death – the death of her who had been bound to him by such close communion in crime – hardly touches him, and seems little more than one additional incident in the weary, meaningless tale of human life.

Dowden's reflections pave the way for an even more ambitious investigation of the workings of *Shakespearean Tragedy* (1904) by A. C. Bradley. In his remarks on *Macbeth*, Bradley observed that

Darkness, we may even say blackness, broods over this tragedy. It is remarkable that almost all the scenes which at once recur to memory take place either at night or in some dark spot. The vision of the dagger, the murder of Duncan, the murder of Banquo, the sleep-walking of Lady Macbeth, all come in night-scenes. The Witches dance in the thick air of a storm, or, 'black and midnight hags', receive Macbeth in a cavern. The blackness of night is to the hero a thing of fear, even of horror; and that which he feels becomes the spirit of the play. . . . In the whole drama the sun seems to shine only twice; first, in the beautiful but ironical passage where Duncan sees the swallows flitting round the castle of death; and afterwards, when at the close the avenging army gathers to rid the earth of its shame. Of the many slighter touches which deepen this effect I notice only one. The failure of nature in Lady Macbeth is marked by her fear of darkness; 'she has light by her continually.' And in the one phrase of fear that escapes her lips even in sleep, it is of the darkness of the place of torment that she speaks.

According to Bradley, Macbeth and his Lady

have no separate ambitions. They support and love one another. They suffer together. And if as time goes on, they drift a little apart, they are not vulgar souls, to be alienated and recriminate when they experience the fruitlessness of their ambition. They remain to the end tragic, even grand.

Eventually critics like L. C. Knights (*How Many Children Had Lady Macbeth?*) and E. E. Stoll (*Art and Artifice in Shakespeare*, published, like Knights's essay, in 1933) would satirize Bradley and his nineteenth-century predecessors for a tendency to treat Shakespeare's characters as if they were real human beings rather than what American scholar Leeds Barroll has referred to as 'artificial persons'. But much of our own century's most penetrating Shakespearean commentary has built on close readings such as Bradley's. A good example may be seen in the following remarks by J. Middleton Murry (*Shakespeare*, 1936).

Perhaps the most marvellous moment in *Macbeth* is when the two actors suddenly emerge from their madness, and look upon their deed with the same naivety as we of the audience. . . . [T]he discrepancy between the character and the act is turned consciously to account. It becomes part of the consciousness which suffuses and animates the drama, as distinct from the consciousness aroused in the spectator by the drama. Suddenly, Macbeth and Lady Macbeth *see themselves*, with an absolute and terrible naivety. This power that is in them to see themselves, manifested as they manifest it, convinces us, as nothing else could now convince us, of their essential nobility of soul. And by this turn the situation becomes bottomless in profundity. That a man and woman should, in the very act of heinous and diabolical murder, reveal themselves as naive and innocent, convulses our morality and awakens in us thoughts beyond the reaches of our souls. So that it seems to us that the wonderful imagination of

> Pity, like a naked new-born babe,
> Striding the blast,

is embodied in the sudden birth of childlike astonishment in the eyes of the murderers themselves.

Murry also offered intriguing speculations about the speech (V.v.17–20) in which Macbeth responds to the news of his wife's death.

I do not profess to know exactly what the first five lines of Macbeth's speech mean; but I am certain that they do not mean what Dr Johnson said they meant:

Her death should have been deferred to some more peaceable hour; had she lived longer, there would have been a more convenient time for such a word, for such intelligence. Such is the condition of human life that we always think to-morrow will be happier than to-day.

Macbeth's meaning is stranger than that. 'Hereafter,' I think, is purposely vague. It does not mean 'later'; but in a different mode of time from that in which Macbeth is imprisoned now. 'Hereafter – in the not-Now: *there* would have been a time for such a word as 'the Queen is *dead*.' But the time in which he is caught is to-morrow, and to-morrow, and to-morrow – one infinite sameness, in which yester-days have only lighted fools the way to dusty death. Life in this time is meaningless – a tale told by an idiot – and death also. For his wife's death to have meaning there needs some total change – a plunge across a new abyss into a Hereafter.

Perhaps I read too much into it; but it seems to me to be the inspired utterance of one 'who lies upon the torture of the mind in restless ecstasy.'

At the same time that Murry was publishing these remarks, a number of other interpreters were beginning to devote new attention to the figurative language of the play. In *Shakespeare's Imagery and What It Tells Us* (1935), Caroline Spurgeon described the poetry of *Macbeth* as 'more rich and varied, more highly imaginative, more unapproachable, by any other writer, than that of any other single play'. She pointed out that 'The idea constantly recurs that Macbeth's new honours sit ill upon him, like a loose and badly fitting garment, belonging to someone else.'

A few years later Cleanth Brooks, one of the leading advocates of the 'New Criticism', took issue with some of Spurgeon's observations. In 'The Naked Babe and the Cloak of Manliness' (*The Well Wrought Urn*, 1947), Brooks said:

there is no warrant for interpreting the garment imagery as used by Macbeth's enemies, Caithness and Angus, to mean that *Shakespeare* sees Macbeth as a poor and somewhat comic figure.

The crucial point of the comparison, it seems to me, lies not in the smallness of the man and the largeness of the robes, but rather in the fact that – whether the man be large or small – these are not *his* garments. Macbeth is uncomfortable in them because he is continually conscious of the fact that they do not belong to him. There is a further point, and it is one of the utmost importance; the oldest symbol for the hypocrite is that of the man who cloaks his true nature under a disguise. Macbeth loathes playing the part of the hypocrite – and actually does not play it too well. . . .

Lady Macbeth abjures all pity; she is willing to unsex herself; and her continual taunt to Macbeth, when he falters, is that he is acting like a baby – not like a man. This 'manhood' Macbeth tries to learn. He is a dogged pupil. For that reason he is almost pathetic when the shallow rationalism which his wife urges upon him fails.

Other interpreters were also examining the play in terms of its image patterns. In *An Approach to Shakespeare* (1938), for instance, Derek A. Traversi was observing that

> As king, Duncan is the head of a 'single state of man' ... whose members are bound into unity by the accepted ties of loyalty. By virtue of this position he is the source of all the benefits which flow from his person to those who surround him; receiving the free homage of his subjects, he dispenses to them all the riches and graces which are the mark of true kingship, so that the quality of his poetry is above all life-giving, fertile. The early, light-drenched scenes of the tragedy are dominated by this rich, vital relationship between service spontaneously given and abundant royal bounty. ... It is in accordance with the spirit of his kingship that Duncan's brief appearances before his murder are invariably invested with images of light and fertility to which are joined, at his moments of deepest feeling, the religious associations of worship in a magnificent, comprehensive impression of overflowing *grace*.

By contrast with the picture the play gives us of Duncan, Traversi noted that

> In practically every one of Macbeth's speeches there is a keen sense of discontinuity, a continual jolting of the sensibility into disorder and anarchy. Macbeth, from the time when the thought of murder first forces its way into his consciousness, moves almost constantly in a remarkable state of nervous tension, a state in which a very palpable obscurity is suddenly and unexpectedly shot through by strange revelations and terrifying illuminations of feeling. This state is fully significant only as an inversion of the rich, ordered poetry of Duncan; it is the natural consequence of his murder, a reflection of the entry of evil both into the individual and the state.

Dame Helen Gardner (*The Business of Criticism*, 1959) commented on the same passage that had provided the title for Cleanth Brooks's remarks on *Macbeth*.

> The naked babe 'strides the blast' because pity is to Shakespeare the strongest and profoundest of human emotions, the distinctively human emotion. It rises above and masters indignation. The cherubim are borne with incredible swiftness about the world because the virtues of Duncan are of such heavenly beauty that they command universal love and reverence. He has 'borne his faculties so meek' and been 'so clear in

his great office.' The word 'clear' is a radiant word, used by Shakespeare elsewhere of the Gods. The helplessness of the king who has trusted him, his gentle virtues, and patient goodness are transformed in Macbeth's mind into the most helpless of all things, what most demands our protection, and then into what awake tenderness, love, and reverence. The babe merges into the cherubim, not because Shakespeare means Macbeth to be feeling both pity and fear of retribution at the same time, but because Shakespeare, like Keats, believes in 'the holiness of the heart's affections.' . . .

In *The Story of the Night: Studies in Shakespeare's Major Tragedies* (1961), John Holloway drew attention to another of the play's powerful images.

At the opening of *Macbeth*, Macbeth is the centre of respect and interest. He is the cynosure, the present saviour of the state. . . . [T]he minion of valour and disdainer of Fortune is sharply before our imagination in all the slaughter of civil war. Yet this image of Macbeth is ambivalent. Only a few lines before, in the explosive opening words of the very first scene (other than that of the witches, no clear part of human life at all), Shakespeare has provided his audience, before their eyes and on stage, with an actual picture that the account of Macbeth in battle . . . disquietingly resembles:

> What bloody man is that? He can report,
> As seemeth by his plight, of the *revolt*
> The newest state.   (I.ii.1)

But insofar as we identify Macbeth with the image of a man stained in blood, and his weapon dripping with blood, he is no image merely of a destroyer of revolt. By a more direct and primitive mode of thought, by simple association, he is an image of revolt itself.

Holloway went on to discuss the disease imagery in *Macbeth*.

That the play depicts disorder spreading throughout a whole society ('bleed, bleed poor country': IV, iii, 32) is a comonplace. So is it, indeed, that this is seen as an infringement of the whole beneficent order of Nature; and that nothing less than that whole beneficent order gears itself, at last, to ending the state of evil ('. . . the pow'rs above / Put on their instruments,' IV, iii, 238). That the coming of Birnam Wood to Dunsinane is a vivid emblem of this, a dumbshow of nature overturning anti-nature at the climax of the play, has gone unnoticed. Professor Knights once suggested that in this scene, 'nature becomes unnatural in order to rid itself of Macbeth,' or rather, that it was 'emphasizing the disorder' by showing the forces of good in association with deceit and with the *un*natural. To a contemporary audience, however, the scene must have presented a much more familiar and less unnatural appearance than it does to ourselves. The single figure, dressed in his distinctive costume (one should have Macbeth in his war equipment in mind) pursued by a whole company of others carrying green branches, was a familiar sight as a Maying procession, celebrating the triumph of new life over the sere and yellow leaf of winter.

A number of twentieth-century critics have focused on the ethical dimensions of the drama. For example, Eugene N. Waith (in 'Manhood and Valor in Two Shakespearean Tragedies', *ELH: A Journal of English Literary History*, 1950), has reminded us that Macbeth's

mental torment grows out of the conflict between the narrow concept of man as the courageous male and the more inclusive concept of man as a being whose moral nature distinguishes him from the beasts. . . . Shakespeare keeps the two concepts before us throughout the play. . . .

Macduff is a complete man: he is a valiant soldier, ready to perform 'manly' deeds, but is neither ashamed of 'humane' feelings nor unaware of his moral responsibilities. . . .

The development of Macbeth's character is a triumph for Lady Macbeth's ideal, for conscience is stifled, and Macbeth, like Hamlet, becomes increasingly 'bloody, bold, and resolute.' His deliberate decision, against the dictates of his better judgment, to be a 'man' in this narrow sense of the word is one of the most important manifestations of the evil which dominates the entire play: to his subjects Macbeth now seems a devil. Shakespeare's insistence upon his narrowing of character is also a commentary on Macbeth's ambition. In 'the swelling act of the imperial theme,' the hero becomes fatally diminished. The final stage of the development is revealed in Macbeth's speeches at the time of Lady Macbeth's death. Here we are confronted by the supreme irony that when she dies, tortured by the conscience she despised, Macbeth is so perfectly hardened, so completely the soldier that she had wanted him to be, that he is neither frightened by the 'night-shriek' nor greatly moved by the news of her death.

In the view of L. C. Knights (*Some Shakespearean Themes*, 1959), the play suggests that listening to the witches

is like eating 'the insane root, That takes the reason prisoner' (I.iii.84–5); for Macbeth, in the moment of temptation, 'function', or intellectual activity, is 'smother'd in surmise'; and everywhere the imagery of darkness suggests not only the absence or withdrawal of light but – 'light thickens' – the presence of something positively oppressive and impeding. Both Macbeth and his wife wilfully blind themselves ('Come, thick Night,' 'Come, seeling Night . . .'), and to the extent that they surrender the characteristically human power of intellectual and moral discernment they themselves become the 'prey' of 'Night's black agents,' of the powers they have deliberately invoked. Automatism is perhaps most obvious in Lady Macbeth's sleep-walking, with its obsessed reliving of the past, but Macbeth also is shown as forfeiting his human freedom and spontaneity.

In '*Macbeth*: The Tragedy of the Hardened Heart' (*Shakes-peare Quarterly*, 1963), Dolora G. Cunningham points out that

Elizabethan moralists frequently discussed the commonly accepted psychology of the hardened heart, in which the sinner becomes so fortified and confirmed in the custom of sin that it becomes a habit, corrupting one's human faculties and, as a popular sermon of the 1580's has it, 'plunging one ever deeper in the stinking puddle of iniquitie. . . .'

Cunningham goes on to observe that

Macbeth, shown in the beginning as having a genuine sense of human kindness, gradually so hardens himself in the custom of evil that he becomes eventually incapable of altering the pattern in which his very being and, for a while, the total action of the play are fixed. . . .
As construed within this play the human person, like the human society, cannot function effectively without sharing in the supernatural energy which is grace; and Macbeth, for whom 'renown and grace is dead,' is accordingly unable to use his mind for the urgent task of restoring himself to working order. The self-inflicted hardening of his nature has raised a deliberate obstacle to grace, so that the understan-ding is darkened and the affections frozen, and the man feeds upon himself . . .
The inability to overcome the surrender to evil and to cope with its consequences is the fundamental tragic pattern of *Macbeth*, as I think it to be, in varying ways, in Shakespearean tragedy generally. . . . Macbeth makes his spirit inaccessible to the light of grace, as do practically all of Shakespeare's tragic heroes, in their various ways. If they had not done so, they would not finally be tragic, and the plays would not be tragedies, but would belong rather with the group often called romances.

Robert B. Heilman (''Twere Best Not Know Myself: Othello, Lear, Macbeth', *Shakespeare Quarterly*, 1964) describes the tragic curve in terms of the classical exhortation to 'know thyself'. Comparing *Macbeth* with another Shakespearean tragedy in which the title character's suffering results in progressive degrees of anagnorisis (self-recognition), Heilman says that

> if Lear yields to knowledge more and more, Macbeth yields to knowledge less and less, and Lady Macbeth seems impregnable to its attacks. Only in retrospect can we measure the pauperizing cost of her apparent invulnerability. When a protagonist 'knows' that his course is morally intolerable, but strains frantically against that knowledge lest it impair his obsessive pursuit of the course, the tension between knowing and willing may itself destroy him. In Lady Macbeth Shakespeare catches the eventual psychic bankruptcy of the assured, plunging personality that can fight off, with a facade of nonchalance, all assaults of a saving self-knowledge, not only for herself but for her husband as well. There is a cumulative, but secret, drain of resources; the prodigal expenditure of will exhausts the soul. . . .
>
> In Macbeth there is nothing of his lady's seemingly passionless closure against irruptive truth. From the beginning the troubles in the psyche break into open consciousness. They are pushed down, and then there they are again, up, presenting, twisting Macbeth into doubt or anguish or horror; and then gone, as if banished. . . .
>
> The play implicitly defines resolution: a denial of consequences and a narcotizing of what one knows. . . .
>
> Conceal knowledge, then eliminate it: it is a major theme of the play in which Shakespeare explores, for the last time in full scale, the complex subject of man's mingled openness to and resistance to self-knowledge. . . . Unlike [Shakespeare's other tragic protagonists], Macbeth does know himself from the start; for him the task is not slowly yielding to knowledge, but getting away from it, making it ever less effective, and escaping, as well as this may be done, into a frenzy of total action that will eventually relieve consciousness by destroying it.

In an essay that first appeared in *Harper's* magazine in June 1962, Mary McCarthy compares 'General Macbeth' to a twentieth-century corporate head.

> What is modern and bourgeois in Macbeth's character is his wholly *social* outlook. He has no feeling for others, and yet until the end he is a vicarious creature, existing in his own eyes through others, through what they may say of him, through what they tell him or promise him. It is he, not Lady Macbeth, who thinks of smearing the drunken chamberlains with blood, so that they shall be caught 'red-handed' the next morning when Duncan's murder is discovered. At this idea he brightens; suddenly, he sees his way clear. It is the moment when he at last decides. The eternal executive, ready to fix responsibility on a subordinate, has seen the deed finally take a *recognizable* form. Now

he can do it. And the crackerjack thought of killing the grooms afterwards (dead men tell no tales – old adage) is again purely his own on-the-spot inspiration; no credit to Lady Macbeth.

It is the sort of thought that would have come to Claudius in *Hamlet*, another trepidant executive. Indeed, Macbeth is more like Claudius than like any other character in Shakespeare. Both are doting husbands; both rose to power by betraying their superior's trust; both are easily frightened and have difficulty saying their prayers.

Other twentieth-century scholars have explored *Macbeth* in terms of its relevance to the time in which it was written. In *The Royal Play of Macbeth* (1950), Henry N. Paul has argued that the tragedy was written with King James in mind and that the earliest performance of it may have been before the king himself in August 1606. Like other scholars who have investigated the play's sources, Paul notes that much of the imagery in *Macbeth* can be interpreted as an allusion to the Gunpowder Plot, the November 1605 conspiracy to blow up the king and Parliament, throw the London government into chaos, and restore Roman Catholicism as the nation's official religion. In what was widely viewed as a providential rescue from the ministers of Satan, the would-be assassins were caught before they could carry out their plans. According to Paul,

> The plot was a deed of darkness in fact as well as in the language of the time. The plotters worked at night to dig their tunnel, got into a vault under the Parliament House, and there hid their powder barrels. There Guy Fawkes was found lurking at night with a dark lantern in his hand and a slow match in his pocket. That evil is associated with darkness is a very old thought, but it became the universal thought of England in the winter of 1605–1606, and this . . . strongly affected the play of *Macbeth*.

Among other things, Paul suggests parallels between the two Thanes of Cawdor in Shakespeare's play and Sir Everard Digby, a 'handsome young friend' of King James who turned out, to the monarch's astonishment, to be among the conspirators. As Paul puts it,

> there was general comment as to this treason committed by a man who had everything to lose and nothing to gain by it. Digby confessed his guilt, received the death sentence, and on Thursday, January 30, 1606, with three others, was dragged on a hurdle to the scaffold in Paul's

churchyard and there hung, drawn, and quartered. It is not at all unlikely that William Shakespeare witnessed this execution so near to his lodging place.

Most of the traitors were defiant or sullen at their trials and executions; but Sir Everard Digby was thoroughly penitent and made a moving speech.

Paul suggests that Digby's story had a lot to do with the passage in I.iv. of *Macbeth* where Malcolm says of the first Thane of Cawdor that

> very frankly he confess'd his Treasons,
> Implor'd your Highness' Pardon, and set forth
> A deep Repentence. Nothing in his Life
> Became him like the leaving it.

In his introduction to *Twentieth Century Interpretations of 'Macbeth'* (1977), Terence Hawkes elaborates upon Paul's thesis.

It would of course be mistaken to argue that *Macbeth* in any sense takes the Plot as its direct subject: the relationship of great art to reality is rarely of that overt order. But it is not surprising that a play dealing explicitly with James's personal ancestry should contain at its core precise references to the trial of one of the alleged conspirators (in the Porter scene) or that the wider social, spiritual, and theological ramifications of the Plot – fully exploited by James in his pronouncement on the subject – should find themselves obliquely embodied in a play whose first performance (the evidence suggests) took place at Hampton Court in his presence and that of his guest King Christian IV of Denmark.

In essence, the Plot's intent was, almost literally, shattering. . . . James was to be the second Brutus, destined to reunify the land founded by the first Brutus, and then riven by him in his folly. And it was that edifice of imminent unity that the Gunpowder Plot seemed designed to reduce to rubble. That the conspirators were foreign-backed Catholics, their confessions appeared to confirm. That they were also (and therefore) agents of the devil intent upon the destruction of God's divine plan for Great Britain and her people followed without question. Inspired by Lucifer, the conflagration they purposed had its analogue in the flames of Hell.

One of the central concerns of *Macbeth* is of course the disunity and disorder that the murder of King Duncan brings to Scotland. 'Confusion hath now made his masterpiece' (II, iii, 68), cries Macduff on discovering the body, and goes on to liken the carnage to 'The great doom's image' (II, iii, 80). Moreover, the play proves quite explicit (and wholly in accord with the spirit of Elizabethan and Jacobean pronouncements on the subject of political rebellion) in the connection it insistently forges between the actions of Macbeth and those of Lucifer.

A number of twentieth-century scholars have noted parallels between the Porter's jests about 'equivocators' in II.iii of *Macbeth* and the comments that one of the accomplices in the Gunpowder Plot made at his trial in March 1606. As Hawkes observes, a Jesuit priest, Father Henry Garnet,

> had dwelt at length on his use of verbal double-dealing, technically termed 'equivocation,' in his own defense. Garnet's subsequent admission that he considered it perfectly acceptable to equivocate 'if just necessity so require' had undoubtedly seemed outrageous to a society already disposed (and encouraged in this by its propaganda) to think the worst of Roman Catholic priests. As a result equivocation had rapidly and popularly become almost the badge of subversion.
> It is important to realize that the question is not one of simple 'lying.' Equivocation of the type allegedly defended by Garnet's Jesuit order involved the deliberate and premeditated manipulation of language in order to obscure the truth and so, as it would appear to Shakespeare's audience, to strike at the foundations of the entire community.

In the play, of course, equivocation begins with the opening scene, and Lawrence Danson notes in *Tragic Alphabet* (1974) that

> The Weird Sisters use a trick that would hardly have been news for the Delphic Oracle: through slight dislocations of normal grammatical or logical relationships, they make simple, even banal, statements sound as difficult as possible. . . . 'When the battle's lost and won' sounds, at first, deeply paradoxical; but the paradox is immediately unraveled, the implicit riddle solved, when we realize that every battle is lost and won: the Weird Sisters, unlike a mortal audience, are simply not engaged on any particular side.
> True, the riddle has still a further dimension, for there is a sense in which Macbeth's temporary victory – the satisfaction of his desires – will prove to be his ultimate loss: but, again, it is a comprehensible statement which leaves the 'rule of unity' unimpaired. . . .
> For the riddle 'Fair is foul, and foul is fair,' is, in miniature, the riddle of the play itself. The entire action of *Macbeth* similarly hovers between a metaphysical horror and a metalinguistic mistake: Has the order of Nature really been destroyed by Macbeth, so that 'nothing is but what is not'? Or do 'measure, time, and place' (those certainties to which Malcolm will appeal in the final speech) still encompass and control the apparent perversion of Macbeth's reign? . . .
> In this *Macbeth*-world of apparently inherent ambiguity, the one

perfectly unambiguous thing is the murder of Duncan. From the start it is conceived as just that: not sacrifice or revenge, but murder. We know from the start that the moral horror which is Duncan's murder cries out for retribution. Hence it is the murderer Macbeth's destiny that we most expectantly attend, and hence (in part) the unrelieved sense of inevitability and directness which gives *Macbeth* its distinctive dramatic concentration. And there is another cause, too, for this sense of concentration: in no other play does language so intimately and immediately reflect the action. Language in *Macbeth* is the mirror and even, in a sense, the cause of the extremity of the moral situation. Macbeth's deed is an overturning of normal values and relationships, and the language of the play (the Weird Sisters' speeches being only the most obvious examples) follows the action into the chaotic world he establishes, into the realm of impossibility, beyond the powers of ordinary conception, beyond the proper sphere of words.

One of the major problems for twentieth-century critics of *Macbeth* has been to account for the way most of us respond to the protagonists in the theatre. Honor M. V. Matthews (*Character and Symbol in Shakespeare's Plays*, 1962) has noted that

Shakespeare adapts his story so as to take from Macbeth all genuine grievances against the king. . . . He selects and arranges his material to ensure that the murdered king is wholly attractive, unlike Richard II or Henry VI, and also gives him worthy heirs of age to rule. . . . He allows Macbeth also a full measure of the popularity, reputation, honour, charm, and also the happiness in marriage which were denied to Richard III. Like Lucifer's, and indeed Adam's, his rebellion lacks any motive other than the rebel's own self-assertion . . .

In Macbeth, moreover, the role of Lucifer is conflated with that of Herod, for when the king's heir has escaped his clutches the tyrant seeks and finds a substitute victim. The outrage of innocence, symbolised by the murder of a child, is an important element in Shakespeare's thought, and here history presented the dramatist with only too much of the material he needed. But the killing of the young Macduff is peculiarly brutal because it is of no possible use to Macbeth; in committing this act he is baser even than his biblical forerunner, for he knew the life he wanted to take was safe from him, and he murdered from mere hysterical vindictiveness.

But if Macbeth is steeped in evil, how does Shakespeare contrive to persuade us that he has enough tragic dignity to sustain our engagement? Alan S. Downer argues (in 'The Life of our Design', *Hudson Review*, 1949) that

One of the achievements of this highly skilful play is the maintaining of interest in, if not sympathy for, the central figure; assassin, evil governor, usurper, and murderer. Shakespeare maintains this interest not merely by portraying Macbeth as a man in the control of wyrd, or to susceptible to uxorial suggestion, but, I think, by making us constantly aware of the armour – the honest warrior's nature – under the loosely hanging robes of a regicide. Until Act II, scene 3, Macbeth is quite possibly dressed as a warrior. From that point, until Act V, scene 3, he is dressed in his borrowed robes. But in the latter scene, with his wife eliminated as a motivating force, and with the English army moving against him, he begins to resume some of his former virtues: his courage returns, his forthrightness, his manliness. 'Give me my armour,' he cries, and in a lively passage with the Doctor, he makes grim jests about the power of medicine as Seyton helps him into his warrior's dress. He is all impatience to be back at the business he understands as he does not understand government. . . . The tragic fall of this good man is dramatically underlined in his attempts to resume his old way of life.

Wayne C. Booth addresses the same issue in 'Macbeth as Tragic Hero' (*Journal of General Education*, 1951), where he says that Shakespeare

has the task of trying to keep two contradictory streams moving simultaneously: the events showing Macbeth's growing wickedness and the tide of our mounting sympathy. In effect, each succeeding atrocity, marking another step towards depravity, must be so surrounded by contradictory circumstances or technical blandishments as to make us feel that, in spite of the evidence before our eyes, Macbeth is still somehow sympathetic.

Our first sure sign that Shakespeare's attention is on the need for such manipulation is his care in avoiding any representation of the murder of Duncan. It is, in fact, not even narrated. We hear only the details of how the guards reacted and how Macbeth reacted to their cries. We *see* nothing. There is nothing about the actual dagger strokes; there is no report of the dying cries of the good old king. We have only Macbeth's conscience-stricken lament. What would be an intolerable act if depicted with any vividness becomes relatively forgivable when seen only afterward in the light of Macbeth's remorse. . . .

A second precaution is the highly general portrayal of Duncan before his murder. It is necessary only that he be known as a 'good king', the murder of whom will be a wicked act. . . . We know almost no details about him, and we have little personal interest in him at the time of his death. All of the personal interest is reserved for Macbeth and Lady Macbeth. . . .

[Banquo's murder] is done by accomplices, so that Macbeth is never shown in any act of wicked violence. When we do see him, he is suffering the torments of the banquet sceno. Our unconscious inference: the self-torture has already expiated his crime.

[Even the slaughter of Macduff's family is staged in such a way that Macbeth] is kept as little to blame as possible. He does not do the deed himself, and we can believe that he would have been unable to, if he had seen the victims as we have. . . .

As a result of these and other dramaturgical devices, Booth says, when the title character observes that his 'way of life' is 'fall'n into the sear,' we as audience 'respond more to Macbeth, the poet of his own condition, whose imagination can still grasp what it has lost, than to the circumstances of his decline'.

SUGGESTIONS FOR FURTHER READING

Many of the works quoted in the preceding survey (or excerpts from them) can be found in modern collections of criticism. Of particular interest are the following anthologies:

Brown, John Russell (ed.), *Focus on 'Macbeth'*, London: Routledge & Kegan Paul, 1982 (see Peter Stallybrass's essay on '*Macbeth* and Witchcraft' for some provocative observations about the social and political functions of Renaissance beliefs about witches, and see Michael Hawkins's essay on 'History, Politics, and *Macbeth*' for a discussion of how the play might have been 'read' politically by Shakespeare's contemporaries).

Halio, Jay L. (ed.), *Approaches to 'Macbeth'*, Belmont, Cal.: Wadsworth Publishing Company, 1966 (a good source for the material quoted or referred to above from A. C. Bradley, Dolora G. Cunningham, Thomas De Quincey, Edward Dowden, William Hazlitt, L. C. Knights, Honor M. V. Matthews, Henry N. Paul, E. E. Stoll, and Derek A. Traversi).

Hawkes, Terence (ed.), *Twentieth Century Interpretations of 'Macbeth'*, Englewood Cliffs, NJ: Prentice-Hall, 1977 (a good source for the material quoted above from Cleanth Brooks, Laurence Danson, Helen Gardner, John Holloway, L. C. Knights, Mary McCarthy, J. Middleton Murry, Caroline F. E. Spurgeon, and Eugene M. Waith).

Lerner, Laurence (ed.), *Shakespeare's Tragedies: An Anthology of Modern Criticism*, Harmondsworth: Penguin, 1963 (contains seven essays on *Macbeth*, including the essay by Alan S. Downer quoted above).

Muir, Kenneth, and Philip Edwards, *Aspects of 'Macbeth'*, Cambridge: Cambridge University Press, 1977 (a collection of articles that originally appeared in *Shakespeare Survey*).

Other studies of Shakespeare that include valuable discussions of *Macbeth*:

Adelman, Janet, 'Born of Woman: Fantasies of Maternal Power in *Macbeth*', in *Cannibals, Witches, and Divorce*; *Estranging the Renaissance*, ed. Marjorie Garber, Baltimore: Johns Hopkins University Press, 1987.

Calderwood, James L., *If It Were Done: 'Macbeth' and Tragic Action*, Amherst: University of Massachusetts Press, 1986.

Campbell, Lily B., *Shakespeare's Tragic Heroes: Slaves of Passion*, London: Methuen, 1966.

Champion, Larry S., *Shakespeare's Tragic Perspective*, Athens, Ga: University of Georgia Press, 1976.

Farnham, Willard, *Shakespeare's Tragic Frontier*, Berkeley: University of California Press, 1950.

Garber, Marjorie, *Shakespeare's Ghost Writers: Literature as Uncanny Causality*, London: Methuen, 1987.

Kahn, Coppelia, *Man's Estate: Masculine Identity in Shakespeare*, Berkeley: University of California Press, 1981.

Knight, G. Wilson, *The Imperial Theme*, 3rd edn, London: Methuen, 1954.

Mack, Maynard, 'The Jacobean Shakespeare: Some Observations on the Construction of the Tragedies', in *Stratford-upon-Avon Studies I: Jacobean Theatre*, London: Edward Arnold, 1960.

Mack, Maynard, Jr, *Killing the King*, New Haven: Yale University Press, 1973.

Mahood, M. M., *Shakespeare's Wordplay*, London: Methuen, 1957.

Norbrook, David, 'Macbeth and the Politics of Historiography', in *Politics of Discourse: The Literature and History of Seventeenth-Century England*, ed. Kevin Sharpe and Steven Zwicker, Berkeley: University of California Press, 1987.

Rosen, William, *Shakespeare and the Craft of Tragedy*, Cambridge, Mass.: Harvard University Press, 1960.

Slights, Camille Wells, *The Casuistical Tradition*, Princeton: Princeton University Press, 1981 (background on 'Equivocation' in *Macbeth*).

Walker, Roy, *The Time Is Free*, New York: Macmillan, 1949.

Background studies and useful reference works:

Abbott, E. A., *A Shakespearean Grammar*, New York: Haskell House, 1972 (information on how Shakespeare's grammar differs from ours).

Allen, Michael J. B., and Kennth Muir (eds), *Shakespeare's Plays in Quarto: A Facsimile Edition*, Berkeley: University of California Press, 1981.

Andrews, John F. (ed.), *William Shakespeare: His World, His Work, His Influence*, 3 vols, New York: Scribners, 1985 (articles on 60 topics).

Bentley, G. E., *The Profession of Player in Shakespeare's Time, 1590–1642*, Princeton: Princeton University Press, 1984.

Blake, Norman, *Shakespeare's Language: An Introduction*, New York: St Martin's Press, 1983 (general introduction to all aspects of the playwright's language).

Bullough, Geoffrey (ed.), *Narrative and Dramatic Sources of Shakespeare*, 8 vols, New York: Columbia University Press, 1957–75 (printed sources, with helpful summaries and comments by the editor).

Campbell, O. J., and Edward G. Quinn (eds), *The Reader's Encyclopedia of Shakespeare*, New York: Crowell, 1966.

Cook, Ann Jennalie, *The Privileged Playgoers of Shakespeare's London*: Princeton: Princeton University Press, 1981 (argument that theatre audiences at the Globe and other public playhouses were relatively well-to-do).

De Grazia, Margreta, *Shakespeare Verbatim: The Reproduction of Authenticity and the Apparatus of 1790,* Oxford: Clarendon Press, 1991 (interesting material on eighteenth-century editorial practices).

Gurr, Andrew, *Playgoing in Shakespeare's London*, Cambridge: Cambridge University Press, 1987 (argument for changing tastes, and for a more diverse group of audiences than Cook suggests).

—— *The Shakespearean Stage,* 1574–1642, 2nd edn, Cambridge: Cambridge University Press, 1981 (theatres, companies, audiences, and repertories).

Hinman, Charlton (ed.), *The Norton Facsimile: The First Folio of Shakespeare's Plays*, New York: Norton, 1968.

Muir, Kenneth, *The Sources of Shakespeare's Plays*, New Haven: Yale University Press, 1978 (a concise account of how Shakespeare used his sources).

Onions, C. T., *A Shakespeare Glossary*, 2nd edn, London: Oxford University Press, 1953.

Partridge, Eric, *Shakespeare's Bawdy*, London: Routledge & Kegan Paul, 1955 (indispensable guide to Shakespeare's direct and indirect ways of referring to 'indecent' subjects).

Schoenbaum, S., *Shakespeare: The Globe and the World*, New York: Oxford University Press, 1979 (lively illustrated book on Shakespeare's world).

—— *Shakespeare's Lives*, 2nd edn, Oxford: Oxford University Press, 1992 (readable, informative survey of the many biographers of Shakespeare, including those believing that someone else wrote the works).

—— *William Shakespeare: A Compact Documentary Life*, New York: Oxford University Press, 1977 (presentation of all the biographical documents, with assessments of what they tell us about the playwright).

Spevack, Marvin, *The Harvard Concordance to Shakespeare*, Cambridge, Mass.: Harvard University Press, 1973.

PLOT SUMMARY

1.1 Amidst thunder and lightning, three witches advance onto an unspecified piece of ground. They vow to meet Macbeth on a heath before sunset, and then leave.

1.2 Near his military camp, Duncan, King of Scotland, and some of his nobles are finding out how the battle against the rebels is going. They have won, and in the fighting Macbeth has distinguished himself. Duncan condemns the captured Thane of Cawdor to death and awards the Thane's title to Macbeth.

1.3 The three witches, on the heath, meet Macbeth and Banquo returning from the battle. The witches prophesy that Macbeth shall first become Thane of Cawdor and then King, and that Banquo shall be a father to kings. After they have vanished, noblemen sent by Duncan arrive and tell Macbeth of his preferment.

1.4 When Macbeth and Banquo arrive at the royal palace in Forres, they are congratulated by Duncan, who announces that his eldest son, Malcolm, shall be his heir. As a mark of favour, Duncan resolves to visit Macbeth's castle in Inverness. Macbeth leaves to prepare for the visit.

1.5 At Inverness, Macbeth's Lady reads a letter from her husband which recounts the witches' prophecies, and then learns from a messenger of Duncan's planned visit. When Macbeth arrives, she declares her hope that Duncan will never leave.

1.6 Arriving with noblemen at dusk, Duncan is welcomed by Macbeth's Lady.

1.7 Sometime later within the castle, while Duncan finishes his dinner, Macbeth debates with himself whether he should kill his King. Macbeth's Lady enters and urges him to do so, suggesting they make Duncan's guards drunk, murder the monarch while he sleeps, and then lay the blame on the guards. Macbeth agrees.

2.1 During the night, Macbeth briefly meets Banquo with his son Fleance. When on his own he meditates on the murder he is about to commit, then sets out to do it.

2.2 Macbeth's Lady, after making the guards drunk, meets her husband as he returns from murdering Duncan. She reprimands him for the regrets and fears he has already begun to feel. Macbeth has forgotten to leave the daggers where they will incriminate the guards; and, as he refuses to return the daggers, Macbeth's Lady does so. As knocking at the castle's doors is heard, she returns to lead Macbeth to their bedroom.

2.3 Macduff and Lenox, two noblemen, have arrived to speak with Duncan, and after the Porter eventually lets them in, Macbeth takes them to the King's door. Macduff goes in, and then raises the alarm for Duncan's murder. While the other noblemen and Macbeth's Lady arrive, Macbeth enters Duncan's room with Lenox, and kills the King's sleeping guards. Duncan's two sons, Malcolm and Donalbain, decide their lives are in danger and resolve to leave Scotland immediately.

2.4 Outside the castle, an old man tells Rosse, another nobleman, of the bad omens that anticipated Duncan's murder. Macduff arrives, and recounts how the guards are thought to have killed Duncan in accordance with Malcolm's and Donalbain's orders. The two sons' guilt is proved by their flight. Macbeth will now be crowned King.

3.1 At the royal palace at Forres, Banquo is suspicious that Macbeth, now King, has gained the crown unfairly. Sensing this, and mindful of the witches' prophecy about Banquo, Macbeth arranges to have Banquo and his son, Fleance, murdered before the evening's feast.

3.2 Macbeth's Lady, herself feeling insecure, attempts to alleviate Macbeth's fears. He tells her that he is taking further action to secure the crown, but refuses to tell her the detail of his plans.

3.3 In fading light, three murderers ambush Banquo and Fleance a little way from the palace. Banquo is killed but Fleance escapes.

3.4 As the banquet starts, Macbeth learns of the murderers' partial success. Then Banquo's ghost appears to him twice at the feast, causing him to lose control of himself in public. Macbeth's Lady assures everybody that such fits are normal, and then dismisses them. Macbeth decides to consult the witches on the next day.

3.5 Amidst thunder, the three witches meet Hecate, who informs them that Macbeth will be coming to see them in the morning. Then music is played and a song sung.

3.6 Elsewhere in Scotland, Lenox discusses with another Lord his suspicions concerning Macbeth's involvement in the recent murders. He learns that Malcolm is at the English court, and that Macduff has gone to request the King of England's help to free Scotland from Macbeth's rule.

4.1 In a cavern, the three witches make charms around a cauldron, and are then joined by Hecate and another three witches. Macbeth enters, and demands that they answer his questions. They summon apparitions who warn Macbeth to beware of Macduff, tell him that he need fear nobody borne of a woman, and assure him that he will only be conquered when great Byrnan Wood moves to Dunsinane Hill. Macbeth wants to know whether Banquo's descendants shall rule the kingdom, and is shown a pageant which proves that they shall. Then the witches dance and vanish. Lenox arrives with the news that Macduff has fled. Macbeth resolves to destroy Macduff's castle and family.

4.2 At Macduff's castle, his wife waits fearfully with her son, unconsoled by Rosse's reassurances. After Rosse leaves, a messenger comes to warn her to flee, but Macbeth's hired murderers arrive almost immediately and kill mother and son.

4.3 In England, near the palace of King Edward I, Macduff tries to persuade Malcolm to return and help save Scotland. Malcolm, having tested Macduff's motives, agrees. He then describes King Edward's God-given ability to cure disease. Rosse arrives, entreats Malcolm to aid Scotland, and then tells Macduff that his family are dead. Macduff resolves to kill Macbeth.

5.1 At Macbeth's castle in Dunsinane, a doctor and a waiting woman watch Macbeth's Lady sleepwalk. She tries to clean her hands and speaks about the murders of Duncan and Banquo.

5.2 In the countryside nearby, Scottish noblemen and soldiers march to Byrnan Wood to meet up with the English forces led by Malcolm.

5.3 In Dunsinane castle, Macbeth is confident, trusting to the witches' prophecies. He urges the doctor to help his wife.

5.4 Near Byrnan Wood, the English forces meet their Scottish allies. Malcolm commands every soldier to carry a branch in order to disguise their true numbers.

5.5 Macbeth, in his castle, prepares to withstand a siege. An officer brings news that Macbeth's Lady is dead. Then a messenger reports that he thinks he has seen Byrnan Wood begin to move. Macbeth decides to fight his enemies.

5.6 The forces led by Malcolm arrive at Macbeth's castle and prepare for battle.

5.7 In the battle, Macbeth kills Young Steward. Macduff seeks out Macbeth. Meanwhile the castle is easily taken. Macbeth meets Macduff, who explains that he was not strictly borne of a woman because he was delivered by caesarian. They fight and Macbeth is killed. Macduff takes Macbeth's head to show Malcolm, whom all now hail as King of Scotland. Malcolm thanks them all, and promises to do all that is necessary to return Scotland to health.

ACKNOWLEDGEMENTS

Acknowledgement is due to the copyright holders of the extracts reproduced in the *Perspectives on Macbeth* section of this edition.

ACKNOWLEDGMENTS